Powerful Literacies

Edited by
Jim Crowther, Mary Hamilton and Lyn Tett

niace

promoting adult learning

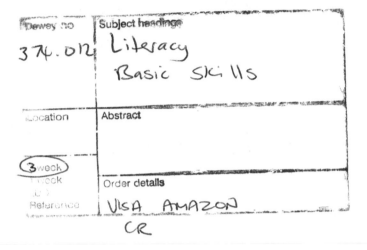

Published by the National Institute of Adult Continuing Education
(England and Wales)
21 De Montfort Street, Leicester, LE1 7GE
Company registration no. 2603322
Charity registration no. 1002775
The NIACE website on the Internet is http://www.niace.org.uk

First published 2001, reprinted 2003

© NIACE

CATALOGUING IN PUBLICATION DATA
A CIP record for this title is available from the British Library
ISBN 1 86201 094 3

Typeset by The Midlands Book Typesetting Co., Loughborough
Cover design by Boldface, London
Printed in Great Britain by Hobbs

Powerful Literacies

Contents

Foreword

This is an important book for literacy educators. It makes a powerful contribution to what is now recognised as a very rich tradition within literacy studies. This centres on the analysis of the fundamentally different, and sometimes 'hidden', ways in which literacy is conceptualised and politicised; and on the generation of 'liberating' educational practice in the light of such work.

It is fitting that this volume derives from the annual Research and Practice in Adult Literacy (RaPAL) Conference in Edinburgh, 1999 [co-sponsored by the University of Edinburgh]. The members of this international network have, since 1985, researched, taught and written extensively about how literacy is used, by whom and for what purposes. They have consistently drawn attention to the relative status of different literacies and to the implications for learners when their literacies are routinely ignored. RaPAL members have been a driving force in the UK in the reconceptualisation of literacy and in the gathering of research data about the undervalued literacies to be found throughout society.

This volume represents a valuable resource for researchers and practitioners in three important respects. First, it provides a succinct critique of the narrow conceptualisation of literacy that continues to underpin UK educational policy in all sectors. Educators who are aware of the real world complexities will find some intellectual nourishment here in the arguments against treating literacy as a narrow skill and in favour of a deeper understanding of real world literacies.

Second, it illuminates some of the daily power struggles to be found at the interfaces between different literacies. Some of the chapters provide graphic examples of how narrowly based but dominant literacy practices have dramatic effects on the personal, social and economic prospects of learners. These accounts underline the urgency of the debate. Literacies coexist but not always equitably. Nor is it always a matter of peaceful coexistence or easy movement between literacies; there are winners and losers. In some contexts the powerful continue to win while in others there are countervailing forces which can check their advance.

The third important aspect of the book is the exploration of how power is experienced and shared within literacy education work. Literacy workers throughout the world have long been aware of the uncomfortable space they sometimes inhabit between funding authorities with narrow agendas and adult learners who must find their own literacy voices. Even so, they have largely developed practice that has focused on acting as 'change agents' and 'empowering' learners. Some of the writers in this volume invite us to re-examine our practice in this respect and to be quite clear about the processes with which we are involved and the kind of power tutors are actually sharing with learners. There is also a useful reference to the relative powerlessness of students with learning disabilities, to the role which deficit views about literacy difficulties play in exacerbating this and to the nature of the processes required for change.

As ever, powerful examples of thinking and practice from international contributors continue to enrich the debates about literacies and they are well represented in this book. It is particularly appropriate to acknowledge the importance of such contributions in a volume about 'powerful literacies', given the seminal contributions on this subject by other international writers such as Freire and Graff.

Margaret Herrington
Chair of RaPAL, 2000

1 Powerful literacies: an introduction

Jim Crowther, Mary Hamilton and Lyn Tett

Introduction

The inspiration for this book originated from a conference sponsored by *RaPAL* and the University of Edinburgh on the theme of powerful literacies. The aim of *RaPAL* is to bring together researchers and practitioners as a way of ensuring that all are informed by developments in their respective fields of work. The Edinburgh conference did just that. It attracted participants from across the UK and also internationally, whose voices can now be heard in this collection. This book has another origin too – but this time a far less positive one. At the beginning of the twenty-first century the issue of literacy (in schools as well as in adult education) dominates the policy agenda in 'developing' as well as 'over-developed' countries. The linking of literacy with the economy and the impact of literacy league tables, as constructed by the International Adult Literacy Surveys, have been powerful forces that have shaped the literacy debate and our understanding of the issues involved. The opportunity for thinking about what literacy means and the issues it involves for developing alternative practices has been squeezed out by the demands of government and global corporations preoccupied with narrowly conceived ideas of human resource development. The space for another vision needs to be created. What is missing is the experiences of practitioners, researchers and broader understandings of literacy and how people use it in everyday ways. The purpose of this book is to contribute towards opening a space for divergent and critical voices to be heard; ones that are grounded in research and practice into the meanings of literacy and what it means to work with literacy students.

Before we can speak about powerful literacies we need to set it against the dominant assumptions made about adult literacy practice. The dominant model systematically fails to address issues of power relations in people's lives and what they can do about them. The selection and distribution of literacy to different social groups is not something that happens neutrally, as it were, above the interests that pattern society. Instead, they are embedded in its infrastructure of power relationships. Literacy is deeply and inescapably bound up with producing, reproducing and maintaining unequal arrangements of power.

The literacy ladder

Definitions of what it means to be literate are always shifting. It is socially constructed and cannot be seen outside of the interests and powerful forces that seek to fix it in particular ways. The common way to think about literacy at the moment is by seeing it as a ladder that people have to climb up. This begins in schooling and adult literacy is the extension of the process in post-school contexts. The emphasis is, therefore, on standardising literacy accomplishments, tests, core skills, and uniform learning outcomes that are specified in advance of the learning process. People are ranked from bottom to top with the emphasis on what they can't do rather than what they can. This leads to a deficit model where those on the bottom rungs are positioned as lacking the skills that they need. Moreover, adults are seen as '[not] even vaguely motivated to do something about their own plight' (Tester, 2000: 42). The frameworks used to define this ladder are top-down ones constructed largely in terms of pre-vocational and vocationally relevant literacy requirements. Consequently, they do not recognise the validity of people's own definitions, uses and aspirations for literacy so they are 'disempowering' in the sense that they are not negotiable or learner-centred and not locally responsive. They define what counts as 'real literacy' and silence everything else. If, however, the emphasis is put on how adults can and want to use literacy then the focus moves to what people have, rather than what they lack, what motivates them rather than what is seen as something they need.

New research and practice has been at the forefront of undermining the conceptual adequacy of the discourse of deficit. It does so by grounding literacies in a social and ecological context. They are no longer disembodied skills but aspects of real people's lives in everyday situations. What has become known as the New Literacy Studies (as in Gee, 1990; Street, 1996; Barton, 1994; Barton and Hamilton, 1998) uses an approach which sets out from a different point – starting from the local, everyday experience of literacy in particular communities of practice. Its approach is based upon a belief that literacy only has meaning within its particular context of social practice and does not transfer unproblematically across contexts; there are different literacy practices in different domains of social life, such as education, religion, workplaces, public services, families, community activities; they change over time and these different literacies are supported and shaped by the different institutions and social relationships. Detailed studies of particular situations can be revealing about these differences and in turn these help identify the broader meanings, values and uses that literacy has for people in their day-to-day lives. We would argue that any research that purports to increase our understanding of literacy in society must take account of these meanings, values and uses – and indeed they are the source of the ideas which statisticians use to interpret their findings. The new literacy studies dispenses with the idea that there is a single literacy that can be unproblematically taken for granted. We have to begin to think in pluralistic terms about the variety of literacies that are used in different contexts in order to make meaning – and in order to make literacy practice meaningful to people.

New modes and conventions for communicating through information and communication technologies are also raising issues about what counts as 'real' literacy. The juxtaposition of icons, imagery and text is presenting new challenges for the process of communication and the literacies associated with it (see Street, this volume). In an information-rich world there is an increasing gap between those with access to information and those denied it. Redistributing information and making it accessible to the 'information poor' is an important educational and political task. Moreover, the demands of a 'knowledge economy' and an 'information society' cannot simply be constrained within the traditional conventions of literacy understanding. Its development exposes the inadequacy of current thinking that constitutes literacy as externally defined rungs on a ladder that has been designed as an extension of initial schooling, rather than in terms of the real shape of literacy practices and goals in adult life. Rather than seeing literacy as a tool for organising our knowledge that is consistent with the economistic vision of the global economy, we need other ways of conceptualising literacy that can embody more democratic visions.

Making power visible

Power that is recognisable is also negotiable (Melucci, 1988: 250)

Literacy that obscures the power relations inscribed in its construction ultimately disempowers. It treats as technical what is in fact socially and politically constructed and is therefore misleading. In one sense, therefore, powerful literacies have to be oppositional. They have to open up, expose and counteract the institutional processes and professional mystique whereby dominant forms of literacy are placed beyond question. They have to challenge the way 'literacy' is socially distributed to different groups. They have to reconstruct the learning and teaching process in a way that positions students in more equal social and political terms. In another sense they should be propositional, in that they have to construct alternative ways of addressing literacy practices and interests grounded in real lives and literacy needs. They need to be critical and political too. The agenda for developing powerful literacies has to be informed by issues of social justice, equality, and democracy in everyday life rather than be limited to a narrow, functional definition primarily addressed to the needs of the economy.

Researchers and practitioners have to construct alliances in order to develop their own agency to act back on the forces that seek to shackle them to a narrow and impoverished vision of literacy. Powerful literacies involve constructing a curriculum that enables workers to learn and share experience. This acts as a counter force against the powerful forces that have dominated the literacy discourse. Increasingly, the stage for these alliances has to be global as well as local. The forces that are impacting on literacy practice are – as many of the accounts here demonstrate – not restricted to national boundaries. Powerful literacies involve opening up the many voices that are silenced in dominant definitions of literacy. It involves people deciding for themselves what is 'really useful literacy' and using it to act, individually and collectively, on their circumstances to take greater control over them. Literacy is a resource for people acting back against the forces that limit their lives. Whilst literacy has to be understood broadly in that it involves social processes of making and communicating meanings, the importance of textual communication always figures prominently. It involves learning to be critical readers and writers in order to detect and handle the inherently ideological dimension of literacy, and the role of literacy in the enactment and production of power (see Lankshear *et al*, 1997).

Powerful literacies speak to an agenda informed by concerns to extend the autonomy of individuals and communities that have been marginalised and ignored. The emphasis is shifted from literacy as a deficit in people to an examination of the literacy practices that people engage in that recognises difference and diversity and challenges how these differences are viewed in society. The deficit, if there is one to be located, is in a society that excludes, reduces and ridicules the rich means of communication that exist amongst its people. The policy discourse both within the UK and the wider world is premised on a basic skills model that prioritises the surface features of literacy and language and we show, through a variety of contexts and practices, how inappropriate this is.

Structure of the book

In this book a variety of voices are heard that subscribe to a variety of positions. The themes that they raise and the conceptual resources deployed reflect a range of perspectives that have a common aim of addressing questions of power, literacy and democratic life. It is divided into three sections that reflect important themes underpinning an analysis of powerful literacies. The first section establishes the theoretical and policy frameworks that underpin the book and shows how literacy is situated in different geographical places, domains and cultural contexts. It also raises critical awareness of the policy discourses around literacy and how they construct the learner, the teacher, the institutional environment for literacy and the goals and outcomes of literacy learning. In the second section, the concern is with reflecting on power not only in terms of the vision behind 'empowering initiatives' but also with the limitations on what has been achieved because of powerful forces in society. It also shows how the purposes and values of literacy in people's lives can be contested. The third section discusses how learners and teachers can be repositioned as active subjects and citizens rather than passive objects. It examines the differential positioning of tutor/student and how these can shift. It emphasises the importance of having another vision, enabling choices for how people can use literacy for their own purposes. The chapters in these three sections are described below.

Theoretical and policy frameworks

Systematic and sustained theoretical critique is needed to shift the literacy agenda away from its current preoccupations and limitations. At the forefront of this work is *Brian Street*, who sets out the conceptual framework for many of the contributions that follow by showing that there are a range of discourses that impact on both what we understand literacy to be and our approaches to it. He shows that what is regarded as 'the basics' needs to be broadened so that the view of literacy is shifted from a focus on rules towards a more creative and user-focused approach.

Mary Hamilton, Catherine Macrae and Lyn Tett offer an overview and critique of the policy context within which the developments described in the rest of this book need to be understood through a focus on the four countries of the UK and Ireland as well as the wider international scene. They suggest that some of the competing policy discourses offer possibilities for more open definitions of literacy than the human resources development model that is dominant. Despite the ascendancy of the latter, the contestation of policy and the opportunity to inscribe in it more socially useful, critical and creative approaches to literacy practice have to be struggled for, as the trajectories of the four countries studied suggest. The dominant policy discourse may set limits and constraints but it also has to be engaged with dialectically to maximise the openings and spaces for more powerful literacies to emerge.

Reflecting on power

Literacy is intrinsically both personal and political and this connection is evident in the most innocuous of literary acts – the signature. *Jane Mace* explores the personal significance of being able to write your own name, especially in the context where literacy is assumed, and the power that this embodies. To be unable to write our own name in a society full of writing is equivalent to being unable to inscribe our selves in that society, she suggests. The author argues that the right to give or to withhold your name is an important civil right. A full literacy life in a lettered world means people not only having the choice of being able to write their name so that it can be read, but also, when they so desire, in the way which is theirs and theirs alone.

The setting for *Geraldine Castleton's* chapter is Australia but the theme addressed is universal. The author systematically and critically examines the way literacy needs are defined by state agencies and professional groups who invariably construct homeless people as deficient and requiring training to reach literacy levels that are assumed to be valued and unproblematic. She shows how literacy can be developed as a social practice based on a curriculum that is relevant because it is rooted in why people *use* literacy rather than why some others think they *need* it.

The power of labelling and its consequences for tutor–student relationships is raised by *Hugo Kerr* in a critique of the literature on developmental dyslexia. He suggests, in a controversial and polemical way, that there is considerable confusion about a definition of dyslexia and indeed about its existence, leading to marked signs of disempowerment or 'learned helplessness' from tutors when faced with a student diagnosed as 'dyslexic'. Developmental dyslexia, it is argued, may be a politically powerful, socially acceptable and sought-after explanation for poor literacy skills. However, it may also be an impediment to learning, leading to reduced confidence, lowered motivation, diminished expectation and passivity from both tutors and students.

The issue of disempowerment and surveillance is raised by *Marcia Fawns and Roz Ivanič* through a consideration of the politics of official forms. They show how form-filling is not just a matter of decoding and spelling, but a complex social practice imbued with issues of identity and power. Drawing on the work of Foucault they suggest that form-filling, through imposing a system of prescribed categories, constitutes a type of self-surveillance whereby our lives are increasingly defined and controlled by such institutionally imposed literacy practices. However, being aware of the ways in which form-filling is imbued with issues of power and identity and taking a critical approach may put power into the hands of even those with the greatest fear and hatred of forms.

The hegemony of literacy for 'human resource development' is structurally powerful and ubiquitous. As *Catherine Kell* points out, the economistic imperative informing government policy in South Africa has replaced the more politically conscious adult literacy that characterised the work of Non-Governmental Organisations in pre-apartheid times. In this context, meaningful literacy learning has been undermined with the result that 'the tail' of literacy outcomes (measured in terms of narrow performance requirements) has been used 'to wag the dog' of literacy practice (teaching to the tests). The argument for a 'third space', between the official versions of literacy and actual literacy use, is made, as a way of recognising cultural difference and creating the capacity for critical thought and action.

The final chapter in this section continues the theme of the uses of literacy in opposition to established practices and ideas by arguing that literacy can contribute to democracy as a *way of life*. Literacy, access to information, and effective communication skills, *Jim Crowther and Lyn Tett* suggest, must be considered as part of the way inequalities of power are systematically reproduced. Literacy education should contribute towards enabling people to interrogate the claims made on their behalf and, in turn, encourage them to develop the skill, analysis and confidence to make their own voice heard. Adult literacy workers with an interest in social purpose have to contest the meaning of citizenship since democracy is too important to be left to the policy makers and politicians. Tutors need to become resources for individuals and collectivities to take some control over their lives by building a broad and rich curriculum that firmly embraces literacy education for democracy.

Repositioning learners and teachers

Working back against powerful forces involves, amongst other things, a repositioning of the 'teacher' and the 'learner'. In contrast to a good deal of literacy work, that starts from individual needs and personal development, the thrust of *Ian Martin* and *Habibur Rahman's* account is with locating adult literacy in the process of collective struggles against inequality and injustice. Drawing on the experience of literacy work in Bangladesh, the authors address how the 'developed' world can learn to link literacy into movements for democratic renewal and social change. Really useful literacy has little in common with dominant understandings of functional literacy that are pervasive in the policy literature. In the rich world, current fashionable interest in lifelong learning and active citizenship have, therefore, much to learn from contexts where the contribution of a politicised understanding of literacy is actually practised and where the meaning is often starker and more visible to see.

If literacy is to be powerful, *Catherine Jamieson* argues that it has to be a resource for less powerful 'communities of interest' to regain some measure of control over their lives. It will involve, in one way or another, inserting literacy into a process of social action and collective organisation. The obstacles to this are often formidable. Narrow definitions of literacy can serve to shackle individuals and groups to a deficit view of themselves and limit their ability to assert, communicate, and act on their own interests with a more positive sense of their identities. The account documents work to develop strategies for people with learning disabilities to acquire a voice and to organise effectively to make their voice heard.

We live in rapidly changing times and this is so clearly evident in the revolution occurring in information technology. The right of access to knowledge, including the infrastructure and use of communication technology, is discussed by *Fiona Frank*. In a world where electronically produced text carries meaning, exclusion from ICT can have disempowering consequences, especially for life in the home, community and workplace. She shows that the developing policy context on literacy and ICT has considerable implications because a good deal of the National Adult Literacy strategy rests on it. This trend, she argues, will have some serious implications on the power relations in the tutor–student relationship and may, in some respects, help to equalise them.

Alan Addison situates literacy in a discourse of cultural politics and how adult learners are positioned negatively by this. He argues that the discourse informing much family literacy work has seen the family as a cultural problem for the school rather than a critical resource for learning. This is more obvious when the vernacular literacy of the home and the dominant literacy of the school are very much at odds with each other. This is a situation experienced in working class communities across Scotland where the 'cultural politics' of the school and those evident in the home and community are sharply divergent. He reflects on work undertaken with adults and primary school children on the creative use of Scots language in order to develop a more relevant and reflexive understanding of literacy practice.

Developing more democratic interpersonal encounters is the theme addressed by *Mary Norton*. She starts from the position that sharing power among teachers and learners is a basic principle of participatory education but illustrates the difficulties that this involves through a detailed account of the organising of a conference with students. A key issue is about sharing power and a framework for understanding power is presented and discussed in terms of 'power-over', 'power-with' and 'power-from-within'. She reflects on how she has applied what she learnt from the conference to practice in the Centre. These include being aware of her personal power and capacity to influence, ensuring that when power is devolved to students they want it, and making explicit the power relations at work within the Centre. Literacy programmes, she concludes, can be places where learners, volunteers and staff experience more equitable power relations.

The theme of 'voice' is continued by *Sue Gardener and Ann Janssen* in the final chapter. They show how bilingual communities are positioned in public policy as having language problems rather than being language resources. Access to public services in multilingual cities is dependent on literacy and language mediators who are at the same time experts and outsiders in the complex process of community interpreting, mediation and advocacy. They argue that the practice of community interpreting and cultural mediation should be respected and developed through research into the way in which texts feature in communicative practices as well as the spoken word. The powerful literacies that are formed within established institutions, they suggest, are a necessary part of an agenda for language and literacy skills that will serve the current social demands of life in the UK.

References

Gee, J. (1990) *Social Linguistics and Literacies: Ideology in Discourses*, London: Falmer Press.

Barton, D. (1994) *Literacy: an Introduction to the Ecology of Written Language*, Oxford: Blackwell.

Barton, D and Hamilton, M. (1998) *Local Literacies: Reading and Writing in One Community*, London: Routledge.

Lankshear, C. with Gee, J.P., Knobel, M. and Searle, C. (1997) *Changing Literacies*, Buckingham: Open University Press.

Melucci, A. (1988) 'Social movements and democratisation of everyday life', in Keane, J. (ed.) *Civil Society and the State*, London: Verso, pp. 245–60.

Street, B. (1996) 'Literacy, economy and society', *Literacy Across the Curriculum*, 12 (3), pp. 8–15.

Tester, N. (2000) 'Blitz on basics', *Guardian Education*, 17 October 2000.

Section One
Theoretical and policy frameworks

2 Contexts for literacy work: the 'new orders' and the 'new literacy studies'

Brian V. Street

Media and government discourses on literacy frequently refer to 'illiteracy' and 'falling standards' and propose ways of 'remediating' the problem, employing approaches to literacy learning that reduce it to isolated units. Alternative discourses that have underpinned much work in adult literacy in the UK over the past two decades include Freirean approaches to 'conscientisation' and 'empowerment' and whole language perspectives on literacy learning (Street, 1996). More recently the New Literacy Studies have proposed theoretical perspectives rooted in critical ethnography and culturally sensitive research, leading to programmes that are negotiated and participatory (Gee, 1991; Heath, 1983; Heath and Mangiola, 1991; Villegas, 1991). I would like to consider these dominant and alternative discourses upon literacy in education in the context of 'new orders' – work, communicative and epistemological. I will then propose that approaches to literacy work be located in terms of new and broader understandings of both literacy and language that take account of these contexts. I begin with a brief account of the 'new orders' within which, I suggest, contemporary work in literacy has to be sited.

The 'new orders': work, communicative, epistemological

What might be termed the 'new orders' – the new work order, the new communicative order and the new epistemological order – require radical rethinking of what counts as literacy. This rethinking is as necessary for academics and researchers as it is for activists and practitioners: whilst the former have to accommodate to the needs of 'knowledge-in-use', the latter are being called upon to take account of knowledge-in-theory.

The new work order

Gee and others (1996; Holland *et al*, 1998), drawing upon the writings of economists and business theorists as well as critical sociologists, have attempted to characterise the new work order associated with globalisation of production and distribution. They consider the implications of these changes for the kinds of language needed in work and in educational contexts. These changes represent the context within which contemporary literacy work is taking place and force us to question the theoretical underpinnings of literacy itself. Work, they suggest, is no longer defined and organised along Fordist lines, with mass production on assembly lines and its Taylorist principles of work organisation and discipline.

> There is now a shift towards forms of production which employ new ways of making goods and commodities, serving more differentiated markets, or niches, through segmented retailing strategies. There is now a great deal more attention paid to the selling environment at every level of production, from design to distribution. So while the old work order stressed issues of costs and revenue, the new work order emphasises asset building and market share. (Gee *et al*, 1996: vii–viii)

Associated with these defining concepts are ideas about proper organisational behaviour, including attention to flexibility and adaptation to change. Procedures are put into place to ensure both flexibility on the one hand and uniformity and guarantee of standards on the other. If consumers are perceived, through market research and company predictions, to demand the same jackets or the same tomatoes in shops across their travelling experience, then mechanisms need to be put into place to ensure that wherever these are produced they conform to those standards. This Total Quality Management (TQM) has been a particular feature of the new work order that has impinged directly on the educational setting. TQM has provided models for quality control there too, imposing reductionist and unitised notions of measurement and of quality on educational outputs and 'products'.

A further organisational change in the new work order that has been of especial significance for language and literacy has been the notion of team working on projects rather than hierarchical forms of organisation that simply pass orders down a chain of command. In the new project-focused work order, all members of a team combine to design, negotiate and develop 'products' for sale and distribution. In order to accomplish this, all members of a team have to be equipped with the discursive skills that such negotiation and development involve, such as ability to present and hear arguments, and to develop material for presentation on communicative devices such as overheads, slide projectors, computer displays, and so on. Radical researchers confronted with these changes have particularly focused on the claims often associated with them that suggest a commitment to democracy. Words like 'collaboration', 'participation', 'devolution' and 'empowerment' – all cherished terms of oppositional groups, such as those working in Freirean literacy campaigns – are now used to indicate a partnership between managers and workers. Gee and his colleagues are highly suspicious of these claims and would have us examine them critically, whilst acknowledging that changes are indeed taking place in both the work order and the communicative demands associated with it. Literacy programmes, then, now need to take account of such shifts and such critiques if they are to handle the complex communicative needs of the new work order.

The new communicative order

A number of writers working in the area of social semiotics and visual design have suggested that in this new context, the reading and writing practices of literacy are only one part of what people are going to have to learn in order to be 'literate' in the future (Kress and van Leeuwen, 1996; Heller and Pomeroy, 1997). They are going to have to learn to handle both the teamwork literacies described above and also the iconic systems evident in many communicative practices. These include the kinds of icons and the signs evident in computer displays like the Word for Windows package, with all its combinations of signs, symbols, boundaries, pictures, words, texts, images et cetera. The extreme version of this position is the notion of 'the end of language' – that we are no longer talking about language in its rather traditional notion of grammar, lexicon and semantics, but rather we are now talking about a wider range of 'semiotic systems' that cut across reading, writing, speech. Kress and van Leeuwen sub-title their book *Reading Images: The Grammar of Visual design* in order to suggest that this new approach to the semiotic order can apply similar 'grammatical' analyses as have been applied to language in its more traditional sense. By this they want to indicate not so much a traditional focus on rules, knowledge of which sets the professional apart from the amateur, but rather grammar as meaning the way in which the people, places and things depicted in images 'are combined into a meaningful whole' (1990: 1). Grammar in this sense is more than a system of rules; it is also a set of possibilities and an active engagement with meaning in which every language user participates. This provides a broader framework for handling questions of literacy and language in both education and the workplace that, again, new literacy programmes are going to have to take into account.

Likewise, Lemke (1998) in a recent edition of *Linguistics & Education* devoted to language and semiotics in education, provides a range of methods for describing and analysing the non-linguistic dimension of learning in maths and science classrooms, museum visits and so on. The authors argue that analysing the semiotic component enables us to 'see' hidden complexities of what children have to deal with; makes explicit processes that are usually implicit; can help explain why some children 'fail'; and can help clarify the cultural dimension of supposedly 'neutral' curriculum and pedagogy. Similar arguments could be used for broadening the range of adult literacy learning and teaching. Indeed, many would argue that such awareness of the non-linguistic has been built into the adult literacy movement from the outset, albeit without the kind of technical apparatus that Lemke, Kress and their colleagues offer.

I would, however, like to enter a warning here: using the term 'literacy', as some of the writers in this field do, in order to encompass these other channels, such as computer literacy or oral literacy, raises a number of problems. Labelling the oral dimension also 'literacy', as Jay does for instance, loses the specificity of the reading and writing dimension. It also loses the methodological advantage of the recent history of new literacy studies for studying those events and practices. It seems to me that if we want to indicate that language, for instance, or literacy as a particular instantiation of language, is always accompanied by/associated with/interwoven with other semiotic practices, such as visual and oral, then it is better to name each of these channels and to find ways of describing the relation between them, than to name them all as 'literacies'. If they are all 'literacies' then we will struggle to differentiate 'literacy' as the reading/writing dimension of a semiotic practice from, say, the oral or the symbolic dimension. Keeping the labels separate conceptually enables us then to describe the nature of the overlaps and the particular hybridity found in, say, maths classrooms, with their mix of notation systems, graphs and diagrams. So I find myself, having argued in favour of a broadening of the term 'literacy', now calling for some narrowing, restricting the term itself to those parts of the communicative repertoire that have traditionally been described as reading and writing. I would like to argue that this strategy has a number of advantages for both research and practice:

- it enables us to see the relationship between reading and writing and other channels, whereas incorporating all of them into the one term 'literacy' hides these internal variations;
- it recognises the continuing social importance of reading and writing in contemporary culture, even amidst the explosion of electronic and visual means of communication;
- it provides a tried and tested language of description that facilitates detailed accounts of varieties of literacy practices;
- it offers a model from the tradition of New Literacy Studies that might then be applied to other channels. This discussion is closely related to the third of the 'orders' I would like to consider, the new epistemological order, in that it entails questioning the very grounds on which we define and learn knowledge in the first place. I will briefly indicate the features of this new 'order' before moving on to consider the implications for theory and practice in the field of literacy.

The new epistemological order

Barnet (1997) and others have referred to crises of knowledge that are leading to a new epistemological order. Within the academy, they suggest, postmodernism and reflexivity have led to a valuing of the local against the universal, including a critique of Enlightenment science and the kind of modernism on which much development work has been founded. Outside the academy, meanwhile, the marketisation of knowledge has likewise led to a challenge to the dominant position previously held by universities as producers and guarantors of knowledge. In this new commercial world knowledge as inert commodity can be bought and sold for profit, measured as though it were inert information, and judged for 'quality' as though it were just another commercial product. As we saw above, 'quality' in the commercial sense now being applied to education refers to the object of knowledge itself but not to the process of learning, questioning and engagement in which receivers relate to it. This new knowledge is based in numerous, non-academic settings, such as large business corporations and leisure industry outlets, for whom the critical perspective of university approaches to knowledge is less important than whether it will sell in the marketplace. The University, then, no longer if it ever did, has a monopoly on the production, guardianship and legitimisation of knowledge.

Faced with this crisis of knowledge from multiple sources, Barnett asks what can be the role of the academy in the new epistemological order. His response is of direct relevance to the projects described in this volume: the role of the researcher is to be that of a 'practical epistemologist', involving critical engagement in real-world projects and action, doing 'participatory' work. At the same time, this involves reworking the university as a forum for debate. This forum offers a discursive space for critique of the bases of knowledge claims and frameworks in ways that for-profit knowledge industries do not. The practical epistemologist engages with knowledge in use, not simply with propositional knowledge, and he or she works *with* partners in real-world contexts in the interests of equity and justice. Combining this task with knowledge of the new work order and of the new communicative order provides the contemporary activist and researcher on literacy with a very different agenda and framework than that envisaged in the modernist era of programmes to 'eradicate illiteracy'.

New literacy studies

The New Literacy Studies (Barton and Hamilton, 1998; Barton, 1994; Gee, 1991; Street, 1984) consist of a series of writings, in both research and practice, that treat language and literacy as social practices rather than technical skills to be learned in formal education. The research requires language and literacy to be studied as they occur naturally in social life, taking account of the context and their different meanings for different cultural groups. The practice requires curriculum designers, teachers and evaluators to take account of the variation in meanings and uses that students bring from their home backgrounds to formal learning contexts, such as the school and the classroom. New Literacy Studies emphasises the importance of 'culturally sensitive teaching' (Villegas, 1991) in building upon students' own knowledge and skills (Heath, 1983; Heath and Mangiola, 1991). The new research and practice are based upon new ideas about the nature of language and literacy and have in turn reinforced and developed these ideas. There are two major tenets to this new thinking:

a)   the notion of 'social literacies';
b)   that language is 'dialogic'.

a) *Social literacies*: this phrase (Street, 1995) refers to the nature of literacy as social practice and to the plurality of literacies that this enables us to observe. That literacy is a social practice is an insight both banal and profound. It is banal, in the sense that once we think about it it is obvious that literacy is always practised in social contexts and that even the school, however 'artificial' it may be accused of being in its ways of teaching reading and writing, is also a social construction. The site of learning, whether school-based or in adult literacy programmes, has, like other contexts, its own social beliefs and behaviours into which its particular literacy practices are inserted. The notion is, in this sense, also profound in that it leads to quite new ways of understanding and defining what counts as literacy and has profound implications for how we learn and teach reading and writing. If literacy is a social practice, then it varies with social context and is not the same, uniform thing in each case.

I have described this latter view as an 'autonomous' model of literacy: the view that literacy in itself has consequences irrespective of or autonomous of context (Street, 1984). In contrast with this view, I have posed an 'ideological' model of literacy, which argues that literacy not only varies with social context and with cultural norms and discourses regarding, for instance, identity, gender and belief, but that its uses and meanings are always embedded in relations of power. It is in this sense that literacy is always 'ideological' – it always involves contests over meanings, definitions and boundaries and struggles for control of the literacy agenda. If that is true, then it becomes harder to justify teaching only one particular form of literacy, whether in schools or in adult programmes – or at least the justification needs to be made explicit. If literacy is seen as simply a universal technical skill, the same everywhere, then the particular form being taught in school gets to be treated as the only kind, as the universal standard that naturalises its socially specific features and disguises their real history and ideological justifications. If literacy is seen as a social practice, then that history and those features and justifications need to be spelled out and students need to be able to discuss the basis for choices being made in the kind of literacy they are learning.

b) *Dialogic language*: new theories of language, closely associated with those regarding social literacies, focus upon the nature of language as a continually negotiated process of meaning-making as well as meaning-taking. In this research tradition, language is viewed as always a social process, as interactive and dynamic (Volosinov, 1973; Hymes, 1977; Halliday, 1978). For Bakhtin (1981), language is both centrifugal and centripetal. By this he means that users are always struggling to extend its boundaries and meanings (the centrifugal perspective), as well as working within prescribed limits (the centripetal view). It is dialogic in the sense that it is always in dialogue – language, even when employed silently by single individuals, is always part of a social interaction, whether with imagined others or with the meanings and uses of words that others have employed at other times and places. As Bakhtin states, 'words come saturated with the meanings of others'. Again this view of language might appear commonsensical at one level – we all know that languages vary, whether that means the differences between French and English, or at a more local level between different dialects, Creoles and Patois. But the implications of this stance, like that of social literacies, are at the same time profound. If language is always contested, negotiated and employed in social interaction, then the appropriateness of particular uses and interpretations have likewise to be opened to debate. It becomes impossible to lay down strict and formal rules for all time, and the authority of particular users – whether teachers, grammarians or politicians – becomes problematised. We all, as it were, take possession of language again rather than being passive victims of its entailments.

Theorists in the New Literacy Studies have tended to root their ideas about reading and writing, as aspects of language, within these broader linguistic theories of a dialogic and constructivist kind. Gee, one of the leading exponents of New Literacy Studies, describes a case study of 'sharing time' in US schools as frequently built upon dominant theories of language that the authors cited above are challenging: 'sharing time, as a literacy building activity, is based solidly on ... a myth: the view of language (deeply embedded in our language and our culture) that meaning is something that is packaged in nice little bundles (words and sentences) and conveyed down a little tube-like channel to someone else who simply undoes the package and takes out the morsel of meaning' (Gee, 1991: 93). In contrast to this atomised view of language that corresponds to the autonomous model of literacy, Gee poses a view of language that corresponds more closely to the ideological model of literacy. From this perspective, language is dynamic in the sense expressed by writers like Bakhtin, Kress and others. 'In fact, language is always something that is actively constructed in a context, physically present or imagined, by both speaker/writer and hearer/reader through a complex process of inferencing that is guided by, but never fully determined by, the structural properties of the language' (Kress and Van Leeuwen, 1996: 28).

Applications

The implications of this view of language are only just being felt in applied studies (*cf* the work and publications of the British Association for Applied Language Studies, BAAL and, of course, the work of RAPAL). With respect to education, these perspectives have recently been conveyed through the notion of critical language awareness (Fairclough, 1995) which argues that learners should be facilitated to engage in debates about the nature and meaning of language, rather than be treated as passive victims of its 'structural properties'. This includes learning some metalinguistic terms, but a more inclusive set of such terms, learned for a different purpose, than those often put forward by State institutions (e.g. the recent Teacher Training Authority proposals for language in the Initial Teacher Training Curriculum and the National Literacy Strategy). I would like to suggest one axis on which these institutions' assumptions about language and literacy differ from those of New Literacy Studies, namely with respect to what counts as 'the basics'.

The National Literacy Strategy sees 'the basics' as surface features of language and literacy, such as rules of grammar in the traditional sense, and rules for phoneme/grapheme relations (Sealey, 1999). The New Literacy Studies, on the other hand, sees 'the basics' as generative, deep structures that facilitate learning and activity, of the dialogic and ideological kind outlined above. Bernstein (1997: 75–6) refers to 'the heart of discourse' as the recognition of ambiguity, creativity, provisionality, recognition of how the rules work, not simply learning of the rules themselves. It is this that lies at the heart of learning and development. In the context of literacy, teaching students to read and write as a set of rules to be learned – rules about sign/sound relationships and about 'phonics' – rather than as a set of possibilities – the ways in which language is always changing and the potential for meaning-making of varieties, across regions and registers – keeps education 'safe'. But this approach undermines its own claims to either equality or access in that it denies students the 'power' to question the rules and procedures and to develop their own uses of language and literacy. Ironically, the current rhetoric of equality and access is currently at its most intense with respect to the communicative requirements of the new work order: here it is precisely the ability of new workers entering the workforce to handle change, ambiguity and variation that employers are asking for. The definition of 'basics' being applied to schooling and to the new adult literacy curriculum, then, contradicts the very possibility of achieving these ends. To the extent that adult literacy schemes are copying schooled practices, as in the Moser Report's recommendations, then adult education too will suffer from the contradictions inherent in the two definitions of 'basics'. Whilst those of us working in New Literacy Studies might agree with politicians and educators that there have to be 'basics' – structures on which learning and activity can be built – we would disagree on content – what counts as basic. Rather than opposing Moser or the National Literacy Strategy outright, many researchers and activists are coming to challenge them at this conceptual level. This involves working in particular to broaden the concept of 'basics' being employed in both child and adult programmes and to shift the view of language from a focus on rules towards a more creative and user-focused approach. This has implications for curriculum, pedagogy and assessment, which many authors in this volume are addressing. I have considered elsewhere these implications with respect to Development (Street, 2000), the National Literacy Strategy (Street, 1999), English in Education (Street, 1997) and Adult Literacy (Street, 1996). The purpose of this chapter has been to put these considerations of practical work in literacy into the broader perspective of what I term the 'new orders' and with respect to the contribution of New Literacy Studies approaches. I hope thereby to have engaged both practitioners and researchers in reflexive debate about these issues and I look forward to continuing the conversation beyond the pages of this book

References

Bakhtin, M. (1981) *The Dialogic Imagination* (ed.) M. Holquist, Austin: University of Texas Press.

Barnett, R. and Griffin, A. (eds) (1997) *The End of Knowledge in Higher Education*, London: Institute of Education.

Barton, D. and Hamilton, M. (1998) *Local Literacies*, London: Routledge.

Barton, D. (1994) *Literacy: An Introduction to the Ecology of Written Language*, Oxford: Blackwell.

Barton, D. and Ivanič, R. (eds) (1991) *Writing In The Community*, Newbury Park, CA: Sage.

Bernstein, B. (1997) 'Social class and pedagogic practice', ch. 2 of *The Structuring of Pedagogic Discourse: vol. IV Class, Codes and Control*, London: Routledge, pp. 63–93.

Fairclough, N. (ed.) (1995) *Critical Language Awareness*, Longman.

Gee, J. (1991) *Social Linguistics: Ideology in Discourses*, London: Falmer Press.

Gee, J., Hull, G. and Lankshear, C. (1996) *The New Work Order: Behind the Language of the New Capitalism*, London: Allen & Unwin.

Halliday, M. (1978) *Language as Social Semiotic*, London: Edward Arnold.

Heath, S.B. (1983) *Ways with Words: Language, Life and Work in Communications and Classrooms*, Cambridge: Cambridge University Press.

Heath, S.B. and Mangiola, L. (1991) *Children of Promise: Literate Activity in Linguistically and Culturally Diverse Classrooms*, Washington DC: NEA/AERA.

Heller, S. and Pomeroy, K. (1997) *Design Literacy: Understanding Graphic Design*, NY: Allworth Press.

Holland, C. with Cooke, T. and Frank, F. (1998) *Literacy and the New Work Order: an International Literature Review*, London: NIACE.

Hornberger, N. (2000) 'Afterword' to *Multilingual Literacies: Reading and Writing Different Worlds* (eds) Martin-Jones, M. and Jones, K., Philadelphia and Amsterdam: John Benjamins.

Hymes, D. (1964) 'Introduction: towards ethnographies of communication', *American Anthropologist,* 66 (6), pp. 1–34.

Hymes, D. (1977) *Foundations in Sociolinguistics*, London: Tavistock.

Kress, G. and van Leeuwen, T. (1996) *Reading Images: the Grammar of Visual Design*, London: Routledge.

Lankshear, C. (1997) *Changing Literacies*, Buckingham and Philadelphia: Open University Press.

Lemke, J. (ed.) (1998) 'Language and semiotics in education', Special Issue of *Linguistics & Education*, 10 (3).

Prinsloo, M. and Breier, M. (eds) (1996) *The Social Uses of Literacy: Case Studies from S. Africa*, Amsterdam: John Benjamins.

Sealey, A. (1999) *Theories about Language in the National Literacy Strategy*, Coventry: Centre for Elementary and Primary Education, University of Warwick.

Street, B. (ed.) (2000) *Literacy and Development: Ethnographic Perspectives*, London: Routledge.

Street, B. (1999) 'New literacies in theory and practice: what are the implications for language in education?', *Linguistics & Education*, 10 (1), pp. 1–24.

Street, B. (1997), 'The implications of the new literacy studies for literacy education', *English in Education*, NATE, 31 (3), Autumn, pp. 26–39.

Street, B. (1996) *Adult Literacy in the UK: a History of Research and Practice*, Commissioned Technical Report for National Center for Adult Literacy, NCAL Technical Report TR95-05, Philadelphia: University of Pennsylvania.

Street, B. (1995), *Social Literacies: Critical Approaches to Literacy in Development, Ethnography and Education*, London: Longman.

Street, B. (1984) *Literacy in Theory and Practice*, Cambridge: Cambridge University Press.

Villegas, A.M. (1991) *Culturally Responsive Teaching*, Princeton: ETS.

Volosinov, V.N. (1973) *Marxism and the Philosophy of Language*, Orlando: Academic Press.

3 Powerful literacies: the policy context

Mary Hamilton, Catherine Macrae and Lyn Tett

Introduction

This chapter offers an overview of the policy context within which the developments described in the rest of this book need to be understood. It focuses on the four countries of the UK and Ireland, but also comments on the wider international scene. It aims to describe briefly the recent history of Adult Basic Education (ABE) in the UK, to compare and contrast developments in the different countries and to identify the main influences that are shaping the field. In 1998 and 1999 new education initiatives in all of these countries raised the profile of, reasserted, or shifted the agenda for literacy programmes. These initiatives, framed with reference to lifelong learning, the knowledge economy and the knowledge society, are set to have a significant influence on practitioners and learners here and may shape future developments elsewhere: in this sense, the literacies they define and promote are powerful literacies. This chapter focuses on the nature of these shifts and their apparent potential to expand or diminish the scope and purpose of literacy programmes.

Some influences on recent ABE policy in the UK and Ireland are international and suggest links with developments in other countries represented in this book as well (for example, South Africa and Australia). The European Union is of obvious importance regionally. A further key influence is the activities of the Organisation for Economic Co-operation and Development (the OECD) and in particular the International Adult Literacy Survey (IALS) which is now routinely cited in government and media publications about adult literacy (OECD, 2000). The OECD has worked with the national governments of its member states to produce a 'league table' of adult literacy standards in each country. The statisticians who have developed the test used in the IALS work with a model of literacy that treats it as a set of unproblematic, information–processing cognitive skills that are independent of the context in which they are used. The test deals primarily with reading and it identifies three dimensions of literacy (prose, document and quantitative literacy). Despite a number of serious critiques of the methodology and validity of the IALS findings (summarised in Hamilton and Barton, 2000), this powerful piece of research has become central to policy discussions. It has framed the terms of the debate, defined the scope and content of 'literacy need', who is deficient in literacy and why, and denied the central role of culture and relationships of power in determining literacy needs and aspirations (see Brian Street in this volume).

In this chapter we begin with brief pen sketches of the history and current situation in each country. The second part is more critical and evaluative. In organising the information about variations in policy we have been guided by four main questions with the aim of getting to the values embodied by a set of practices in ABE which for the most part are only implicitly stated in government documents:

- What concept of literacy underpins recent policies?
- How are learners and teachers positioned by the policies?
- What kinds of learning activities/processes are programmes or initiatives expected to engage in?
- What outcomes are literacy programmes and learners expected to achieve?

Adult basic education in the countries of the UK and Ireland

We use the term United Kingdom here as the generic name for the union of England, Scotland, Wales and Northern Ireland. Each of these countries is currently moving toward greater autonomy, and there are distinctive differences among them in the history and organisation of their educational provision[1] which may well become more pronounced in the near future.

England and Wales

The Right to Read literacy campaign in the early 1970s was the first time that adult literacy was identified as a national policy issue in the United Kingdom. The public awareness campaign was initiated by volunteer activists and supported by politicians and the broadcasting services, especially the BBC. Community, adult and further education throughout the country began to offer 1:1 and small group tuition. (For overviews see Withnall, 1994; Hamilton, 1996; Street, 1997.) A central resource agency for adult literacy (now known as the Basic Skills Agency) was set up by the central government in 1975 with a remit covering both England and Wales. The central resource agency produced materials for students and tutors, organised training events, supported new developments and disseminated good practice.

Now, as in the 1970s and 1980s, the majority of those working in ABE do so in part-time or voluntary posts. There has been, however, growth in the number of paid staff and an increasing emphasis on professionalism.

In the late 1980s, an accreditation framework for ABE (*Wordpower and Numberpower*) was introduced. This established a set of basic skills standards and assessments that continue to be developed. The framework is related to a unified system of national vocational qualifications (NVQs) that are tied to a set of national training targets and quality assurances. This system is designed to provide a means of determining equivalence amid the maze of different vocational qualifications and to bridge the divide between academic and vocational qualifications. Teacher credentials have also been linked with the NVQ system.

The Further and Higher Education Act of 1992 made ABE part of the system of further education in England and Wales which is mainly concerned with providing accredited vocational qualifications. As a result of these developments, ABE has become more firmly established, increasingly formalised and less rooted in the interests and experiences of people in communities. About two-thirds of the approximately 320,000 ABE students in England and Wales (Further Education Funding Council, 1998) now study within further education colleges, and less than a quarter in local authority adult and community-based programmes. This reverses the proportions at the start of the 1990s (BSA, 1997). This reorganisation of practice has been part of a policy focus that seeks to link education more closely with initial education and the economy and to provide clearer measures for evaluation and achievement.

Under the previous Conservative government, the arguments used to justify the need for ABE were framed in terms of global economic competitiveness: creating a skilled workforce rather than an informed citizenry. The European experience counters this to some degree with the concept of social exclusion, arguing that society is threatened by a dispossessed minority who are systematically excluded not only from the good jobs but also from participation in their community. In England, long years of isolation and conflict with its European partners prevented this concept from entering the policy discourse. The 1997 change of government brought the UK more in line with other European countries.

The present New Labour government strongly supports the concept of lifelong learning (Department for Education and Employment, 1998) and concerns about the effects of social exclusion are increasing, as highlighted in a series of important reports (Kennedy, 1997; Tomlinson, 1996; Fryer, 1997). In 1999 the government carried out a major review of Adult Basic Education as part of a National Literacy Strategy addressing the needs of both children and adults (Moser, 1999). The vision behind Moser is of a much tighter, quality controlled system of provision with a core curriculum, new national qualifications, a baseline national literacy test and better teaching training. It uses the language of entitlement (alongside 'functional illiteracy') – but this seems to mean first and foremost an 'entitlement to be assessed', for example through the New Deal Gateway for unemployed people. The plans for the new strategy include national targets for a vastly expanded service with a heavy reliance on computer-based learning technologies for both teacher training and learner provision and the use of local partnerships between different agencies (DfEE, 1999). Better quality and inspection systems are also promised and provision will link with other initiatives to increase adult participation in lifelong learning, such as the University for Industry, all under the control of the new funding agency, the Learning and Skills Council. This integrated approach is designed to avoid the marginalisation of ABE that has limited it – but possibly enabled it to occupy a creative space – so much in the past. Moser's final recommendation is on research, but no link is proposed between research and professional development in the field so there are no mechanisms proposed for this development.

Adult literacy in Wales has been patterned on that in England and is under the remit of the BSA. The main difference has been the inclusion of Welsh as an official language for educational provision, resulting in bilingual materials and tuition. A new National Strategy for Basic Skills in Wales (BSA, 2000) has been written in consultation with Welsh colleagues, and it directly parallels the English literacy and numeracy strategies. Although there are no detectable differences in this document, there are differences in the way the education system operates in Wales that may affect the future shape of ABE, allowing the development of a distinctively Welsh model. Control of education has recently been delegated from the Welsh Office to the new Welsh Assembly. There is a separate Welsh Inspectorate (OHMCI) run on the same lines as the English Ofsted. There is more flexibility and local discretion in school-based literacy teaching strategies and there are no primary school league tables or compulsory literacy hour. A separate curriculum accommodates Welsh language teaching into secondary schools.

Scotland

Adult literacy emerged as a field of work in Scotland as a result of the BBC's 'On the Move' campaign in the early 1970s. Although there was much scepticism that the initiative was as pertinent to Scotland (where educational standards were thought to be superior to the rest of the UK), large numbers of viewers responded, even after programmes went off the air. The Scottish Adult Literacy Agency worked to secure what they describe as 'well established and thriving adult literacy schemes' in virtually all regions. By 1983 there were 17,850 literacy students in Scotland, mainly learning 1:1 with a volunteer tutor in the home or a local centre in programmes organised by local authorities' community education services. Programme organisers found that many learners were more interested in developing writing or numeracy rather than reading. Programmes began to broaden out from their original focus on reading in response to this and tutors and organisers began to develop more adult learning material. Some Regional Councils developed an English as a Second Language provision.

The Scottish Adult Literacy Agency was succeeded by another government-funded body, the Scottish Adult Literacy Unit, and then in the early 1980s by the Scottish Adult Basic Education Unit (SABEU). SABEU encouraged providers to move away from the individualised, remedial model of the early literacy campaign and introduced the term EAL (essential adult learning) alongside the term ABE. These terms were not (as elsewhere) euphemisms for literacy and numeracy but an attempt to encourage councils to develop broader 'positive action' type adult learning programmes covering a range of skills such as life management, confidence building, learning about health issues and learning for democratic participation.

At a time of increasing local government funding cuts, the regional councils generally ignored the advice and continued to provide literacy provision but often as a 'remedial' and temporary adjunct to mainstream community education. Other councils understood the advice as providing a rationale for incorporating their literacy staff and budget into mainstream community education and reversing their commitment to literacy. A small minority of councils continued to expand and develop literacy and numeracy programmes alongside other adult learning within community education.

In the mid-1980s, SABEU was absorbed into the Scottish Community Education Council (SCEC) with accompanying staff losses. Since then, Scotland has not had a national agency responsible for promoting adult literacy. By the end of the 1980s there were wide disparities in the nature and extent of literacy and numeracy provision across different areas of the country and generally programmes continued to rely heavily on volunteer tutors working with individual students, although increasingly these met in centres rather than at home.

By the early 1990s education providers looked to the government for clearer guidance on their role and several developments guided their thinking. New guidance to college principals stated that a poor match between students' literacy skills and course demands should be avoided via better guidance and admission systems, but where these were not fully effective, subject teachers could offer help and if necessary refer the learner to ABE classes. While colleges were being discouraged from taking on a role in literacy, local authorities were allowed to deliver programmes although their duty to provide remained very general. The Further & Higher Education (Scotland) Act laid a new duty on colleges to provide ESOL. At the committee stage of this new Bill, the Secretary of State for Scotland issued a statement to authorities that 'extensive provision of basic skills education and provision for other special groups currently made through the community education services can continue'. Around the same time the Scottish Adult Basic Education Forum (1989–1992) continued to encourage a broad definition of ABE as referring to 'literacy, numeracy *and the other basic skills* necessary for life in a modern society'.

The HMI Report on ABE in all post-school education sectors (SOED, 1993) evaluated a range of provision operating under the title of ABE. Programmes varied from access/return to learn courses to computing, sewing or driving courses. The Report argued that whilst the number of adults with literacy and numeracy difficulties was unclear, it was clear that the majority 'had come to terms with their handicap' and therefore recommended that literacy and numeracy provision become 'an integral and inseparable strand of a much wider educational provision'. Many local authorities responded to the Report by further withdrawing funding from dedicated literacy programmes, reducing staffing levels and prioritising ICT and other 'more attractive' basic skills programmes under the heading of 'Essential Skills'. These changes were also responses to the impending Local Government Reorganisation and the funding constraints it was expected to bring.

By 1998 research quoted in the Convention of Scottish Local Authorities (COSLA) Report (COSLA, 1998) suggested that the numbers of students participating in ABE across all sectors had fallen by at least 40 per cent compared with 1992 figures. Recent research (carried out by the National Development Project referred to below) suggests that there may now be only around 6,000 adult students, the majority in local council organised community education programmes and the remainder in FE colleges and voluntary organisations. The National Development Project's Survey of Programmes (NDP, 2000) suggests that the quality of programmes is as much a matter of concern as their limited capacity. The Project has emphasised that poor capacity and quality need to be understood as an outcome of several factors. These are: the structural variety of adult literacy provision in Scotland over the last 25 years, the lack of specific guidance from the national agencies or government and the uneasy relationship between literacy provision and under-funded local authority services.

The low priority placed on adult literacy and numeracy in Scotland is now being addressed in recent policy developments, with a new visibility within the wider agendas of lifelong learning, social inclusion and active citizenship. A number of recent government documents have referred to adult literacy and basic skills. These include: the review of community education (SOEID, 1998a) and subsequent written guidance to local authorities, the Green Paper on lifelong learning, *'Opportunity Scotland* (SOEID, 1998b), the Strategic Framework for Further Education (Scottish Executive, 1999a) and the Skills Strategy *Skills for Scotland* (Scottish Executive, 1999b). Although these documents have little to say on strategy and policy, local authorities are now expected to produce Community Learning Strategies along with all the relevant partners in their areas (from colleges and voluntary organisations to health agencies and enterprise bodies) incorporating explicit targets for adult literacy and numeracy. A National Development Project, 'Adult Literacies in Scotland', has produced a pack of resources for programme managers and practitioners, *Literacies in the Community* (Macrae, 2000). This pack includes a quality framework with good practice guidelines, as well as guidelines on tutoring and guidance in literacy programmes and on staff development and training. In a policy context which has previously been silent or hostile to adult literacy and numeracy provision, the newly devolved government has just announced a task group, 'Literacy 2000', to provide a focus for the development of national policy and strategy on adult literacy and numeracy.

Northern Ireland

In Northern Ireland provision developed in Further Education Colleges, with each college appointing an adult literacy organiser and group tutors. Volunteer tutors were recruited to provide 1:1 tuition in the college or at home if necessary. ABE provision is still mainly located in the Further Education sector, although since 1990 basic skills support has been offered as part of vocational courses run by recognised training organisations through the Training and Employment Agency (T&EA). Voluntary and community groups together meet a growing need for literacy and ABE provision in the non-formal community sector and ABE is offered in all four prisons in Northern Ireland.

The Adult Literacy Liaison Group (ALLG) was formed by the Northern Ireland Department of Education in 1975 to provide a discussion forum for representatives of agencies and groups involved in adult literacy work such as the library service, broadcasters, prison service, referral agencies. The ALLG and its successor organisation, the Adult Literacy and Basic Education Committee (ALBEC), have supported provision through publishing tutor guides and teaching materials, arranging training courses and promoting the BSA's quality standards for tutors and programmes. In 1999 a Basic Skills Unit for Northern Ireland was established to promote and develop quality provision in basic skills education among adults but to date has established little independent leadership.

Northern Ireland's general approach to education is similar to that followed by the DfEE; the major exception being that Northern Ireland retained the 11+ with the related grammar school system (40 per cent of children having grammar school places). The other schools are known as secondary highs though recently many have renamed themselves as colleges. Most of the schools are denominational and many are single sex. The political context of Northern Ireland, involving long-term conflict between the two religious communities (Catholic and Protestant) and the military involvement of the British State, has prevented much organic change within education.

As in Scotland, Northern Ireland has not in the past had a separate agency responsible for promoting adult literacy. Such policy as has been explicitly developed follows that of England and Wales quite closely. Two main policy documents have been published recently: Sweeney *et al* (1998) report on the findings of the IALS for Northern Ireland and the government Green Paper, *The Learning Age* (DENI, 1998), outlines a strategy for Lifelong Learning. Both parallel the equivalent documents in England. There is an economistic emphasis in the government documents with references to 'basic skills' rather than literacy.

The IALS research report includes an especially commissioned chapter on the literacy skills in the Catholic and Protestant communities showing that 'on all three literacy scales, Protestants had higher mean scores than Catholics'. It also suggests, however, that the gap is declining, with differences less pronounced within the youngest age groups and a mean score among youth in Northern Ireland that is higher than the international average. This literacy differential in the two communities, which has been known for some time, has enabled funding to be sought under the European Union Special Programme for Peace and Reconciliation (EGSA) for a number of community development projects. The sectoral partners mainly concerned with the distribution of this funding for adult literacy support have been the Educational Guidance Service for adults who have always provided the ABE referral service. This funding has often been distributed directly to community development organisations to put together their own forms of support within communities. The focus of the projects funded through this route has been very different from that provided through the FE colleges where the emphasis has been on delivering a pre-set curriculum focused on 'skills' requirements determined mainly by the providers.

Ireland

Ireland has a long history of voluntary literacy schemes. It was not until 1980, however, that a National Adult Literacy Agency (NALA) responsible for developing policy and good practice in adult literacy was created. NALA received government funding in 1985 when the Adult Literacy and Community Education (ALCE) budget was introduced. Subsequently, paid literacy organisers were appointed throughout the country by the Vocational Education Committees (VECs) and funding was made available for group tutoring hours.

The vast majority of literacy tuition still takes place in the locally based VEC schemes and literacy is integrated in other adult education and training programmes. Throughout the 1990s NALA has co-ordinated a programme for training and development for literacy schemes and carried out a national research project on participation and access. In 1999 it hosted an EU project to consult on and develop a quality framework for adult literacy and to address the inconsistencies of provision around the country. The project on quality standards 'revealed a wide interest but lack of consistency in the development and monitoring of standards of ABE. Only the vocational programmes had developed a consistent approach to quality assurance, and approach that encourages self-evaluation' (NALA, 1999). Since 1997, student numbers have risen from 5,000 to 13,000.

Key recent government policy documents are 'Adult Education in an Era of Lifelong Learning' (DES, 1998), the first-ever Green Paper on adult education, and the subsequent White Paper *Learning for Life* published in July 2000; the National Development Plan, 2000–6 and the National Anti-Poverty Strategy, 1999. All give a high priority to adult literacy. The Green Paper argues that 'the most urgent task is that of confronting the literacy problem in Ireland' (p. 8) and suggests that 'education and skill deficiencies must not pose a barrier to any person in accessing a livelihood' (p. 7). This response has been partly a reaction to the IALS survey that pointed to 'Ireland lagging significantly behind other countries (except Poland) in terms of literacy performance' (p. 32). The concept of literacy underpinning these documents has been described by NALA as 'more than functional literacy, trying to embrace the holistic approach but falling short of the critical reflection aspect'. Currently Ireland has low participation rates. The main influences apart from the IALS have been OECD policy and the skilled labour shortages cause by Ireland's booming economy. The White Paper is underpinned by three principles: a systemic approach to lifelong learning, equality and inter-culturalism that recognises the diversity of the population to be served. It also develops the notion of 'lifewide' as well as 'lifelong' learning to emphasis the broad, multidimensional approach that is necessary to support learning in the many situations in which it occurs (DES, 2000).

A comparison of policies addressing four key questions

What concept of literacy underpins recent policies?

In England (and by implication in NI and Wales as well) an earlier discourse of individual rights and welfare in educational and social policy had coexisted with a narrow functional definition of literacy. However, the discourse of human resource development now dominates the literacy agenda with managerial, technicist and corporate notions (see Hamilton, 1996, 1997; Gee *et al*, 1996; Hamilton and Merrifield, 1999). This has resulted in an increasingly standardised definition of literacy that is linked to formal educational structures and methods of assessment at both initial and post-school levels. The new Labour government has overlaid this approach with a rhetoric that draws on concepts of lifelong learning and social exclusion. This reflects an increased sensitivity to European and other international thinking in the field. The vocational rationale is still powerful, however, and the Basic Skills Agency works with a functional definition: '*the ability to read, write and speak in English and use mathematics at a level necessary to function and progress at work and in society in general'*.

The policy emphasis in Northern Ireland generally follows England and Wales, but there is a special concern with community development resulting from civil and religious conflict.

In Scotland, policy and practice have largely been influenced by the same forces as above. However, the concept underpinning literacy may be more open at the moment. The best signals we have of future developments are found in the papers produced by the NDP which acknowledges the value of a socio-cultural approach to literacy and identifies three aspects of community learning: lifelong learning, social inclusion and active citizenship (see *Communities: Change through Learning* (SOEID, 1998a). These may provide a basis for a model of literacy provision that seeks to raise literacy levels through dedicated tuition and community development and recognises both individual and collective gains.

Government documents from Ireland recognise that there are different ways of conceiving of 'literacy' and are careful to avoid the narrowly economistic definitions, arguing for a broader view. Literacy learning is viewed as being not only the acquisition of a technical competence but also the development of the learner in many other ways. NALA, in their response to the Green Paper, state that 'all good adult literacy work starts with the needs of individuals. Literacy involves the integration of listening, speaking, reading, writing and numeracy. It also encompasses aspects of personal development – social, economic, emotional, cultural, political – and it is concerned with improving self-esteem and building self-confidence. It goes far beyond the mere technical skills of communication. The underlying aim of good adult literacy practice is to enable people to understand and reflect critically on their life circumstances with a view to exploring new possibilities and initiating constructive change'.

In its explicit commitments to equality and inter-culturalism (diversity), the Irish strategy is most distanced from the market-driven rhetoric that is otherwise dominant. Ireland currently has the least formally developed state provision of all the countries considered here (still relying largely on voluntary provision) but is arguably the furthest on in defining its future policy strategy for literacy. It is therefore making an interesting leap from a situation that has stayed close to the adult literacy of the 1970s to a contemporary vision that responds to current national and international agendas but avoids the narrowness that has characterised notions of ABE over the past two decades in the UK.

How are learners and teachers positioned by the policies?

The influence of the IALS can be seen in how adult learners are constructed by policy in the different countries. In the IALS adults are treated as one undifferentiated mass of people whose basic skills needs have been defined by experts and who may or may not recognise the difficulties that they face. The assumption made is that people with literacy problems have a deficit that needs to be rectified – primarily because of the needs of the economy. There is a strong tendency for this approach to be reflected in the policy statements that draw upon the IALS findings. The emphasis is on the huge scale of the 'problem' rather than a fine appreciation of its many dimensions in terms of diverse cultural groups and more nuanced understandings of literacies (see introduction to this book). Despite reference to particular target groups and some specific commitment to cultural diversity (e.g. Ireland), the overall impact is an homogenising one that projects an inadequate mass in need of help.

The English documents most strongly follow the IALS in characterising learners as reluctant and deficient recipients who must be lured into programmes designed to address needs they may not yet be aware of. The Moser report (1999: 1.8) states that 'people with difficulties are often understandably reluctant to acknowledge, or are unaware, that they have a problem' and suggests that 'persuasive publicity' will be needed to encourage people into ABE programmes. Ireland is distinctive in that it promotes a student-centred model, reminiscent of England in the 1970s, which emphasises individual student input and negotiation. Students are construed as willing, voluntary participants with rights to determine what they get within an ABE programme and views of what they need. In Scotland, too, the Good Practice Framework produced by the National Development Project (2000) is underpinned by a principle of learner participation in the curriculum.

Teachers are unevenly present in the policy documents. Their role is defined very much in terms of how the learners are seen (joint partners in the learning process or receivers of knowledge). In the English policy documents, the teacher is positioned as technician, rather than as a professional who is to be 'upskilled' through short, prescriptive training programmes; there is sporadic consultation, but no rights to be involved in the process or representative bodies able to put forward the perspectives of practitioners. In Scotland, the NDP consulted extensively but was also hampered by the lack of bodies representing practitioners. Only in Ireland are tutors' needs for professional development and accreditation given top priority and this is in a situation where 85 per cent of tutoring is currently by volunteer staff.

Nowhere do tutors appear as powerful actors shaping ABE provision. The dominant assumption is that a strong, pre-formed framework for delivery is needed to ensure systematic and effective learning, rather than relying on the judgements of securely funded, high-level professional staff.

What kinds of learning activities/processes are programmes or initiatives expected to engage in?

There are big differences between the institutional frameworks of the different countries reviewed here. The institutional possibilities are very wide for ABE. This is unlike almost any other kind of education or training, where there are usually clear-cut institutional affiliations and bases (e.g. school is the only widespread institutional setting available for children's initial education). This is extremely important for understanding the shape of ABE provision and how it might develop (see Hamilton, 1997) and is one of the focal points for policy debate and strategy. The constraints and possibilities for an ABE situated within a formal Further Education college are different from that taking place in a prison setting, a workplace or a community project. The relationships of co-operation and competition between these different agencies are also crucial. In England, Wales and Northern Ireland provision is mainly in the formal FE College sector. In Scotland it is mainly in the LEA-run community education sector staffed by paid tutors and volunteers whilst in Ireland informal volunteer-run programmes are the norm. However, despite these different starting points there is rhetoric common to all the policy documents referring to partnerships between institutions, with local learning plans being formulated by consortia of organisations.

Institutional structures also affect the learning processes that are possible or easy to support. In England, Wales and Northern Ireland most learners are taught in a college setting, either in groups or in open learning centres. There is an increasing reliance on on-line resources, closely structured by the accreditation and curriculum frameworks. In Scotland, tuition is currently mainly 1:1 or in small groups. New guidance to local authorities on community learning strategies and plans emphasises literacy and numeracy in the context of core skills and it is unclear to what extent formal accreditation will be available through the Core Skills Units introduced in the new 'Higher Still' initiative.

In Ireland, tuition is also 1:1 and in small groups, supported mainly by volunteer tutors. Control of programmes is still very light and de-centred. Tutors are seen as being in partnership with students and are encouraged to carry out self-assessments, and there is a concern to develop robust consultation processes. A learner-centred approach is advocated with built-in progression opportunities, including accreditation. Participation for learners is voluntary and there is an emphasis on the importance of guidance and flexibility of learning opportunities. Future plans include family literacy programmes, an adult ICT Basic Skills programme, and use of TV and radio for both awareness raising and tuition.

All countries are under pressure to develop on-line learning rather than face-to-face contact with tutors and other students. This trend, plus decisions about formal versus community-based informal learning provision are key issues in determining the nature of the learning process that will be common in the ABE of the future. What may at first glance seem to be simple technical decisions, made for reasons of efficiency and easy dissemination and monitoring of programmes, have important consequences also for the kinds of learning activities that adults can engage in. In particular the content and curriculum of literacy learning and the motivational and social aspects of learning will be influenced by a greater reliance on the use of information technologies. There is presently little evidence that governments are considering these consequences of their decisions. Neither is there much discussion of other measures that can be taken to develop and support a literate culture, for example through a more comprehensive language policy (see Lo Bianco and Freebody, 1997) or through supporting local resources for informal learning, rather than concentrating solely on expanding formally structured learning opportunities to develop literacy (see Hamilton, 2000).

What outcomes are literacy programmes and learners expected to achieve?

In all countries, the IALS is used to justify the need for increased participation rates in education and training with the ultimate aim of achieving increased levels of literacy/numeracy in the population. In England and Wales these aims are realised with target numbers to be met by specific dates.

In England and Wales, there is a very strong emphasis on standardised tests and learner qualifications that fit with the National Vocational Qualification system and will follow seamlessly from the Key Skills now embedded within initial education. Quality standards and accountability to funders are also important outcomes. In addition to these outcomes, in Northern Ireland, conflict reduction and mutual understanding are goals of the European Union Peace and Reconciliation funding. Whilst the placement of ABE in the formal, Further Education sector results in an emphasis on vocational outcomes, there is currently no real consistency or close monitoring of outcomes and a reliance on self-assessment on the part of providers.

In Scotland, a number of different outcomes are signalled as being important for the future. As well as targets for increased participation rates and increased levels of literacy/numeracy in the population, the value placed on social inclusion and active citizenship may well lead to important outcomes that are collective and social rather than primarily individual and vocational. The policy also refers to targets for participation and literacy and numeracy as core skills, implying that programmes should be accredited.

In Ireland, empowerment and critical reflection and the fulfilment of individual needs are at the forefront of NALA's strategic vision. The new adult education strategy foregrounds equal opportunities and cultural diversity and a systemic approach to lifelong learning, and collective as well as personal advancement. There is a concern for progression, and flexible learning and accreditation opportunities, quality and greater consistency of learning opportunities.

Discussion

It is possible from the detail offered above to draw out some main themes that will determine the shape of the ABE of the future.

A renewed policy interest in ABE prompted by international influences

As a service mandated by legislation, ABE now has a secure funding and institutional base in England and Wales. Scotland, NI and Ireland have yet to achieve this security but in all the countries there is currently a renewed policy interest in and commitment to ABE and priority is being given to improving the quality, extent and coherence of provision. Things are changing swiftly in all four countries and it is important to understand where the impetus for this change is coming from and who is involved in shaping the future of ABE in these countries. The publication of the International Adult Literacy Survey 'league tables' for international literacy and numeracy rates has played a major role in the drive to increase participation rates in the adult population with a corresponding deficit view of people's existing capabilities. The IALS survey has to be seen as part of broader OECD and EU influences which are also reshaping the larger schooling and training system as part of an agenda of human resource development (Hamilton and Barton, 2000). This agenda emphasises both literacy and lifelong learning for their assumed contribution to economic prosperity and aims to integrate basic skills provision across all educational and training sectors. The result is the strongly controlled and narrowly focused approach to literacy and numeracy evident in all the countries reviewed here.

The marketisation of literacy: standardising frameworks

One consequence of the renewed interest in literacy is a common concern with the quality, consistency and coherence of provision and accountability to public funders. In England and Wales a substantial part of the new funding so far released is being used to put in place a standardised national curriculum and tests for adult literacy, underpinned by a limited and limiting standards framework. Despite the new rhetoric of social inclusion and citizen participation, this system is driven by a market ideology and a vision of the needs of global economic competitiveness. The imperative is to create a skilled workforce and an active consumer, rather than an informed citizen. It is based on a top-down definition of literacy where need is defined for learners rather than negotiated with them on the basis of their perceived needs. However subtle and flexibly designed the curriculum is, it cannot transcend this fundamental feature: it is designed for learners rather than with them or by them. To this extent, the more open and humanistic possibilities of a lifelong (and lifewide) system of learning opportunities for literacy are weakened and obscured.

Ideological and structural dominance of the English system

Despite the histories of each country which reveal diverse approaches to literacy and the organisation of ABE, the dominance of the English educational and policy frameworks both structurally and ideologically are evident across the UK. ABE in England is still the most systematised and narrowly defined first and foremost as part of education or training (rather than a social or community development issue). This vision also drives mainstream developments in Northern Ireland and Wales and is in contrast to the community development approach which has figured most strongly in Scotland and the EU-funded projects in Northern Ireland targeted at improved conditions within the religious communities.

The discourse of the national adult literacy agency in Ireland is still reminiscent of that prevalent in the 1970–80s with a strong emphasis on individual rights to literacy and an emancipatory goal, though with less emphasis on mutual learning and support or collective outcomes. As the present international pressures come to bear on the field more strongly, the impulse toward conformity will increase. The contrary trend of devolution of political power to individual countries and regions is the main assurance against this happening and the future shape of ABE will be one test of the robustness of the autonomy that has been achieved.

The role of the ABE professional

In none of these settings does there appear to be a strong professional voice moderating the official policy agendas. This is in contrast to what has happened in school-based reforms over the past 10 years, where teachers have influenced the development of new assessments and curricula. The reasons for this are clear: a fragmented and low status workforce, including many volunteers and part-time workers; lack of training and no representative professional associations or stable networks that could develop such bodies. This means that ABE practitioners are ill equipped to move into more powerful positions in the expanded provision that is currently envisaged. They are used to working creatively 'in the cracks' with inadequate funding or formal structures that do not support the understandings that they have gained from their experience about what good practice entails. However, they are not used to being involved in the wider processes of policy formation or designing structures that can work, to arguing their case in public or systematically documenting their achievements.

There also appears to be little influence from educational or organisational research about learning and literacy. This means that the imperatives of the economic arguments advanced by both national and international bodies tend to claim undisputed sway over policy rationales in the field of ABE. Recent research by Thomas Sticht (2000) suggests the dangers and insecurities of this situation. He argues that new evidence in the US suggests that developed industrial nations may be facing a 'literacy surplus' rather than a deficit in terms of work-related skills and that this undermines arguments for the expansion of adult literacy on the grounds of human resource development needs. He suggests that the implications of this are that policies must argue on the basis of the wider benefits and rights of the population to literacy and play down the employment connection. For such alternative arguments to have persuasive force in policy circles, they need to be well articulated and based on a coherent model of literacy such as that advanced by the research work of the New Literacy Studies (see Street, this volume).

The role of national agencies

A key issue is the role of the national agencies in the policy development process. In Ireland, NALA sees itself as operating by carrying out consultations with learners and students and feeding these back to government, in order to help develop high quality literacy programmes including tutor training and the provision of a referral service. The role of the Basic Skills Agency in England and Wales, however, is seen as being much more top-down and there is a very real danger that the corporatist vision of ABE promoted by international bodies like the OECD will come to dominate the UK at the expense of more locally defined and appropriate responses. It will be particularly interesting to see what kind of infrastructure Scotland adopts in its new policy and how far it can preserve local autonomy in this process.

Models of the consultation process

Models for consultation are available from the NALA project on quality (see Bailey, 2000) and from the Equipped for the Future project in the US (Merrifield, 1998). The pace of change is such that it is difficult to engage in a proper consultation process, even where respect for the rights of students and teachers to be involved is a strong core value. This difficulty is exacerbated where there are no, or only weak, mechanisms for consultation and few opportunities for collective voicing of opinion. Consortial partnerships are not the same as a democratic consultation process, as democratically accountable bodies like the LEAs have only a marginal role to play in them and there are no existing organisations that can represent either staff or learner views.

Conclusion

In Scotland and Ireland especially, and in community-based literacy in all countries, there is evidence of attempts to build in respect for some of the core values of ABE within transparent, consistent frameworks for improving access and quality in the context of a consultative and empowering policy process. How powerfully these values will be represented in the ABE of the future depends on the larger social policy context in each country and the possibilities for democratic control of the policy process. As always, there are competing policy discourses that may pull adult literacy in different directions. In this case, the lifelong learning, active citizenship and social inclusion agendas, if they are creatively and critically understood, offer possibilities for more open definitions of literacy than the human resources development model still dominant within initial education.

This is a moment of opportunity for ABE in the UK and in Ireland in which we can build on our history of participatory approaches to adult learning, the strong tradition of voluntary associations, and new research which can underpin and justify a broadly based and sustainable approach to practice (see Street, 1995; Barton and Hamilton, 1998). It remains to be seen how the different perspectives of potential learners, students, providers and policy makers will be heard about what adult literacy and numeracy are, where they stand in relation to other aspects of lifelong learning and in what ways they will contribute to the vision of the countries of the UK and Ireland as dynamic learning societies.

In developing the field of ABE, individual countries can exert a strong national steer, but this will inevitably be within a wider framework of interconnected social polices and international agendas. As practitioners and researchers we need to understand this complexity and how it shapes day-to-day practice and funding opportunities. We need to be clear about where our commitments and underpinning values and assumptions about literacy lie, and skilful in articulating these within the policy arena.

Acknowledgements

We are grateful to the following individuals and organisations who provided us with information for this chapter: Judy Pringle of Young Help Trust, Belfast; Inez Bailey, NALA; Julia Clarke, Open University and NALA/SOCRATES project; Sylvette Jones, Coleg Menarc.

Note

As the National Literacy Trust has pointed out, the national press tends to write as if every utterance of the English DfEE were statutory throughout the UK. But the Department for Education and Employment only deals with education in England; in Wales its equivalent is the Education Department within the Welsh Office; in Scotland it is The Scottish Office Education and Industry Department; and in Northern Ireland it is the Department of Education for Northern Ireland (DENI). Each of these departments has a different approach to education and therefore may use some different terminology to describe the various policy initiatives, programmes and sectors; this is particularly so in Scotland (see www.literacytrust.org.uk/Update; Clark and Munn, 1997; Cantor and Roberts, 1995).

References

Bailey, I. (2000) 'Ireland's evolving quality framework for ABE: an account of NALA's piloting process', *RaPAL Bulletin*, 41, Special Issue on Quality, pp. 17–22.

Barton, D. and Hamilton, M. (1998) *Local Literacies: A Study of Reading and Writing in One Community*, London: Routledge.

Basic Skills Agency. (1997) *Annual Report 1996/7*, London: BSA.

Basic Skills Agency (2000) *Improving Standards of Literacy and Numeracy in Wales: A National Strategy*, London: BSA.

Cantor, L. M. and Roberts, I. F. (1995) *Further Education Today: a Critical Review*, 3rd edn, London: Routledge and Kegan Paul.

Clark, M. M. and Munn, P. (eds) (1997) *Education in Scotland: Policy and Practice from Pre-School to Secondary*, London: Routledge.

COSLA (1998) *Promoting Learning – Developing Communities*, Edinburgh: COSLA

Department of Education for Northern Ireland (1998) Green Paper *The Learning Age,* Belfast: DENI.

Department for Education and Employment (1998) *The Learning Age: a Renaissance for a New Britain*, London: The Stationery Office.

Department for Education and Employment (1999) *Better Basic Skills*, London: The Stationery Office.

Department of Education and Science (1998) 'Adult education in an era of lifelong learning', Green Paper on *Adult Education*, Dublin: Stationery Office.

Department of Education and Science (2000) White Paper on Adult Education, *Learning For Life*, Dublin: Stationery Office.

Fryer, R. (1997) *Learning for the Twenty-First Century: First Report of the National Advisory Group for Continuing Education and Lifelong Learning* (NAGCELL1. PP62/3111634/1297/33), London: Government Stationery Office.

Further Education Funding Council (1998) *Basic Skills Curriculum Area Survey Report*, London: Government Stationery Office.

Gee, J., Hull, G. and Lankshear, C. (1996) *The New Work Order: Behind the Language of the New Capitalism*, Sydney and Boulder, CO: Allen & Unwin and Westview Press.

Hamilton, M. (1996) 'Adult literacy and basic education' in Fieldhouse, R. (ed.), *A History of Modern British Adult Education*, Leicester: National Institute of Adult Continuing Education.

Hamilton, M. (1997) 'Keeping alive alternative visions' in Hautecoeur, J.P. (ed.), *ALPHA 97: Basic Education and Institutional Environments*, Hamburg, FRG: UNESCO Institute for Education, and Toronto, Canada: Culture Concepts.

Hamilton, M. (2000) *Sustainable Literacies and the Ecology of Lifelong Learning*, paper presented at the Global Colloquium for Lifelong Learning, www.ou.lifelonglearning

Hamilton, M. and Barton, D. (2000) 'The International Literacy Survey: what does it measure?', *International Journal of Education*, UNESCO, Hamburg.

Hamilton, M. and Merrifield, J. (1999) 'Adult basic education in the UK. Lessons for the US', Commissioned Review Article in *National Review of Adult Learning and Literacy*, 1 (1), National Center for the Study of Adult Language and Literacy, San Francisco: Jossey-Bass.

Kennedy, H. (1997) *Learning Works: Widening Participation in Further Education*, Coventry: Further Education Funding Council .

Lo Bianco, J. and Freebody, P. (1997) *Australian Literacies: Informing National Policy on Literacy Education*, Melbourne: National Languages and Literacy Institute of Australia.

Mace, J. (ed.) (1995) *Literacy, Language, and Community Publishing: Essays in Adult Education*, Clevedon: Multilingual Matters.

Macrae, C. (1999) *Literacy and Community Education: Adult Literacies in Scotland. Project Paper 1*, Edinburgh: Scottish Office.

Macrae, C. (2000) *Literacies in the Community: Resources for Practitioners and Managers*, Edinburgh: Scottish Executive, Enterprise and Lifelong Learning.

Merrifield, J. (1998) *Contested Ground: Performance Accountability in Adult Basic Education, NCSALL Report No. 1*, Cambridge, Mass: National Center for the Study of Adult Learning and Literacy.

Moser, C. (1999) *A Fresh Start: Improving Literacy and Numeracy*, London: Department for Education and Employment.

National Adult Literacy Association (1999) *NALA-SOCRATES Project Evolving Quality Framework for Adult Basic Education*, Dublin: NALA.

National Development Project (2000) *Good Practice Guidelines*, Edinburgh: Scottish Executive, Enterprise and Lifelong Learning.

Organisation for Economic Cooperation and Development (2000) *Literacy in the Information Age*, Paris: OECD.

SOED (1993) *Alive to Learning*, Edinburgh: HMSO.

SOEID (1998a) *Communities Change Through Learning*, Edinburgh: Scottish Office.

SOEID (1998b) *Opportunity Scotland. A Paper on Lifelong Learning*, Edinburgh: Stationery Office.

Scottish Executive (1999a) *Strategic Framework for Further Education*, Edinburgh: Scottish Office.

Scottish Executive (1999b) *Skills for Scotland. A Skills Strategy for a Competitive Scotland*, Edinburgh: Scottish Office.

Sticht, T. (2000) *Are We Facing a Literacy 'Surplus' in the Workforces of the United States and Canada?*, Research Note 3/21/00, e-mail 10 August 2000.

Street, B. (1995) *Social Literacies: Critical Approaches to Literacy in Development, Ethnography and Education*, London: Longman.

Street, B. (1997) *Adult Literacy in the U.K.: A History of Research and Practice*, National Center for Adult Literacy Policy Paper Series, Philadelphia: University of Pennsylvania.

Sweeney, K., Morgan, B. and Donnelly, D. (1998) *Adult Literacy in Northern Ireland*, Belfast: Northern Ireland Statistics and Research Agency.

Tomlinson, S. (1996) *Inclusive Learning: Report of the Learning Difficulties and/or Disabilities Committee*, London: The Stationery Office.

Withnall, A. (1994) 'Literacy on the agenda: the origins of the adult literacy campaign in the United Kingdom', *Studies in the Education of Adults*, 26 (1), pp. 67–85.

Useful contacts

For information on Ireland: National Adult Literacy Agency (NALA), 76 Lower Gardiner Street, Dublin 1. Tel: (01) 855 4332; Fax: (01) 855 5475; e-mail nala@iol.ie; Web: http://www.iol.ie/~nala

For information on England and Wales: Basic Skills Agency (BSA), Commonwealth House, 1–19 New Oxford Street, London WC1A 1NU, UK. Access to all BSA publications and many other sources referred to in this chapter is provided by the agency's resource centre Web site: [http://www.ioe.ac.uk:library/bsa.html]. Institute of Education Library and Media Services, 20 Bedford Way, London WC1H 0AL, UK.

For information on Northern Ireland: Adult Literacy and Basic Education Committee (Northern Ireland). Contact Hilary Sloan, 344 Stranmills Road, Belfast BT9 5ED. Tel: 0213 268 2379. Adult Basic Skills Resource Centre: c/o Young Help Trust, 23–31 Waring Street, Belfast BT1 2DX. Tel: 01232 560120; fax: 01232 530016; e-mail: [adultbasic@unite.co.uk].

For information on Scotland: Community Learning Scotland (CLS), Rosebery House, 9 Haymarket Terrace, Edinburgh, Scotland EH12 5EZ. Tel: 0131 313 2488; fax: 0131 313 6800; Web site: [http://www.communitylearning.org]. Scottish Executive, Enterprise and Lifelong Learning Department, Adult Literacy 2000, Europa Building, 450 Argyle Street, Glasgow G2 8LG. Tel: 01412 420219; fax 01412 420251; Web site: [http://www.scotland.gov.uk/who/elld/alt.asp].

Department for Education and Employment, Lifelong Learning Web site: [http://www.lifelonglearning.co.uk].

For information about European Basic Skills [Eurobasic skills site: http://www.eurobasicskills.org/].

Federation of Worker Writers and Community Publishers, PO Box 540, Stoke-on-Trent ST6 6DR, England. Web site: [http://www.fwwcp.mcmail.com]. Useful for links with writers' groups and community publishing projects around the country.

Further Education Development Agency, Dunbarton House, 68 Oxford Street, London W1N 0DA, UK. Web site: [http://www.feda.ac.uk]. For access to policy information and downloadable publications.

Further Education Funding Council (FEFC). Web site: [http://www.fefc.ac.uk]. For access to policy information and downloadable publications.

Further Education National Training Organisation (FENTO) for information on professional development and qualifications in ABE.

Gatehouse Books, Hulme Adult Education Centre, Stretford Road, Manchester M15 5FQ, UK. Tel: 0161 226 7152.

Lancaster Literacy Research Group, c/o Department of English and Modern Languages, Lancaster University, Lancaster LA1 4YL, UK. Web site: [http://www.literacy.lancaster.ac.uk].

London Language and Literacy Unit, Southwark College, Southampton Way, London SE5 7EW, UK. For publications on ESOL and family literacy.

Macrae, C., Literacy and Community Education: Project Paper 1 Adult Literacies in Scotland. Scottish Office.

National Association for Teaching English and Other Community Languages to Adults (NATECLA), South Birmingham College, 520–524 Stratford Road, Birmingham B11 4AJ, UK. [Regular journal: *Language Issues*].

National Institute of Adult Continuing Education (NIACE), 21 De Montfort Street, Leicester LE1 7GE, UK. Web site: [http://www.niace.org.uk]. For publications: www.niace.org.uk/publications.

National Literacy Trust, 59 Buckingham Gate, London SW1E 6AJ, UK. Web site database and information service: [http://www.literacytrust.org.uk]. E-mail: [contact@literacytrust.org.uk].

Research and Practice in Adult Literacy (RaPAL), Old School, Main Street, Tilton-on-the-Hill, Leicester LE2 9LF, UK. Web site: [http://www.literacy.lancaster.ac.uk.rapal/RaPAL/htm].

UNISON Centre, 137 High Holborn, London WC1 IV6PL, UK. For information on trades union education.

Workplace Basic Skills Network, c/o Fiona Frank, CSET, Lancaster University, Lancaster LA1 4YL.

Write First Time. Archive 1975–1985. Contact the Librarian, Ruskin College, Oxford University, Oxford. Student-published newspaper.

Section Two
Reflecting on power

4 Signatures and the lettered world

Jane Mace

To be able to write your own name is the first literacy ambition. To begin with, you copy it, forming the letters. Later, when it comes easy, you doodle a little, play with a different way of crossing the *t* or looping the *g*. You are writing your name independently. You may even be able to do it in front of witnesses. This written version of your name, at another time, might have appeared in a public register and formed the basis of a calculation as to how many people in your village could read and write. It is evidence that yours is a hand capable of manipulating pen or pencil and therefore of writing other signs and symbols, like a tick on a voting slip. It signifies that you are a person who can scribe your self on a page without recourse to your thumb.

When I stop to think about it, I seem to have been puzzling about the meaning of signatures for some time. In 1994, when I was invited to give a keynote speech at a national conference on adult literacy in Australia, this was the topic that I worked on. I wanted to have another look at the ways in which literacy achievement is measured, and the strange concept of using marriage register signatures as a measurement tool for literacy would not leave me alone (Mace, 1995). In the course of thinking about those things, I was reminded of the many ways in which the signature features in public and private settings – often, in fact, signals an overlap between the two. During that time, too, I had begun my own kind of historical research, seeking out accounts from living memory of the literacy lives of mothers bringing up children in the late nineteenth/early twentieth centuries (later published in Mace, 1998); and among many stories, came pictures of women who kept autograph books. Reading about and visiting literacy programmes in African countries for the first time a couple of years later helped me to think about *franchise* and literacy, the difference between the print of a thumb and the mark of a pen. So it is that in this chapter, I have chosen to bring together some of these lines of thought and invite you to consider with me the different meanings that signatures and name-writing hold in the lettered world of the early twenty-first century. At a time when the technologies of writing allow us to transmit texts in all kinds of fonts and formats across great distances in a matter of seconds, it continues to be (I suggest) a literacy practice which has a deeply symbolic importance as a tool for empowerment.

I begin with some examples of how the signature has featured in the work of historians. I then consider what it means as a form of writing which is different from simply writing a name, and what that means for the owner of the name. By the end, I want to have shown you that the act of writing a signature remains a donation: the gift of our consent, agreement and commitment.

The historian

From the mid-1800s until the early twentieth century, one source above others was used as an indicator of literacy: the marriage register. Throughout Europe, the practice of recording a marriage in a register had been prevalent since the sixteenth century, but only from the early nineteenth century did it become common to require that both bride and groom should write their names on it (Houston, 1988: 123). The first national report on literacy in England, made in 1840, was based on statistics of signatures in marriage registers. On this evidence, it concluded that 67 per cent of males and 51 per cent of females were literate (Altick, 1983: 170). Today, as then, we have serious misgivings about a signature being an indicator of any such thing. But it is worth considering today what attractions it had then.

To discover the extent of literacy in a past beyond living memory historians have had to rely on what has been written: school attendance figures, sales of published writing, autobiographies, and so on. They may also, in the case of some European countries, turn to data provided by self-assessments – a source which can only ever tell part of the story. If you or I opened our door to a stranger asking if we could or could not read and write, our answer would have been a chosen version of a very relative matter, coloured by the mood we happened to be in, what we were in the middle of doing, when the questioner arrived, and so on. The likelihood of the answer being anything near an objectively measurable 'truth' seems to be fairly remote. No wonder that historians read statistics based on these statements with caution. How much more straightforward must the signature on a register appear. It is, surely, authentic evidence of at least the writer's ability to write his or her own name. But of course, it will say no more than that; and in fact, as a measure of literacy, it says almost nothing. Even if it can suggest the ability to read and write, the signature cannot tell the reader whether the writer actually *did* either of these things. Being able to write your name on one occasion, as well, does not mean you could write it again. In addition, in the absence of any witnesses who could confirm this either way, it's impossible to know how many people *copied* their name. (In seventeenth- and eighteenth-century France, it was apparently common for the writing teacher to copy out the pupil's name on a slip of paper so that it could be copied when the need arose: a *modèle* (Houston, 1988: 126). 'The task of signing the marriage register', writes David Vincent,

> was the only examination the great majority of the population would ever face. Those who signed displayed both their identity and their independence; those who did not remained anonymous until the register was completed by another hand. (Vincent, 1993: 21)

'Anonymous' – well, not to those who were there, of course. To the witnesses, family, friends and spouse, the groom or bride who picked up the pen and made a cross on the page was very much a person with an identity, a history and a future. It is to the rest of us, those not present, examining the records, that this person lacks existence.

In unlettered company, the question of whether you could or could not write your name, compared to other abilities, may have little importance. For researchers reading such signatures from within another time and place, there is a deceptive simplicity about them. The signature, we assume, must be the writing of someone who can write his or her name. But what of the cross, or mark? Is that always the sign of someone who cannot? Or might it be possible, just occasionally, to think that a person who could write their name actually chose to pretend that they could not? In a culture that prizes literacy, we might find that surprising. Yet here is a story in which, apparently, a woman did just that.

On the one hand, there are the 'facts'. In 1852, it seems, the parish of St Albans in Hertfordshire had a population of 18,000 men, women and children. Of the couples who got wed that year, apparently, just over half signed their names, and just under half signified their names with a mark or cross (Stephens, 1987: 324). Now for the 'fiction'. It is the description of a scene which, by coincidence, is set in a village church not far from St Albans, at a time (by chance) just a year or two earlier than 1852. The scene is observed through the eyes of someone called Esther:

> The bridegroom, to whom the pen was handed first, made a rude cross for his mark; the bride, who came next, did the same. Now, I had known the bride when I was last there, not only as the prettiest girl in the place, but as having quite distinguished herself in the school; and I could not help looking at her with some surprise. She came aside and whispered to me, while tears of honest love and admiration stood in her bright eyes. 'He's a dear good fellow, miss; but he can't write, yet – he's going to learn of me – and I wouldn't shame him for the world!' Why, what had I to fear, I thought, when there was this nobility in the soul of a labouring man's daughter!

This episode occurs in *Bleak House*, the novel which Charles Dickens published between 1852 and 1853 in 19 monthly parts. For Dickens (through the character of Esther) its dramatic interest lies not so much with the groom's 'rude cross' but with that of his bride. Here is a woman who is able to write her name but yet who is choosing to pretend that she cannot. Here, as he put it, is the 'noble soul' of a labourer's daughter covering up for her man's illiteracy. Here, too, however, is a marriage register mark which has to be read, not as the sign of an illiterate, but as that of a literate pretending illiteracy; and if one person might have done that, what are we to think of the rest of the writing in that register?

Another story adds possibilities to this one. Among the Mass

Observation Archive writers who contributed to my own research on the literacy lives of mothers rearing children in the late nineteenth/early twentieth centuries, one recalled contrasting uses of signature and mark by the same woman. Her grandmother, she recalled, married in 1896 and signed the marriage register. A year later (in 1897), the same woman registered the death of her mother. This time, she did not give her signature, but made the mark of a cross on the register. The woman who had been born in 1874 of an 'extremely poor' family had grown up in Lancaster, later moving to Manchester. The question which intrigued her granddaughter was: why did she write her name one year, and the next resort to a mark? These were her speculations on the matter:

Either

1. she hadn't learned to write her married name, or
2. she was too shocked and upset to write, or
3. she did not want to put her name to what was on the death certificate (it was not all correct information).
    (J931 quoted in Mace, 1998: 114)

As for the *Bleak House* scene, it appears that Dickens was (as so often) echoing a prevailing concern of his time. Victorian researchers had their own doubts about the validity of signatures:

> There was some concern that the pressures surrounding the marriage ceremony might cause a literate bride or groom to make a mark out of nervousness, or out of fear of embarrassing an illiterate spouse. (Vincent, 1993: 17)

David Vincent, in reporting this, goes on to say why he does not share this concern – and would presumably read the actions of Dickens' 'noble soul' as a fiction in the full sense of the word. In a closely argued chapter on family literacy in the early nineteenth century, he rejects the association of shame with illiteracy – largely on the grounds that illiteracy was too ordinary to carry any stigma:

> In households, in the informal relationships in the neighbourhood, literate and illiterate were everywhere in each other's company. (1993: 23)

– and evidently, marriage ceremonies were no exception. From an analysis of signatures and marks in marriage registers between 1839 and 1854, Vincent found that while only three out of ten newlyweds could sign their name, as many as three in four weddings managed to include at least one literate individual in the ceremony. Witnesses to marriages, Vincent argues, are as important to the literacy historian as the bride and groom themselves. Using a study of witness marks and signatures, he looked to see if there was evidence that literate spouses felt they should avoid illiterate witnesses. Instead of finding this, he found literate couples accepting illiterate witnesses as often as he found illiterates seeking out literates (*ibid*: 31–32). 'The issue of embarrassment,' he concluded, 'was not as acute as observers sometimes assumed' (1993: 17).

We cannot be sure either way. To confuse the picture still further, here is a story cited by Richard Altick. He writes of W.I. Sargant, a Victorian commentator who was concerned at the high number of marks in marriage registers as a valid measure of literacy. Like Dickens, Sargant suggested sentimental reasons for someone who could write to disguise their literacy – this time, with a different gender slant. In the 1867 *Journal of the Statistical Society* Sargant suggested that when a literate man took an illiterate bride 'he chivalrously wrote his X instead of his name to save her embarrassment' (Altick, 1983: 170).

The owner of the name

So far I have been exploring a little of the mystery behind the apparent simplicity of signatures as a measure of literacy. Far more mysterious than this, I believe, is the personal significance of being able to write our own name. Given the opportunity, we learn young to make marks and draw, later – with help – turning these into the shapes and lines which might, later still, correspond to our own names. Once we can do this, many of us repeat the experience over and over again, in idle moments during lessons or meetings – copying, re-copying, trying out styles and shapes until we find the one that pleases us. But what if we find ourselves unable to do it, *and others can*? What, then, might be our sense of loss? Ursula Howard has a suggestive answer. In her study of self-educated working class women and men in the nineteenth century, she writes of the determination (and evident loneliness) of some of these individuals to teach themselves, in the absence of any other teachers. Reflecting on their autobiographical writing, she concludes:

> The self who lived without a signature and without a voice in a lettered world was a different self than one who could write. (Howard, 1991: 107)

For any one of us who happens to have grown up in a society full of writing, she suggests, to be unable to write our own name is equivalent to being unable to inscribe our selves in that society; for to write our names is to write our selves into the world.

If, on the other hand, we can write our names, and write them in public places, readers may have very different reactions to this, according to different contexts. Sometimes we read these names as romantic inscriptions; at other times, we see them as defacements. Debbie Pounds, in her poem *Same as it ever was*, captures something of this contrast in the reactions of the reader:

> We carved our names on trees of oak
> Scratched true love on legs of desks
> Whittled away the world's wood.
>> Romantics.
> They spray paint initials on corrugated iron
> Scribble dirty jokes on plastic tables
> Deface flats with felt tip pens.
>> Vandals.

> (Pounds, 1989)

The petty vandalism of lovers is innocent, part of a nostalgic past; their writing material the oldest kind. The inscriptions of 'scribblers' and 'defacers', by contrast, are shown as offensive; whether of dirty jokes or of their own names, theirs are alive and present; the spray paint may be barely dry. Mary Wolfe's analysis of the challenges posed by urban graffiti sees these as a private dialogue in public spaces; a deliberate contradiction. The 'tagging' by the graffiti artist is his or her personal signature, intelligible only to those in the know. In this sense, she argues, the graffiti artist is making his or her own challenge to conventions, maintaining a secret identity to all but the initiates:

> This is writing as counter culture; in a prohibited public space, it is the personal made public. (Wolfe, 1998:19)

Whether seen as romantics or vandals, these writers are writing in secret; whittling away their names or scrawling defiant jokes in private for others to read later in public. Not for them the twentieth century 'conceit of cultivated illegibility' (Vincent, 1993: 21). Each letter in the words (for instance) 'Gary loves Sharon' is etched so that it can be read. 'Vandals' who have other purposes than romantic ones may indeed choose to write anonymously; but (unlike those who really can only write a mark to represent themselves in the register) this anonymity is a choice.

Our signature is the way we write our name which is distinctive to us and us alone. In writing it, we ask ourselves to do two things at once: to produce a version which no one else can, and at the same time write it so that we ourselves will be able to repeat it in exactly the same way every time. In contrast to the secret name-writing of lovers, formal name-writing is a very public matter to which there are, very often, witnesses – there to ensure that the signature is authentic. At its most extreme, the publicly witnessed signature is part of a very public ceremony, where signatories are representatives of whole peoples. In her study of media images of literacy, Mary Hamilton refers to the 'legal power' of this kind of signature writing, in which the writing of the signature not only confers authority to the document but is a performance for public purposes 'within political and business deals'. To sum up the kind of literacy this is, she chooses the useful term '*literacy as ritual public gesture*' (Hamilton, 2000: 21). These are gestures which carry the burden of history with them, as this example suggests. The story is of two public signature rituals, over a century apart, deep in the cultural history of Aoreatora (New Zealand). The first and most recent is that of the British monarch. In 1995 the Queen signed a document formally recording the apology of her government to the Maori people for the historic damage made by its predecessors to their lands and ancestors. In doing so, she was acting out the same symbolic literacy event which her antecedents had imposed on the Maori leaders more than a century before.

The second, nearly two centuries ago, is that of 240 Maori chiefs, who, on 6 February 1840, signed the document at Waitangi transferring ownership of Maori lands to the British crown. (Later, seven more copies had had to be dispatched around the country at the order of William Hobson, then British Governor General.) To the Maori leaders, a mark of particular significance had been felt necessary for this transaction. With customs which transcended documentary promises and silent writing, the chiefs were agreeing to pledge their allegiance to a Queen living on the other side of the world. In choosing how to mark their consent, for the benefit of the Governor General's men standing beside them, a few chose European-style signatures. Many, however, preferred the authority of their own marks: those which derived from each chief's particular *moko* or facial tattoo. This facial signature had a depth of meaning which those of us who are illiterate in Maori symbolic and cultural life can only guess at (Hailstone, 1993).

In the years between these two historical moments, the newspaper image of heads of state grasping Parker fountain pens and signing peace treaties has become commonplace. Caught up in the bureaucracies of industrial society, it is easy to forget the significance of such pictures. Whether it be written by a Queen in apology for her people's historic crimes, or by a single parent claiming the benefit to which she is entitled, the signature is symbol. It stands as the writer's agreement to all that has gone before, as if the writer is saying: all this is true, and my own name written here by me shows, not only that I am not lying in what this says, but also that I give my consent to it. Only with a signature is the legal document made valid. Globalisation may run on the Internet but the hand-made inscription is still necessary for transactions to be complete. For those between the individual and the state, a kind of public ceremony is called for: in person, the beneficiary of pension or income support must queue up to sign at a counter in front of others. The person as well as their signature must be present.

To be unable to write your name, to sign it in your own idiosyncratic way, is to be deprived of the choice *not* to give your name to something. One adult literacy learner, looking back on a time before he had achieved 'nominal literacy', expressed it like this:

> If I don't agree with the contents of the document … I just don't sign.
> Whereas before, one could never refuse to sign. (Nelson, 1981: 87)

To have the right to give or to withhold your name is an important civil right.
For a democracy to function, the need for a population to be able to write
their own name may not be absolutely essential (we do not write when we
vote); but the need to be able to hold a pen and make a mark may make the
difference between a wasted ballot paper and a vote. The print of a thumb
may blur the line between one box and the next. Naigaga Irene Ouma, a
local councillor in the county of Bugiri, Uganda, told me recently:

> The Council has supported adult literacy because they want votes in the
> future. In the last elections in 96, many votes were spoilt with so many
> people using the thumbprint. (Mace and Keihangwe, 2000)

She and others with whom I spoke during a short visit to her country spoke
of rural people increasingly feeling 'disgusted' at being forced to use their
thumbs to signify their choice or their agreement. During those few days that
I was there, I visited women in villages who were participants in literacy
classes and, with the help of an interpreter, asked them to tell me something
of what they had learned. At each interview, I asked first if the woman would
write her name for me in my notebook, so that I would be sure not to
mistake the spelling of it. Each time, I witnessed the writing of the speaker's
name. I was a witness, she the signator, slowly scribing her name to help me
know her. These were women who until recently had had to rely on thumbs,
and who, in the course of learning the act of writing, had also been learning
much else, building on what they already know about their communities and
their lives to make new possibilities happen, for water supplies, for food
production, for their own health.

In UNESCO's catalogue of posters published to celebrate International
Literacy Year there is a particularly striking image on this theme. Produced
by the Directorate of Education in Jaipur, India, it shows a large thumb
planted firmly on a page of script. Beneath the poster is a translation of the
text, half-concealed beneath the thumb:

> We borrowed one hundred rupees. We gave our thumbprint on a paper.
> For many years we have been paying interest. But the debt still remains
> unpaid. (Giere, 1992: 47).

This is an image of betrayal. The literate stand accused. If we had been able
to read the small print of your paperwork (say the thumb-owners) we would
never have given our agreement to it. You claim we owe you money; but you
owe us your literacy: you, the world's rich, are using yours to cheat us. The
thumbprint here is not only the mark that risks spoiling a ballot paper. It is
a humiliation.

So?

I began this essay by noting that writing your name is not the same as signing your name. For myself, I *write my name* (Jane Mace) clearly, so that it can be read. When I *write my signature* (Jane S. Mace), however, the curve and push of the lines are almost entirely out of alignment with the shape of the letters they purport to represent. The *J* swoops up from bottom to top, across the upright and back, making a lassoo of the *a*. This doubles back to push a track in which neither of the letters (*n* and *e*) due to follow can be discerned. Then comes the forward snake of an *S* (my middle initial). Up rushes the *M*'s great wave, a breaker tumbling down into the ripple which ends it all (and could not possibly be taken for the three letters which spell out the rest of the name).

I have been writing my signature like this for years, although I could not be sure when it got fixed in that shape. Some days I have reason to write it several times. I sign letters; I write cheques; I fill in forms and sign my name at the bottom. And each time my hand (more or less) reproduces the same combination of loops and ripples. It is my signature, the graphic me, as near-impossible as possible to reproduce. Accept no substitute: only I can write my name like that. Woe betide me if I suddenly take it into my head to loop the J differently. The clerk in front of me, if she is doing her job, would compare it with the scrawl on my card and see an unacceptable difference. (Worse still is the moment when, on a form designed to be machine-read, I so write my signature that some part of it trespasses outside the box set out for it — as I recently did, not once, but three times before I got it right on the form I had to fill out to renew my passport.) But I can also write my name so that it is clear and legible, in carefully joined up writing, keeping to a straight line. The reason I do not have to write the legible form very often is either that there is a typed version already there, or that I have written the printed version alongside the signature.

Literacy classrooms across the world are full of stories about name-writing. Day after day in this 'lettered world' decisions have to be made as to where and how to sign a name. Literacy learners know that they may be able to get help to fill in the form, but only they can sign it, and in signing it they have committed themselves. Let me offer a couple of possibilities we might use, any of us, among a group of people interested in literacy:

1. Let each person write their name, putting down all the names they have, whether or not they use them every day. Invite each person to tell the group about these names, about who chose them, about which ones they like or don't like, and get them to teach the rest of the group the proper spelling. Write the preferred names of the group on a whiteboard or flipchart sheet of paper. Consider them.
2. Give everyone in the group two cards, of two different colours. Ask them

to write their name on one in their best handwriting. Then ask them to write on the other in the way they feel is most personal to them. Exchange cards. Spend some time wondering about handwriting style. Invite people to try out the style of their neighbour's signature. Reflect on this.

We expect signatures to be unique to their owner. And we expect the signer to reproduce the same version of the signature every time they write it. These two expectations have not always been there; they are the creature of our times. To be able to inscribe your name in full is indeed a primary literacy ambition: to write it in a way that no one else could reproduce is about showing that the name is yours and yours alone. Here, from among the stories offered by Mass Observation writers for my research on mothers in the 1890s, is a picture which captures the special activity this represents:

> Although she was a great reader, her writing skills were almost non-existent. I always took this for granted, but can clearly remember how, whenever she had to write her name, anyone who was around was called in to assist; and the only picture in my mind that I have of her writing is of her surrounded by a small crowd holding their breaths, (R446 quoted in Mace, 1998: 113)

This is the writing of the name as a performance, complete with audience, breathless with anticipation; a good moment to end with, in this collection of thoughts about signatures and name-writing. It seems to me to portray something of the fundamental importance that the ability to write our own name represents; an ability which is, or should be, a human right. Each one of us should have the right to write our names in at least two ways – legibly and illegibly – and to have the choice not only as to *how* we write it but also as to *whether* we do so. A full literacy life in a lettered world means a person having the choice of being able to write her or his name so that it can be read, but also, when she or he so desires, in the way which is theirs and theirs alone.

References

Altick, R. (1983) *The English Common Reader: a Social History of the Mass Reading Public*, Chicago: University of Chicago Press.

Giere, U. (1992) *Worlds of Words: an International Exhibition of Literacy Posters*, Stuttgart: UNESCO.

Hailstone, M. (1993) 'Te tiriti' (The treaty) in *Visible language*, Summer, 27, pp. 302–19.

Hamilton, M. (2000) 'Exploring literacy as social practice through media photographs' in Barton, D., Hamilton, M. and Ivanič, R. (eds), *Situated Literacies*, Routledge, pp. 16–34.

Houston, R.A. (1988) *Literacy in Early Modern Europe: Culture and Education 1500–1800*, London: Longman.

Howard, U. (1991) 'Self, education and writing in nineteenth-century English communities' in Barton, D. and Ivanič, R. (eds), *Writing in the Community*, Newbury Park: Sage, pp. 78–109.

Mace, J. (1995) 'The politics of measurement: from signatures to significance' in Palfreeman, A. (ed.), *Critical Issues, Essential Priorities: Conference papers* – *18th National Conference*, Melbourne: Australian Council for Adult Literacy, pp. 35–43.

Mace, J. (1998) *Playing with Time: Mothers and the Meaning of Literacy*, London: UCL Press.

Mace, J. and Keihangwe, S. (2000) *'We are together, we are many': adult literacy in rural Uganda*, World University Service (UK) (Web site: www.wusuk.org).

Nelson, A.J. (1981) *On the Importance of Being Literate*, Melbourne: Australian Council for Adult Literacy.

Pounds, D. (1989) 'Same as it ever was' in Federation of Worker Writers and Community Publishers, *Once I was a Washing Machine: The Working Class Experience in Poetry and Prose*, London: FWWCP, p. 44 (reproduced with permission of the author).

Stephens, W.B. (1987) *Education, Literacy and Society: 1830–1870 – the Geography of Diversity in Provincial England*, Manchester: Manchester University Press.

Vincent, D. (1993) *Literacy and Popular Culture: England 1750–1914*, Cambridge: Cambridge University Press.

Wolfe, M. (1998) 'Shake, rattle and write', *RaPAL Bulletin* 35, Spring, pp. 17–20.

5 The role of literacy in people's lives: a case study of its use amongst the homeless in Australia

Geraldine Castleton

Introduction

This chapter explores the significance of literacy in the lives of homeless people who are clients of a welfare centre located in a large Australian city. The work reported here is similar to an earlier study conducted in the United Kingdom (Hamilton and Davies, 1996) that also set out to examine how various official versions of adult literacy need intersect with the views held by the very people seen to have these needs.

The centre at the focus of the study has been operating for 24 years. It aims 'to provide a better quality of life for homeless, destitute and socially isolated people within their own framework. While self-reliance and participation is strongly encouraged, clients are accepted and supported unconditionally' (Annual Report, 1999: 1). Operating from Monday to Friday, the centre offers a number of services, including the provision of meals; showering and washing facilities; mail distribution; first aid/health services; emergency housing; counselling; and the distribution of financial and material support. A strong emphasis is placed on social networking to expand clients' horizons, minimise social isolation and improve self-esteem by providing support, contacts and avenues for change leading to improved quality of life and relationships with the wider community. According to the Centre's latest annual report, it assisted 'over 19,000 people with food, rental payments, utility payments, travel assistance, clothing, medication and fares [while having] to decline financial assistance to a further 16,000 people' (Annual Report, 1999: 6).

It would be doing a grave injustice to both the organisation and the people it serves to try to describe the centre's clients as a homogeneous group of socially disadvantaged people, other than to note that people use the centre because of pressing need, either short or long term. Many of the groups found within the wider community, that have frequently been categorised in various Australian-based reports produced over the past decade as 'disadvantaged' and in need of adult literacy services, are represented within the centre's client base. These groups include:

- people of non-English speaking background;
- indigenous people;

- unemployed, particularly men;
- youth;
- intellectually and physically disabled;
- women (though in limited numbers).

With respect to indigenous peoples, these centre clients may best be defined as fitting within the category of 'Urban' (National Aboriginal Education Policy, 1984). This term describes indigenous people who are highly geographically and economically embedded in non-indigenous society, but, because of the ways in which they may be seen as 'different' from the mainstream culture, experience considerable social separation (Nagi Binanga, 1995: 29). The British study (Hamilton and Davies, 1996) found a similar socio-cultural mix among the group of unemployed people they worked with in the United Kingdom. While the vast majority of people who used the centre involved in this study were unemployed, there were a small number of clients who held casual, part-time jobs, all of which required low levels of skill.

Who are the homeless?

In writing about homelessness within the city of Toronto in Canada, Trumpener (1997: 7) has noted that definitions of this phenomenon need to be broad enough to reflect the reality of contemporary urban life. From this perspective, she described it as including 'people who are homeless, transient, staying in emergency shelters, or underhoused in substandard apartments and rooming houses'. She then went on to note that '[p]eople who are homeless also tend to be living in extreme poverty and excluded from opportunities for employment, education, recreation and social contact'. The conditions of homelessness in Toronto reflect the same realities for homeless people in the Australian city referred to in this account, and, no doubt, many other cities around the world. Coare and Jones (1996: 105), for example, describe a similar population in their work with homeless people in Brighton, UK, the city identified as having the highest number of street homeless, pro rata, in the whole country. Certainly, Trumpener's (1997) definition aptly depicts the actuality of everyday life for the majority of the people who use the centre.

What is literacy?

The meaning of the term 'literacy' is highly contested within political, economic and educational circles. Contemporary understandings have come to recognise the relative and socially contingent nature of literacy so that it can be interpreted as what people need, or want to do, often in interaction with other people, to be able to go about their daily lives. According to

LoBianco and Freebody (1997: 26), 'literacy is … for acting on and in the world'. This conceptualisation encompasses notions of literacy as not just skills, but rather as 'value defined practice[s] within a cultural context (which must be defined) from community to community and not across the nation' (cited in McNaught et al, 1996: 3). From this perspective literacy can also be viewed as a communal resource, utilised by family, community groups as well as by individuals (Barton and Hamilton, 1998: 5). Interpretations of 'what is literacy' given by centre clients, staff and people who work with the homeless emphasise that aspect of literacy as a shared resource, accounting for it in the numerous ways in which people rely on each other to complete such routine tasks as reading instructions for prescription drugs, interpreting correspondence from bureaucracies and clarifying details of rental agreements.

Within official discourses on literacy in Australia and other western nations, found in various reports and documents originating from governments and other authoritative sources, however, literacy is typically framed as an individual, functional, employment-related skill. From this viewpoint people with low literacy skills are often construed as being 'deficient', and then may be held accountable for a range of social ills (Graff, 1987; Wagner, 1998), including a nation's difficulty in trading competitively in the international marketplace (Castleton, 1999; Moser, 1999).

How is literacy need defined?

Just as definitions of literacy must capture the dynamic nature of literacy practices, so too must descriptions of literacy need be viewed as a changing continuum, 'with the variability over the stages of a person's life. … Such needs are not constant, but may arise at different intervals, and in different intensities and forms in work and in community or family life' (McNaught et al, 1996: 3–4), reflecting its role as a social practice.

A number of reports produced in Australia over recent years have dealt with the difficulty of distinguishing between the concepts of 'need' and 'demand' for literacy provision while the situation can be further complicated when distinctions are drawn between the terms 'need', 'unmet need' and 'demand': do the latter terms mean one and the same, for example? Interpretations of these concepts will differ according to *who* is doing the asking, *how* the questions are asked, for *what* purpose is the information being collected and *what* stakeholders are involved in the process, illustrating Foucault's (1980) claims that knowledge can be traced to different discourse practices that enclose the knowledge formulated from within them.

The following distinctions of need, devised by McNaught and colleagues (*op cit*: 4), were adopted to examine the literacy needs of people using the centre:

apparent   estimated from quantitative data sources including population statistics from census data, extrapolations from government department data bases and large-scale research surveys;

perceived   interpreted by service delivery agents, researchers, community welfare officers and interested/informed stakeholders, usually qualitative in nature;

expressed   typically obtained from clients or from people with direct access to clients.

According to these distinctions, 'demand' is best understood as 'expressed need'; however, it is worth noting that there can be considerable overlap across these different categories of data.

Apparent need established

Australian Bureau of Statistics (ABS) (1997) census data (1996) and information taken from the survey of Aspects of Literacy (1997) provided macro-level data on the literacy skills of people in the target area that establish 'apparent' need for literacy provision. Census information showed higher proportions of:

- people born overseas from countries where English is not the first language;
- Aboriginal people and Torres Strait Islanders;
- unemployed people, including youth;
- people with no post-compulsory qualifications;
- people living alone;

than figures reported as the national averages for these categories.

Interpretations of the findings of the Survey of Aspects of Literacy support concerns made available from census data that many of the clients of the centre would fit within the group of people 'at risk' because of their low literacy skills, a concern that is typically explained through a mix of cultural factors such as ethnicity, gender, socio-economic status and schooling experiences. Throughout these official discourses people with low literacy skill are contrasted with those with higher levels of literacy who, in consequence, enjoy better levels of education, social status and employment. An implication that can be drawn from these discourses is that education and training, particularly literacy training, is viewed as a solution, at least in part, to the problems faced by people with low literacy skills.

This assertion is supported by the National Strategy of the Australian National Training Authority (ANTA), *A Bridge to the Future* (1998), which identifies access for all Australians as an essential principle of vocational education and training. It recognises that particular groups of people may be under-represented in the vocational education and training sector because of individual factors including limited skills in literacy, membership of a specific group, geographic and/or social isolation, or a combination of these. This need for people to be involved in training is clearly related within the document to widely held economic rationalist discourses on national productivity and prosperity. Again, the various groups that make up the client base of the centre are included within ANTA's categorisation of 'under-represented' groups.

Perceived need established

Official recognition of concern for levels of literacy among Australia's adult population, that has grown since the late 1980s, has resulted in a plethora of reports that restate the case made by the official data: there is a clearly made case of 'perceived' need among people who fit the category of 'homeless' and may be clients of the centre. Various causes are offered for this need, including people's poor schooling experiences; lack of opportunities to attend school; the nature of physical and/mental disabilities or their state of health; lack of access to the provision of services; and lack of appropriate literacy skills. There is general agreement that the consequences of these factors in people's lives are the perceived 'need' for adult literacy provision to counter personal, cultural and institutional barriers to full community participation and citizenship. Hamilton and Davies (1996: 7) have noted related concerns being expressed in reports in the United Kingdom over the past decade or so, with a similar case being made for training as the solution.

The common premise underlying much of this literature is that literacy provision is essential for all people within the community. Many of the reports ground their arguments in particular 'official' definitions of literacy that emphasise its essential personal and social benefits, and its relationship to wider societal economic goals. In this sense the literature may be seen as presenting 'popular and prevailing conceptions of literacy [that] equate its acquisition with positive and unproblematic outcomes' (Prinsloo and Breier, 1996: 16).

What can be overlooked in this process, however, is consideration of what literacy means for the intended recipients of literacy support. This point has been made clearly by Prinsloo and Breier (1996) who have argued that there is an existing bias in research about adult literacy on literacy provision – what literacy do people *need* – rather than on acquisition – what do people *want* to use literacy for. Furthermore, they contend that the discourses and practices of policy makers and providers have received most attention in this literature. They maintain that attention must focus more directly on discourses that are centred on the people said to be in need of literacy support. This focus on the intended recipients of literacy provision then leads into a consideration of how expressed need can be established.

Establishing expressed need

The expressed need of people accessing the centre was sourced through interviews with a range of informants familiar with, or employed by, the centre as well as clients of that organisation. Interviewees were selected for the various perspectives they could offer to the examination of the relationship between 'literacy' and 'homelessness' in its various forms. In their talk about homeless people and literacy, the informants drew on a cultural history of professional and community interpretations that enabled them to give various accounts of the relationships they perceived between homelessness and literacy. From such a working knowledge certain beliefs about 'homelessness' have emerged, namely that many homeless people had low levels of literacy that could be addressed through some form of literacy support.

Talking up the category of 'homelessness'

The category of 'homelessness' was clearly evidenced in interviewees' talk and presented as an established category from traditional discourses including those of social welfare. 'Homeless' people were typically depicted as:

- low in self-esteem;
- lacking in motivation;
- lacking skills;
- more likely to be male than female;
- more likely to be middle-aged than youthful;
- likely to have health problems;
- lacking insight into their own situation;
- lacking strategies to affect change in their situation.

This talk in general reflected the stereotypical categorisation of homeless people presented in official discourses and demonstrates commonly held beliefs and institutional points of view about this category of people. Working within this established category, and its characteristics, emanating from existing social welfare discourses on homelessness, enabled the interviewees to establish links between these discourses and other readily available discourses on adult literacy. These discourses, evidenced both in policy and practice, have characteristically identified adults with limited literacy skills with a similar range of attributions as those ascribed to homeless people. This link thus enabled informants to describe various ways in which homeless people had a problem that may be addressed through some form, or forms, of literacy support.

Accounting for homelessness and the need for literacy

The correlation between homelessness and literacy was realised in the talk by recourse to a complex set of causal relations. Invariably the link between being homeless and literacy was related to an intricate pattern of culturally determined attributes pertaining to experiences of schooling, race, health and socio–economic status. This assembly of people with a specific range of cultural attributes thus allowed for the formulation of taken–for–granted propositions that informants then took up in their explanations of the causes and consequences of homelessness, and its link with literacy. Typically, informants grounded explanations of the conditions of 'homelessness' in personal and behavioural factors, such as poor skills, lacking motivation and self–esteem. In the words of one staff member of the centre, for example, homeless people were described as being 'totally unmotivated … it's part of the culture that they've become' while another interviewee likened lack of motivation to a lack of hope, and, in her words, showed that homeless people were 'in a sense being realistic about what their chances are'. Rarely were explanations given in systemic terms such as the nature of schooling, the state of the labour market, opportunities for retraining, perceptions and treatment of mental health problems in the general community, or the contraction of boarding house accommodation for low income earners. While the existence of homeless people, with their various characteristics, is seen as not a good thing for society, this same 'society' is generally not held responsible for this condition.

In terms of expressing the significance of the literacy status of homeless people, informants were in agreement that, while it was an important issue among the mix of factors that impacted on the lives of homeless people, it was not seen as the most significant element in their lives, and neither was it described as the cause of homelessness. Rather than seeing lack of literacy as a precipitating factor in homelessness, informants generally identified limited literacy skills as an integral part of a range of characteristics of homelessness that included low socio–economic status, poor employment opportunities, limited disposable income, poor accommodation, lack of self–esteem and motivation for learning.

Within many interviewees' accounts, literacy was presented as the key to equipping individuals and groups of people to make various transformations in their lives. In this sense, the talk resonated with a number of the major themes presented in official discourses not only around literacy but also those discourses that link literacy and work (Castleton, 1999; Moser, 1999; Wagner, 1998). Notably, however, centre clients did not necessarily talk of literacy as being a central concern, being rather more focused on just making it through each day. This finding is consistent with work reported by

Hamilton and Davies (1996: 10) from the United Kingdom who found that half the unemployed people they interviewed did not perceive a problem with their own reading and writing competencies, while the other half admitted having a problem but did not regard it as the most significant barrier to securing employment. When asked to elaborate further on their circumstances, many centre clients did acknowledge some ways in which better literacy skills would assist, perhaps in dealing with social service organisations or boarding house managers. Importantly, centre clients felt at ease about asking other homeless people, or the staff of the centre, to assist in these tasks. Within one particular group, for example, one man was clearly identified as 'the literacy person who helps with those things'. Hamilton and Davies (1996: 16) likewise reported that unemployed people with limited literacy skills regularly relied on informal networks of people to assist them with literacy tasks, such as completing forms.

While there was some agreement with the causes and effects of poor literacy skills, and the unquestioned benefits of literacy training depicted in official discourses, there was, however, also acknowledgement of the extent to which these discourses did not reflect the reality experienced by many of the homeless. Among centre clients who defined themselves as 'job seekers', for example, there was a lived understanding of the actuality of the current economic situation in which jobs, particularly jobs requiring low skill levels, were difficult to find. According to the majority of the participants, including centre clients, most jobseekers were resigned to this situation, while others, mostly youth, were angry because 'we've been brought up on a diet of get educated and we'll give you a job'.

The limited compliance with and trust of those official discourses that promote a belief in the unquestioned good of literacy and therefore in the benefits of literacy training displayed by many informants was regularly substantiated by the calling up of those discourses with which they were more familiar. For example, one welfare worker noted that 'literacy training won't stop them being thrown out of their boarding houses because of urban renewal'. This finding serves to highlight Street's (1995) concerns over how literacy has become valorised in certain discourses and caution about literacy taking on a signification that far outweighs what features of social life can be adequately and appropriately explained in terms of its actual role in people's lives.

Existing literacy practices and a role for literacy support

Having stated a reason for caution when presenting literacy training or support as some kind of panacea for a whole host of social ills, there were, however, various indications in informants' talk that provide some directions for the type of literacy provision that may be worthwhile for homeless people. The talk of people who work with the homeless frequently reinforced links made in the literature (Freebody and Freiberg, 1997; Jayne, 1999; Trumpener, 1997) between health factors and low literacy. The need, and indeed the stated desire in some cases, for many homeless people to be able to take more responsibility for their health and well-being was seen to create an appropriate way of making literacy relevant in their lives. One interviewee who works with homeless youth, for example, described the importance of working 'from a harm minimisation frame to help young people to maximise their health'. There was general agreement, however, that such a focus must go beyond a superficial treatment of these issues. Programmes designed to address both literacy and health must be about more than 'it's for your own good'. There was an acknowledged need for programmes that equip young people to better understand the consequences of their own actions at a personal and societal level; to recognise risks involved and how to minimise harm to themselves; to learn how to communicate in effective, positive ways and how to control frustration and anger. This work may require literacy providers to reconsider traditional means of delivery, and develop what Coare and Jones (1996: 106) have called 'dynamic partnerships'. According to them, partnerships require adult educators to 'work with a team of people whose primary role and function is social rather than educational' so that all involved can establish trust amongst participating agencies, educators and clients.

While there were some jobseekers among the homeless people using the centre, it was clear that many of them were not looking for work, nor ever likely to do so. For those who are looking for support in developing job skills, identified as mainly younger people, this support must be flexible and responsive to accommodate the lifestyles of homeless people and should include case management and job placement services. Hamilton and Davies (1996: 13) have identified three core ingredients of the support needed for jobseekers, namely 'accessibility, trust and quality specialist knowledge'. They have claimed that support systems must be accessible in the sense that users are aware that the provision exists; it is readily available and users feel comfortable about using it (that is, without fear of being stigmatised). Furthermore, it is important that clients can approach the support without fear of there being any kind of hidden agenda; and finally the support that is given must be of a good quality and be a specialist service that provides a range of options.

A disturbingly high proportion of people using the centre were receiving various forms of disability payments. Many of these people were living in poor quality boarding house accommodation, and came to the centre not only for social contact, but also for support in dealing with various social security-related reading and writing tasks as well as sound advice.

Generally speaking, the homeless people interviewed did not describe themselves as wanting literacy training as a way to access employment and/ or more training, but rather looked to it as a means of enabling them to achieve greater personal and collective responsibility over their lives. There was a genuine desire among the homeless to be productive citizens, to be doing things in and for the community, but there was a noticeable sense of helplessness and lack of any sense of power in their talk of how to achieve such goals — 'it doesn't matter what we do, everyone is down on us'. A number of older men talked animatedly and enthusiastically about a programme that brought teenage boys from a local school into the centre for activities such as playing pool and football and working collaboratively on crosswords and puzzles. These men all stated they felt they had a lot to offer the boys, apart from being able to beat them at pool and 'teach them a thing or two about rugby', but many lamented that they didn't know how to establish and maintain such contacts away from the centre.

A common feature of the talk of all informants was frequent reference to the various networks that exist among homeless people, both within this centre and beyond. Moreover, these networks were characterised by accepted norms of behaviour, established and maintained by the members of those networks — 'if you don't behave, you're out'. Within these networks particular people are known to take on various roles, including, as already mentioned, the role of 'literacy broker', a term used by Hull (1997) and others to describe someone who applies his or her literacy skills on behalf of others. The networks may be seen as manifestations of the 'communities of practice', identified by researchers such as Barton and Hamilton (1998), Hull (1997) and Prinsloo and Breier (1996), as existing in a range of contexts from workplaces to community settings. Such communities are characterised by the mutual exchange of skills and practices, and reflect the ways in which people in various contexts take up their roles as particular kinds of citizens. An example of the power of such a network in operation, perhaps in a 'negative' sense, was given by indigenous clients and staff of the centre. For these clients, and for many Indigenous People in Australian society, alcohol has become a unifying, though destructive element in their lives, with much of the social contact they have with family members and peers revolving around alcohol. Even though there is general acknowledgement, including among many indigenous organisations, that inappropriate use of alcohol is a serious problem, there is also recognition of its cohesive role. As one informant put it: 'You say to them "Okay give up the grog", that's not what you're saying, you're saying "Give up your family and the other people you know"'.

These existing, though informal structures were still seen to offer the best possible base upon which to build any useful form of literacy support as these networks already exist for specific purposes, determined by the network members themselves. This point underlies the basic premise of beginning with the clients and what they have already in place, and working from there towards better equipping them for self-determination. What then becomes indisputable is the need to take up seriously Street's (1996: 4–5) point that discussions about literacy and literacy provision should focus more on the notion of 'change' rather than on that of 'access', as this leads to a different view on the nature of that support. If the focus is put on 'change', that is, how people can and want to use literacy to bring about change in their lives, then literacy, and consequently the people looking for support, can be viewed in a far more positive light. Emphasis is then given to what clients have, what contributions they can make, and perhaps are making already within their networks, rather than on what they lack. Such a framing allows for recognition of the ways in which people use literacy as a resource shared by members of communities of practice in which participants assume different roles for different purposes.

Changing the focus of discourses on literacy and homelessness

Discourses on literacy for the homeless therefore need to be less about providing the means by which people can access training, and maybe employment, and more about helping them 'build the bridges' so that 'homeless people can access mainstream services', move out into the community and assume some measures of choice and control in their lives. In terms of the framing used in this study, this involves ensuring that claims made for the 'need' of literacy training are grounded not only in the accepted, official discourses of 'apparent' and 'perceived' need, but also suitably reflect the third perspective of 'expressed' need that comes closer to the lived experiences of the individuals and groups framed within these discourses. There are many disparities between the various ways in which literacy need is represented in official discourses and is present in people's lives. Official discourses on literacy and the needs of homeless people may not adequately portray the realities of how the consequences of low levels of literacy can be played out in the everyday lives of homeless people. They may also be shown not to recognise the many literacy practices that exist and flourish outside official discourses, such as those of schooling and work, but which result in making many people competent communicators (Street, 1997). Other discourses that challenge the dominant representations of literacy must be heard not only because they offer more realistic representations of everyday literacy users and their practices, but because they challenge the inherent power structures that exist within such dominant discourses.

More attention must be given to the connection between improving literacy skill and better quality of life outcomes for the homeless. In particular, this quality of life relates directly to the ability to have greater personal control over issues such as health, financial management, housing, and day-to-day interactions with government and welfare agencies. It also means being able to feel a sense of 'belonging' to the community, of being recognised as active citizens, exercising their full rights and responsibilities. Due recognition must therefore be given to literacy as a vehicle for innovation and knowledge dissemination (Wagner, 1998), with 'knowledge' being interpreted as that gained in both formal and informal ways. This can happen through greater collaboration, or 'dynamic partnerships' (Coare and Jones, 1996: 106) between the various agencies that come into day-to-day contact with homeless people. Personnel involved in functional operations within welfare agencies and literacy providers must work together so that the relationship between literacy and daily life is better understood. This could mean that every contact with homeless people would not only be used to mediate and facilitate better lifestyle outcomes, but also become an opportunity to increase skill levels at the same time.

The challenge therefore rests in bringing to homeless people the kind of literacy support that will enable them to effect change in their everyday lives, and take up their rightful opportunities for greater participation in community life, enabling them to be the kinds of citizens they want to be. Setting full citizenship participation as a goal for homeless people acknowledges the multiple ways in which literacy serves individuals and groups in all aspects of life in today's world.

References

Annual Report 139 Club Inc (1999), Brisbane: 139 Club.

Australian National Training Authority (1998) *A Bridge to the Future*, Brisbane: Australian National Training Authority.

Australian Bureau of Statistics (1997) *Aspects of Literacy: Assessed Skill Levels, Australia 1996*, Canberra: ABS Catalogue No. 4428.0.

Barton, D. and Hamilton, M. (1998) *Local Literacies: Reading and Writing in One Community*, London: Routledge.

Castleton, G. (1999), *Understanding Work and Literacy: (E)merging Discourses at Work*, Melbourne: Language Australia.

Coare, P. and Jones, L. (1996) 'Inside-outside a homeless people's writing project', *Adults and Learning*, January, pp. 105–106.

Foucault, M. (1980) *Power/Knowledge: Selected Interviews and Other Writings 1972–1977*, Gordon, G. (ed.), New York: Pantheon Books.

Freebody, P. and Frieberg, J. (1997) *Adult Literacy and Health: Reading and Writing as Keeping-Well Practices*, Melbourne: Language Australia.

Graff, H. (1987) *The Labrinths of Literacy: Reflections on Literacy Past and Present*, London: Falmer Press.

Hamilton, M. and Davies, P. (1996) 'Literacy and long-term unemployment: options for adult guidance support and training', *British Journal of Education and Work*, 6 (2), pp. 5–19.

Hull, G. (ed.) (1997) *Changing Work, Changing Worker: Critical Perspectives on Language, Literacy and Skills*, Albany: SUNY.

Jayne, S. (1999) 'The effect of education on health' in Wagner, D., Vensky, R. and Street, B. (eds), *Literacy: An International Handbook*, Boulder, Co: Westview, pp. 294–99.

LoBianco, J. and Freebody, P. (1997) *Australian Literacies: Informing National Policy on Literacy Education*, Melbourne: Language Australia.

McNaught, C., Candlin, C., Plimer, D. and Pugh, R. (1996) *Unmet Need and Unmet Demand for Adult English Language and Literacy Service*, Sydney: NCELTR, Macquarie University.

Moser, C. (1999) *Improving Literacy and Numeracy: A Fresh Start*, Sudbury, Suffolk: DfEE.

Nagi Binanga Strategic Plan: A Plan to Increase Training and Employment Opportunities for Aboriginal and Torres Strait Islander People (1995), Brisbane: Nagi Binanga, Department of Training and Industrial Relations.

National Aboriginal Education Policy (1984), Canberra: Australian Government Printing Service.

Prinsloo, M. and Breier, M. (eds) (1996) 'Introduction', *The Social Uses of Literacy: Theory and Practice in Contemporary South Africa*, Bertsham, SA and Amsterdam: John Benjamins, pp. 11–30.

Street, B. (1995) *Social Literacies: Critical Approaches to Literacy in Development, Ethnography and Education*, London: Longman.

Street, B. (1996) 'Preface' in Prinsloo, M. and Breier, M. (eds), *The Social Uses of Literacy: Theory and Practice in Contemporary South Africa*, Bertsham, SA and Amsterdam: John Benjamins, pp. 1–10.

Street, B. (1997) 'The implications of the "New Literacy Studies" for literacy education', *English in Education*, 31 (3), pp. 45–49.

Trumpener, B. (1997) *Gimme Shelter: A Resource for Literacy and Homelessness Project*, Ontario: National Literacy Secretariat.

Wagner, D. (1998) *Literacy and Development: Rationales, Myths, Innovations and Future Directions*, Literacy Online. Papers from the 2nd Asia Regional Literacy Forum, New Delhi. 9–13 February.

6 Dyslexia and adult literacy: does dyslexia disempower?

Hugo Kerr

... the history of dyslexia research is littered with theories that were once widely supported but now lie abandoned on the scrap heap... It is vital that we should continue to treat everything *as questionable and to regard nothing as beyond dispute. Certainty is for tele-evangelists, not scientific researchers or teachers. (Ellis et al, 1997: 13–14, their emphasis)*

A small survey of adult basic education (ABE) providers

In 1998 an in-depth questionnaire survey was carried out among 12 professional providers of ABE, exploring their attitudes towards, and behaviour in respect of, developmental dyslexia (hereafter simply dyslexia) in their students (Kerr, 1999). The sample was small but this research appears to be the first of its kind and particular interest is thereby claimed for it though such a preliminary piece of research can only be suggestive and exploratory. All respondents were on the same M. Ed. distance learning course as was the author, forming therefore a straightforwardly 'convenience sample'. All respondents taught, or had until recently taught, ABE. Two had become managers, one managing workplace literacy initiatives, the other ABE and family literacy provision county wide. The remainder all taught ABE as follows: two worked in the prison service, one as a volunteer tutor with elderly people in the US and the remaining seven with the general 16+ population in, or through the auspices of, colleges. My sample population was reasonably representative of ABE provision. Eight of the respondents held teachers' certificates and four held City and Guild certificates relevant to ABE (9282 or 9285 or both).

Results were interesting but disconcerting. The most outstanding finding was variance among, even within, respondents' opinions, overtly recognised by almost every respondent. There was almost universal, and very considerable, confusion as to what dyslexia might be, what might indicate it, what might cause it, what to do about it and even whether it existed at all. Almost all respondents were muddled and insecure on the subject of dyslexia, but recognised this clearly and overtly in their questionnaire responses. There was a considerable tendency to use the term 'dyslexia' very loosely; to mean simply 'difficulty with literacy', irrespective of aetiology (the assignment of causation). The spread of opinion among respondents was substantial. One respondent estimated the prevelance of dyslexia, for example, at over 25 per cent, another at under 5 per cent. One respondent considered six times as many signs to be indicative of dyslexia as did another. Intelligence/achievement discrepancies were overwhelmingly chosen as pathognomic for dyslexia (as that sign which, absolutely and alone, indicates dyslexia beyond doubt). Five respondents could not provide a definition when asked and only one coherent definition emerged. Many respondents accepted extremely wide variation in possible aetiologies and effects. Emotional problems were suggested by eight respondents as a commonplace, alternative explanation for poor literacy skills. Five respondents stated that they did not believe psychometric tests were useful or reliable, particularly in ABE. Six respondents claimed to consider dyslexia when assessing students, but six said they did not. Only two respondents routinely screened for dyslexia, one by performance assessments adopted from Klein (1993) and one using a battery of psychometric tests. Four responses claimed that the apparent effect of a diagnosis on a student could be positive (e.g. 'relief') but two that it could be negative (e.g. 'doom'). A quarter of the sample stated that they were fully persuaded that dyslexia existed, another quarter were absolutely sure that it did not. Half the sample were uncertain, and said so.

Perhaps the most practically important finding was that respondents almost universally showed marked signs of disempowerment, or learned helplessness, in respect of students with the diagnosis. Faced with a 'dyslexic' student, respondents' language grew grey and pessimistic. Only two respondents confidently expected progress. The remainder considered that progress would be unlikely or uncertain and would take much longer, with an increased tendency to regress. Any progress made would, most respondents wrote, be very insecure, with learned skills much less likely to be applied outside the 'classroom'. The language of respondents in respect of their tuition policy, faced with a student diagnosed as dyslexic, became abruptly behaviourist. Almost all respondents dramatically altered tuition under these circumstances. What they said they offered a 'dyslexic' student was repetitive, highly structured and controlled, depersonalised and skill-focused. Methodologies and expectations were instantly and drastically restricted, according to respondents' own accounts, following a diagnosis of dyslexia. Only two respondents were satisfied with such an approach, but nonetheless almost all felt obliged to adapt their tuition in these ways. These findings suggest that it is important to review what we know of dyslexia; to review what the evidence says and perhaps particularly what it does not say.

Why review this issue?

The most important purpose of education may be the inculcation ... of a deep, even raucous, scepticism. (J.K. Galbraith, 1969)

The term *dyslexia* is used, by most of us, very casually. We use it without properly defining it, or we define it so broadly as to be next to pointless. We apply the term even when we are perfectly well aware that we have no clear definition of it, or explanation for it. The word is commonly used to mean nothing more scientifically exact than a difficulty with written language which appears to be inexplicable. We tend to use the term to denote a problem with reading and/or writing and/or spelling (and sometimes much more besides) which we find hard to understand – especially where there appears to be a discrepancy with what we would otherwise expect from a particular person. We find such discrepancy so peculiar, so personally threatening, so deeply and intimately offensive that we are driven to believe, almost to hope, that there is something constitutionally wrong with the victim, that the cause must be a specific neurological deficit, beyond blame, safely located among all the other medical conditions beginning with 'dys-'.

Dyslexia is sometimes sought after as an empowering diagnosis, in that it may open particular educational opportunities. The diagnosis may also be considered to be desirable as preferable to the alternative, which may simply be considered unintelligent. There is an established dyslexia industry and very considerable vested interest in it. There seem to be as many wonderfully special assessment methods, remedial schemes and distinguished gurus as the market will carry. There are illogicalities and inconsistencies in much of the reported science (and see later). Weird and colourful creatures appear fleetingly through the muddied waters – are they fish, fowl or beast? Mostly, they soon disappear again. None of this seems to *bother* us nearly enough.

Why all the fuss? Does it matter whether there really is such a syndrome, so long as people who need appropriate help get it? I suspect that it matters fundamentally, and for several reasons. Much discussion about dyslexia is careless, or at least carefree. Many are willing to make the diagnosis, though rather fewer are qualified so to do. And what about those students who don't achieve the label? Are they simply (and publicly) to be designated as stupid? And then, we do not see over or around dyslexia, once the diagnosis has been invoked we stop looking for other aetiologies. Simpler, more everyday, scientifically duller (and much less lucrative) explanations are not sought once a diagnosis of dyslexia has been made. While dyslexia may be aspired to as a more socially acceptable and politically powerful aetiology it may also prove extremely disconcerting. 'That was another big shock, finding out you're disabled!' cried one student (Whitehouse, 1995). Dyslexia is accepted as a disability by the DfEE, and the law. In the face of a diagnosis we may act and believe differently – we may perceive a need for deficit-focused and limited practice, and we may experience abruptly depressed expectations. This is, indeed, almost inevitable once we have attributed a student's problems to a single, conceptually simple (albeit imperfectly understood), seemingly innate and fundamentally unalterable cause. This is classic soil in which to grow another important disability – 'learned helplessness' – and assuredly not only in the student (Agne *et al*, 1994; Butkowsky and Willows, 1980; Chan, 1994, 1996; Fang, 1996; Holt, 1984a, 1984b; Johnston, 1985; Kerr, 1999; Maier and Seligman, 1976; Peterson *et al*, 1993; Westwood, 1995).

Some science

To begin at the beginning, with definition.

> Definitions of dyslexia are notoriously varied and no single definition of dyslexia has succeeded in gaining a scientific acceptance which even approaches unanimity .... Definitions ... soon become muddied when the researcher or clinician is confronted with a variety of adult cases exhibiting highly heterogenous profiles. (Beaton *et al*, 1997: 2)

Writers often feel free to define very loosely, or give up altogether without a blush.

> The fact that no exact definition [of dyslexia] has yet been produced is of little consequence ... *there is another quite distinct group* who have difficulty with reading yet are very able in other ways ... for convenience we refer to them as being *dyslexic* or having *dyslexia*. Parents, teachers and others understand these words and find them to be an easy form of verbal shorthand to describe the children with whom we are concerned. (Doyle, 1997: 82. his emphasis)

Assessment varies, depending on who does it and to what end. There are many assessment schemes designed for practitioners in literacy teaching, based on assessment of performance on a variety of skills involved in, or said to relate to, literacy (see Klein, 1993; Miles, 1983; Nicolson and Fawcett, 1997). Such schemes are intended for dissemination to educationalists specifically to enable them to diagnose dyslexia on the run, for immediate educational purposes, with the implicit (indeed often explicit) presumption that both tuition and expectations will differ importantly should the syndrome be found. It remains unclear, though, to what degree the measurement of literacy or related skills measures anything other than these skills themselves; in particular it is not at all clear whether such performance tests are able to tell us anything whatsoever about the aetiology of literacy failure.

Assessment for dyslexia for the purposes of scientific research continues to regard the intelligence/achievement discrepancy criterion as the single pathognomic indicator of dyslexia and researchers use it themselves, or rely for diagnosis on educational psychologists who use it. Diagnosing dyslexia simply on a finding of a particular discrepancy between measured IQ and performance on norm-referenced literacy tasks is problematic on two counts. The first is the increasingly frequent finding that a population defined as dyslexic by IQ/achievement discrepancy may not, in the event, differ reliably or importantly from the general population (see Miles and Miles, 1999; Samuelsson *et al*, 1999; Siegel and Himel, 1998; Stanovich and Stanovich, 1997). IQ/achievement discrepancy certainly indicates the existence of a problem (it is a discrepancy after all) but the measure probably says nothing useful about its aetiology. Much frontline scientific theory, however, rests on the definition of sample populations as distinct, different and dyslexic by invocation of this criterion (e.g. Brooks and Weeks, 1998; Fisher *et al*, 1999; Hanley, 1997; Hogben, 1997; Hynd *et al*, 1995). Such studies may thus be fundamentally, perhaps even fatally, flawed.

The second, and perhaps more basic, difficulty lies in the concept of IQ itself. As Stanovich (1991: 9) says, '... one would be hard pressed to find a concept more controversial than intelligence in all of psychology'. Some writers (e.g. Turner, 1997) claim to measure IQ in a multitude of different cognitive domains and with great precision, though even Turner himself says that:

> It has often been said that the best indicator of dyslexia in young children is the performance of the father on a reading test. As 80% of cases may be identified in this way, it would compare favourably with more elaborate screening exercises! (1997: 224)

The gene for dyslexia?

There is much interest in the 'gene for dyslexia'. (e.g. Cardon *et al*, 1994, Fisher *et al*, 1999). This strand to the argument raises fundamental questions. Biologically speaking there can be no gene(s) for literacy *per se*. The first literate acts (clay tablet invoices) were only about 6,000 years ago. This is some 94,000 years too short a time for a skill or aptitude to be encoded into our DNA. It would be about as sensible to propose genes for driving ability as for literacy *per se*. However, it *is* feasible to imagine that a gene or genes affecting a skill or skills related to literacy might have evolved. That is to say; dyslexia, if it exists at all, will never show itself as pure literacy failure – it will be accompanied by consistent failure at a fundamental, related ability or abilities. The 'dyslexic' who is absolutely 'normal' in every other respect is, in other words, mythical. The search for consistent diagnostic signs (ranging widely, e.g. from perceptual defects through postural weakness to post-mortem neuropathology) other than literacy failure *per se* continues, with extremely variable results and no sign of consensus (Everatt, 1997; Galaburda, 1993; Hulme and Snowling, 1997; Nicolson and Fawcett, 1999; Pumfrey and Reason, 1991; Rack, 1997).

The incidence of dyslexia is consistently reported to be three to four times greater in boys than in girls, and yet a genetic sex-linkage has not been demonstrated. It should be simple to do this if such a linkage existed. This is a wobble and not a trivial one; as Stein and Talcott (1999: 60) say, it is 'surprising' and 'still lacks an explanation'. The pure 'gene for dyslexia' theory is considerably flawed at this point.

What might innate deficits which related to literacy consist of? They might be genetically determined deficits, or deficits induced *in utero* or at birth or thereabouts. A number of interesting candidates have been considered for such deficits. (It should be noted that studies considered in this section define 'dyslexics' by invoking the IQ/achievement discrepancy criterion, as does almost all such research.)

First, a tentative dip into the phonological awareness debate. There is good evidence that 'dyslexics' have relatively poor linguistic phonological skills (Ellis, 1993; Goswami, 1997; Snowling, 1995; Snowling and Nation, 1997). There is also the finding that literacy training in an alphabetic system rapidly improves phonological awareness. This is an important carts and horses question that has been well aired in the literature (Goswami and Bryant, 1990; Perfetti and Zhang, 1995; Smith, 1994; Taft, 1991; Thompson, 1999). Given the phenomenal, phonological fuzziness of spoken language, however, it is not astonishing that those with poor literacy skills have poor phonological skills, nor that the latter swiftly improve with targeted tuition, nor that such improvement supports subsequent spelling performance. There is circularity here: learning literacy (in English) causes phonological awareness, something only rather good spellers have.

The 'magnocellular deficit' is an interesting proposal (Eden *et al*, 1996; Hogben, 1997; Stein and Talcott, 1999; but also Goulandris *et al*, 1998; Johannes *et al*, 1996). Magnocells, as a result of the speed at which they conduct stimuli, play an important part in the control of rapid, accurate eye movements (e.g. saccades) and the stabilising of eye fixations. A magnocellular deficit will clearly affect reading. It will, though, similarly affect all those other activities for which magnocellular systems were evolved. Diagnostic signs, in neurological fields unrelated to literacy, should be consistently obtained. However, findings are generally contradictory and contradicted.

Different brains?

Brain scans show exciting, if crude, differences between 'dyslexics' and 'normals' (Duara *et al*, 1991; Eden *et al*, 1996; Larsen *et al*, 1990). However, the normal and literate brain inevitably differs from the normal but less literate brain in important functional ways. This is absolutely unremarkable – they have had radically different experiences (e.g. Castro-Caldas *et al*, 1998). The Matthew effect (the differential effect on ability or performance of variation in the quantity of practice – see Stanovich, 1986 and Matthew, XV: 29), naturally enough, eventually shows up as a difference in functional organisation on brain scan; how could it be otherwise? We need not invoke neuropathology to explain these findings.

Geschwind and Galaburda (1987) proposed a general, overarching theory of 'anomalous cerebral dominance' (which they suggested was primarily due to a testosterone imbalance *in utero*). This theory, which can only be described as grand, links a vast array of syndromes and conditions such as most language disorders, including dyslexia, and many immune disorders. Evidence is wildly mixed and the theory remains disputed (Bryden *et al*, 1994). Problems of measurement and definition bedevil the elucidation of this theory, and findings frequently contradict previous findings.

In other studies, the macro–anatomy of brains is measured and far-reaching conclusions drawn (e.g. Hynd *et al*, 1995). Unusual symmetry of the planum temporale (a part of the brain which, on the left side in most people, deals with much language management), for example, has been claimed as diagnostic (Galaburda *et al*, 1994; Galaburda *et al*, 1985). It is not clear how far this 'weights-and-measures' approach takes us. Sample sizes are often very small and 'dyslexics' are discrepancy defined. Brain micro-anatomy likewise, some research claims, shows a plethora of different abnormalities in 'dyslexics' (e.g. Galaburda, 1993). How abnormal such macro- and micro-abnormalities really are is uncertain and so is how, if at all, they relate to observed abilities or behaviours (e.g. Pumfrey and Reason, 1991).

To say that this theoretical area is unresolved is an understatement. No theory has reached anything like consensus and theories which have been intensively researched are frequently not supported, or not strongly supported.

Is the diagnosis benign?

Learned helplessness (Butkowsky and Willows, 1980; Maier and Seligman, 1976) refers to an unconsciously mediated mental state characterised by reduced confidence, lowered motivation, diminished expectation and passivity. In the educational context it is frequently engendered by maladaptive attribution (the attribution of an effect – such as poor literacy – to a cause which is debilitating – such as low ability, or in this instance to an innate, neurological defect). Learned helplessness is disempowerment.

Is a diagnosis of dyslexia a neutral thing? May it have a subtle but malign influence? Learned helplessness, or disempowerment, as a result of maladaptive attributions, is well recognised among ABE students (Charnley and Jones, 1981; Du Vivier, 1992; Levine, 1986; Mace, 1979; Wallis, 1995). Occasionally it is consciously apparent.

> I was very unhappy. I was told I'd never be able to read or write – I was told this by an educational psychologist. (Open Learning Project, nd: 37)

Also:

> Dyslexia is a disability or specific learning difficulty which needs to be identified and clarified with the student. This is not because of some desire to label students, but because students need to understand that their difficulties will not go away with tuition, practice, hard work, etc. (Klein, 1993: 54)

My own research, though, in addition, appears clearly to demonstrate a strong disempowerment effect among *providers* of ABE tuition, in respect of students with a diagnosis of dyslexia (Kerr, 1999).

Given the clear maladaptive attribution that a diagnosis of an innate, irreversible, neurological handicap inevitably entails, how could it be otherwise? (Bar-Tal, 1984; Chan, 1994, 1996; Fang, 1996; Johnston, 1985; Muthukrishna and Bordowski, 1995; Peterson *et al*, 1993; Stanovich, 1986). Maladaptive attribution inevitably engenders learned helplessness. Dyslexia, whatever else it may or may not be, is clearly a maladaptive attribution. A diagnosis of dyslexia, to the precise degree it is accepted, may therefore function on a conscious level as a politically powerful, socially acceptable and hence desirable explanation for poor literacy skills, on a less conscious level as a potent, but generally unnoticed, impediment to learning those skills – and developmental dyslexia itself may yet prove to be non-existent.

Dyslexia is politically powerful. '... the media have accepted (why I wonder?) that the case is proven ... .' (Martin, 1989: 19). The teacher of literacy works in an environment where public, student and management firmly believe that dyslexia is real. As Galbraith ironically asserted, in a different context, 'Anything so convenient must be right' (J.K. Galbraith, 1969). Dyslexia is nothing if not convenient; it blames the victim, which is such a comfort to everyone else. If only because of the highly particular political convenience of the syndrome presently sweeping us all along, dyslexia surely demands our deep, even raucous scepticism.

References

Agne, K.J., Greenwood, G.E. and Miller, L.D. (1994) 'Relationships between teacher belief systems and teacher effectiveness', *Journal of Research and Development in Education*, 27, pp. 141–52.

Arnold, J. (ed.) (1994) *Affect in Language Learning*, Cambridge: Cambridge University Press.

Bar-Tal, D. (1984) 'The effect of teachers' behaviour on pupils' attributions – a review' in Barnes, P., Oates, J., Chapman, J., Lee, V. and Czerniewska P. (eds), *Personality, Development and Learning*, Milton Keynes: Open University Press.

Beard, R. (ed.) (1993) *Teaching Literacy, Balancing Perspectives*, London: Hodder and Stoughton.

Beaton, A., McDougall, S. and Singleton, C. (1997) 'Humpty Dumpty grows up? Diagnosing dyslexia in adulthood', *Journal of Research in Reading*, 20 (1), pp. 1–12.

Brooks, P.L. and Weeks, S.A.J. (1998) 'A comparison of the responses of dyslexic, slow-learning and control children to different strategies for teaching spellings', *Dyslexia*, 4 (4), pp. 212–22.

Bryden, M.P., McManus, I.C. and Bulman-Fleming, B. (1994) 'Evaluating the empirical support for the Geschwind-Behan-Galaburda model of cerebral lateralisation', *Brain and Cognition*, 26, pp. 103–67.

Butkowsky, Irwin S. and Willows, Dale M. (1980) 'Cognitive-motivational characteristics of children varying in reading ability: evidence for learned helplessness in poor readers', *Journal of Educational Psychology*, 72 (3), pp. 408–22.

Cardon, L.R., Smith, S.D., Fulder, D.W., Kimberling, W.J., Pennington, B.F. and De Fries, J.C. (1994) 'Quantitative trait locus for reading disability on chromosome 6', *Science*, 266, pp. 276–79.

Castro-Caldas, A., Peterson, K.M., Reis, A., Stone-Elander, S. and Ingvar, M. (1998) 'The illiterate brain: learning to read and write during childhood influences the functional organisation of the adult brain', *Brain*, 121, pp. 1053–63.

Chan, L.K.S. (1994) 'Relationship of motivation, strategic learning and reading achievement in grades 5, 7 & 9', *Journal of Experimental Education*, 62 (4), pp. 319–39.

Chan, L.K.S. (1996) 'Combined strategy and attributional training for 7th grade average and poor readers', *Journal of Research in Reading*, 19 (2), pp. 111–28.

Charnley, A.H. and Jones, A.H. (1981) *The Concept of Success in Adult Literacy*, London: ALBSU.

Davis, Sir Peter (1997) *Annual Report of the Basic Skills Agency 1996/7*, London: Basic Skills Agency.

Doyle, J. (1997) *Dyslexia: An Introductory Guide*, London: Whurr.

Du Vivier, E., (ed.) (1992) *Learning to be Literate: A Study of Students' Perceptions of the Goals and Outcomes of Adult Literacy Tuition*, Dublin: Dublin Literacy Scheme.

Duara, R., Kutsch, A., Gross-Glenn, K., Barker, W., Jallad, B., Pascal, S., Lowenstein, D.A., Sheldon, J., Rabin, M., Levin, B. and Lubs, H. (1991) 'Neuroanatomic differences between dyslexic and normal readers on magnetic resonance imaging scans', *Archives of Neurology*, 48, pp. 410–16.

Eden, G.F., Van Meter, J.W., Rumsey, J.W., Maisog, J. and Zeffiro, T.A. (1996) 'Functional MRI reveals differences in visual motion processing in individuals with dyslexia', *Nature*, 382, pp. 66–69.

Ellis, A.W. (1993) *Reading, Writing and Dyslexia: a Cognitive Analysis*, Hove: Lawrence Erlbaum Associates.

Ellis, A.W., McDougall, Sine J.P. and Monk, A.F. (1997) 'Are dyslexics different? IV. In defence of uncertainty', *Dyslexia*, 3 (1), pp. 12–14.

Everatt, J. (1997) 'The abilities and disabilities associated with adult developmental dyslexia', *Journal of Research in Reading*, 20 (1), pp. 13–21.

Fang, Z. (1996) 'A review of research on teachers' beliefs and practices', *Educational Research*, 38 (1), pp. 47–65.

Fisher, S.E., Marlow, A.J., Lamb, J., Maestrini, E., Williams, D.F., Richardson, A.J., Weeks, D.E., Stein, J.F. and Monaco, A.P. (1999) 'A quantitative-trait locus on chromosome 6p influences different aspects of developmental dyslexia', *American Journal of Human Genetics*, 64, pp. 146–56.

Galaburda, A.M., Sherman, G.F., Rosen, G.D., Aboiz, F. and Geschwind, N. (1985) 'Developmental dyslexia: four consecutive cases with cortical anomalies', *Annals of Neurology*, 18, pp. 222–33.

Galaburda, A.M. (ed.) (1993) *Dyslexia and Development: Neurological Aspects Of Extra-Ordinary Brain*, Cambridge, MA: Harvard University Press.

Galaburda, A.M., Menard, M.T. and Rosen, G.D. (1994) 'Evidence for aberrant auditory anatomy in developmental dyslexia', *Proceedings of the National Academy of Science of the U.S.A.*, 91, pp. 8010–13.

Galbraith, J.K. (1969) *The Affluent Society*, London: Penguin.

Geschwind, N. and Galaburda, A.M. (1987) *Cerebral Lateralisation*, Cambridge (Mass.): MIT Press.

Goswami, U. and Bryant, P. (1990) *Phonological Skills and Learning to Read*, Hove: Lawrence Erlbaum Associates.

Goswami, U. (1997) 'Learning to read in different orthographies: phonological awareness, orthographic representations and dyslexia' in Hulme, C. and Snowling, M. (eds), *Dyslexia: Biology, Cognition and Intervention*, London: Whurr Publishers.

Goulandris, N., McIntyre, A., Snowling, M., Bethel, J. and Lee, J.P. (1998) 'A comparison of dyslexic and normal readers using orthoptic assessment procedures', *Dyslexia*, 4 (1), pp. 30–48.

Hanley, J.R. (1997) 'Reading and spelling impairments in undergraduate students with developmental dyslexia', *Journal of Research in Reading*, 20 (1), pp. 22–30.

Hogben, J.H. (1997), 'How does a visual transient deficit affect reading?', in Hulme, C. and Snowling, M. (eds) (1997), *Dyslexia: Biology, Cognition and Intervention*, London: Whurr Publishers.

Holt, John. (1984a) *How Children Fail*, London: Penguin.

Holt, John. (1984b) *How Children Learn*, London: Penguin.

Hulme, C. and Snowling, M. (eds) (1997) *Dyslexia: Biology, Cognition and Intervention*, London: Whurr Publishers.

Hynd, G.W., Hall, L.J., Novey, E.S., Eliopolus, D., Black, K., Gonzales, J.J., Edmonds, J.E., Riccio, C., and Cohen, M.J. (1995) 'Dyslexia and corpus callosum morphology', *Archives of Neurology*, 52, pp. 32–38.

Johannes, S., Kussmaul, C.L., Munte, T.F., and Mangun, G.R. (1996) 'Developmental dyslexia: passive visual stimulation provides no evidence for a magnocellular processing defect', *Neuropsychologia*, 34 (11), pp. 1123–27.

Johnston, P.H. (1985) 'Understanding reading disability: a case study approach', *Harvard Educational Review*, 55 (2), pp. 153–77.

Kamin, L. (1974) *The Science and Politics of IQ*, Potomac, Lawrence Erlbaum Associates.

Kerr, H. (1999) *Dyslexia in ABE: Beliefs and Consequences*, M.Ed. Dissertation: Sheffield University Library.

Klein, C. (1993) *Diagnosing Dyslexia: A Guide to the Assessment of Adults with Specific Learning Difficulties*, London: ALBSU (BSA).

Larsen, J.P., Hoien, T., Lundberg, I., and Odegaard, H. (1990) 'MRI evaluation of the size and symmetry of the planum temporale in adolescents with developmental dyslexia', *Brain and Language*, 39, pp. 289–301.

Levine, K. (1986) *The Social Context of Literacy*, London: Routledge and Kegan Paul.

Mace, J. (1979) *Working with Words*, London: Writers and Readers Publishers Cooperative.

Mace, J. (ed.) (1995) *Literacy, Language and Community Publishing: Essays in Adult Education*, London: Routledge.

Maier, S.F. and Seligman, M.E.P. (1976) 'Learned helplessness: theory and evidence', *Journal of Experimental Psychology: General*, 105, pp. 3–46.

Martin, T. (1989) *The Strugglers*, Milton Keynes: Open University Press.

Miles T.R. (1983) *The Bangor Dyslexia Test*, Wisbech, Cambs: LDA.

Miles, T.R. and Miles, E. (1999) *Dyslexia One Hundred Years On*, Buckingham: Open University Press.

Muthukrishna, N. and Borkowski, J.G. (1995) 'How learning contexts facilitate strategy transfer', *Applied Cognitive Psychology*, 9, pp. 425–46.

Nicolson, R.I. and Fawcett, A.J. (1997) 'Development of objective procedures for screening and assessment of dyslexic students in higher education', *Journal of Research in Reading*, 20 (1), pp. 77–83.

Nicolson, R.I. and Fawcett, A.J. (1999) 'Developmental dyslexia: the role of the cerebellum', *Dyslexia*, 5 (30), pp. 155–77.

Open Learning Project (undated) *'We've Tried – You Try!'* Lancaster: the Literacy Research Group and London: Goldsmiths College.

Perfetti, C.A. and Zhang, S. (1995) 'The universal word identification reflex', *The Psychology of Learning and Motivation*, 33, pp. 159–89.

Peterson, C., Maier, S.F. and Seligman, M.E.P. (1993) *Learned Helplessness: a Theory for the Age of Personal Control*, Oxford: Oxford University Press.

Pumfrey, Peter D. and Reason, R. (1991) *Specific Learning Difficulties (Dyslexia): Challenges and Responses*, London: Routledge.

Rack, J. (1997) 'Issues in the assessment of developmental dyslexia in adults: theoretical and applied perspectives', *Journal of Research in Reading*, 20 (1), pp. 66–76.

Samuelsson, S., Bylund, B., Cervin, T., Finnstrom, O., Gaddlin, P., Leijon, I., Mard, S., Ronnberg, J., Sandstedt, P. and Warngard, O. (1999) 'The prevelance of reading disabilities among very-low-birth-weight children at 9 years of age', *Dyslexia*, 5 (2), pp. 94–112.

Siegel, L.S. and Himel, N. (1998) 'Socioeconomic status, age and the classification of dyslexics and poor readers: the danger of using IQ scores in the definition of reading disability', *Dyslexia*, 4 (2), pp. 74–90.

Smith, F. (1994) *Understanding Reading*, Hove: Lawrence Erlbaum Associates.

Snowling, M. (1995) 'Phonological processing and developmental dyslexia', *Journal of Research in Reading*, 18 (2), pp. 132–38.

Snowling, M., Nation, K., Moxham, P., Gallagher, A. and Frith, U. (1997) 'Phonological processing skills of dyslexic students in higher education: a preliminary report', *Journal of Research in Reading*, 20 (1), pp. 31–41.

Snowling M.J. and Nation K.A. (1997) 'Language, phonology and learning to read', in Hulme, C. and Snowling, M. (eds.), *Dyslexia: Biology, Cognition and Intervention*, London: Whurr Publishers.

Stanovich, K.E. (1986) 'Matthew effects in reading: some consequences of individual differences in the acquisition of literacy', *Reading Research Quarterly*, 21, pp. 360–406.

Stanovich, K.E. (1991) 'Discrepancy definitions of reading disability: has intelligence led us astray?', *Reading Research Quarterly*, 26, pp. 7–29.

Stanovich, K.E. (1994) 'Annotation: does dyslexia exist?', *Journal of Experimental Child Psychology and Psychiatry*, 35, pp. 579–96.

Stanovich, K.E. and Stanovich, P.J. (1997) 'Further thoughts on aptitude/achievement discrepancy', *Educational Psychology in Practice*, 13 (1), pp. 3–8.

Stein, J. and Talcott, J. (1999) 'Impaired neuronal timing in developmental dyslexia – the magnocellular hypothesis', *Dyslexia*, 5 (2), pp. 59–77.

Taft, M. (1991) *Reading and the Mental Lexicon*, Hove: Lawrence Erlbaum Associates.

Thompson, M.E. (1999) 'Subtypes of dyslexia: a teaching artefact?', *Dyslexia*, 5 (3), pp. 127–37.

Turner, M. (1997) *The Psychological Assessment of Dyslexia*, London: Whurr Publishers.

Wallis, J. (1995) '"You can't write until you can spell". Attitudes to writing among adult basic education students' in Mace, J. (ed.), *Literacy, Language and Community Publishing: Essays in Adult Education*, London: Routledge.

Westwood, P.S. (1995) 'Teachers' beliefs and expectations concerning students with learning difficulties', *Australian Journal of Remedial Education*, 27 (2), pp. 19–21.

Whitehouse, G. (1995) 'Dyslexia: an FE student's experience of assessment, *RaPAL Bulletin*, 27, pp. 19–21.

7 Form-filling as a social practice: taking power into our own hands

Marcia Fawns and Roz Ivanič

Introduction

In today's business world and day-to-day life it seems as though most of our affairs are regulated by form-filling. We can't even receive a parcel without having to add our signature to a specially designed form to provide official confirmation that it has been delivered. Such administrative transactions are part of an information society which increasingly controls and dominates us – not through force or exploitation, as in the past, but through the need to engage in institutionally imposed literacy practices, through what Foucault calls 'technologies of power' (1979).

Forms have become a familiar part of our lives, yet people often feel disempowered by the requirement to fill them in. This applies not only to people who consider themselves as having difficulties with literacy, but to almost everyone. How is it possible that someone can read and write 'perfectly well', yet feel frightened of, resistant to, and incompetent at form-filling? In this chapter we will suggest that what people do, think and feel when required to fill in forms reveals that literacy is not just a matter of decoding and spelling, but a complex social practice through which bureaucratic documents can strip people of their identities.

The focus of this chapter is an investigation into the NHS HC1 form, *'Claim for help with health costs'* (1998 version), looking at how six university students completed this form, the constraints it forces upon users' identities, and the ways in which users can take more power into their own hands when faced with forms to fill in. We will suggest that the relations of power and issues of identity surrounding form-filling could usefully be addressed in Adult Basic Education classes. In the main part of the paper we will present Marcia's account of her research revealing what people do and think while filling in this form.[1]

Marcia's research on form filling: aims of the study

Form-filling is a complex social practice imbued with issues of identity and of power. By putting our pen mark (which we are usually told has to be black) in a particular place on the form we are instantly categorising ourselves as one thing and not another. Often with forms there is no place for us to represent ourselves as we truly are; we are forced into conforming to one of the prescribed boxes which frequently reflect neither ourselves nor our personal circumstances. In highlighting how we are 'bullied' by public documents I hope to make people aware of how they are being positioned by the forms, so that they can utilise this knowledge to challenge the existing conventions in ways which enable them to reclaim their identity while still being able to apply for the benefit. The aim of the study was also to look at the practices used when completing a form, seeing how conflicts arise and are overcome. Errors are easily made, often through no fault of the users, and can have frightening repercussions.

Other research relevant to the study of form-filling

The design of forms has received considerable attention from psychologists (see, for example, Wright, 1979, 1980, 1981a, 1981b), and from public and private service organisations, prompted by the work of The Plain English Campaign. The ways in which forms exercise power over people seeking

TO ACHIEVE SMOOTH PROGRESSION THROUGH A FORM	1) Principle of *linear progression*:	Work through the questions in the order they appear on the form.
	2) Principle of *least reading effort*:	Read only what seems to be necessary to maintain form-filling progress.
	3) Principle of *question routing*:	Jump directly to a new question if the form tells you to.
	4) Principle of *question omission*:	Miss out questions which don't seem to apply to you.
TO RESPOND TO CONFUSION CAUSED BY THE FORM	5) Principle of *question preview*:	If in doubt about the meaning of the current question, read the subsequent question.
	6) Principle of *question review*:	If in doubt about your interpretation of the previous question, review that question and the answer provided.
	7) Principle of *topic scan*:	If in doubt about the relevance of the current question topic, scan the local topic context.

Figure 7.1: Frolich's seven principles for successful form-filling (adapted from Frohlich, 1986:56)

employment have been discussed by Davies (1994), and numerous examples of how they pervade people's everyday lives are described by Barton and Hamilton (1998). Frohlich (1986) investigated how people fill in a 'public service' form and identified four components of forms: titles, questions, explanations and instructions. He found a discrepancy between what material was available to read and what was actually read. He also looked at routing behaviour. 'Routing behaviour is the activity of navigating through the questions on the form' (1986: 52) and is an important area of study within public service forms because they are designed to be used by a wide audience whose members differ greatly. Frohlich identified a pattern of form-filling behaviour based on seven 'principles'. These are summarised in Figure 7.1, and I will draw upon them in the discussion of my findings.

Although my study is similar to Frohlich's it differs in its focus on individuals and their identity. He noticed that each person's form-filling behaviour is idiosyncratic but did not relate this behaviour to the person's identity, nor did he look at how people take their life experiences to the text (Barton, 1994). In completing forms people have to recall things about their lives, constituting a type of self-analysis, which Frohlich did not comment upon. Another difference between the two studies is the 'power relations' dimension. Frohlich did not consider the power relations embedded in the form, but I looked at the relationship between people and bureaucracy within the form. I will highlight how it fails to do the job it sets out to do – to be applicable to a cross-section of society.

How I did the research: the HC1 form (1998 version)

The HC1 form '*Claim for help with health costs*' is a National Health Service form used by people on a low income, to gain help with paying for health costs. The form asks questions about personal circumstances to establish eligibility and need. It asks about finances, family, living arrangements and employment, and uses the information provided to work out entitlements. It is A4 in size, and has two sides of notes for users before the questions begin. The form itself consists of 11 parts, each with between 3 and 10 questions, 12 pages in all. Finally there is a back cover with notes on both sides of it. There is an extract from a completed version in Figure 7.2.

One reason why I chose the HC1 form was that I wanted participants' form-filling behaviour to be as true to reality as possible, so I chose one relevant to their own situation. I was a student myself at the time, and I had personal experience of the form. The form has a section specifically for 'People in full-time education', but, as the form is addressed to a wide and diverse audience, there are also many parts of it which do not apply to students.

Part 4   About where you live

| **1** | Do you or your partner live in a residential care home or nursing home? | NO | ✓ | GO TO QUESTION 2 |
| | | YES | | GIVE DETAILS BELOW |

| HOW MUCH DO YOU PAY? *You might pay this direct to that home or to a Local Authority.* *If you have a partner who lives with you in that home please include what they pay.* | £ |
| | EVERY |

| | Is this a temporary arrangement? | NO | | PLEASE GO TO **Part 6** PAGE 7 |
| | | YES | | GO TO QUESTION 2 |

IN THE REST OF THIS PART only tell us about your share and your partner's share of anything you pay for the place where you live.

Tick YES if someone pays for something on your behalf. Also tick YES if someone gives you money to pay for something.

| **2** | Are you or your partner a joint owner or joint tenant of the place where you live? | NO | ✓ | GO TO QUESTION 3 |
| | | YES | | GIVE DETAILS BELOW |

| WHO WITH (NAME)? | |
| WHAT IS THEIR RELATIONSHIP TO YOU OR YOUR PARTNER? | | GO TO QUESTION 3 |

| **3** | Do you or your partner pay rent or money like rent for the place where you live? | NO | | GO TO QUESTION 4 |
| | | YES | ✓ | GIVE DETAILS BELOW |

If you pay money to parents, other relatives or friends, tick No and go to part 6, page 7. We do not need to know about any money that you pay to them.

| HOW MUCH DO YOU PAY? **Do not include** *water rates, Council Tax, or arrears.* *If you pay for heating, lighting, cooking or hot water with your rent, tell us the amount of the rent alone. Take off Housing Benefit if you get it.* | £ | 40 |
| | EVERY | week |

DOES YOUR RENT INCLUDE ANY OF THESE THINGS? *If it does not, or if you have already taken any of these off your rent, leave the box blank.*	HEATING	✓	✓
	LIGHTING	✓	✓
	COOKING	✓	✓
	HOT WATER	✓	✓

| DO YOU HAVE JUST ONE ROOM? *Don't count rooms you share with people who are not members of your family.* | NO | |
| | YES | ✓ |

| DOES YOUR RENT INCLUDE ANY MEALS? | NO | ✓ | GO TO QUESTION 4 |
| | YES | | GIVE DETAILS BELOW |

HOW MANY BREAKFASTS EACH WEEK FOR EACH PERSON?	
HOW MANY MIDDAY MEALS EACH WEEK FOR EACH PERSON?	
HOW MANY EVENING MEALS EACH WEEK FOR EACH PERSON?		GO TO QUESTION 4

| **4** | Do you or your partner have to pay Council Tax? | NO | ✓ | GO TO QUESTION 5 |
| | | YES | | GIVE DETAILS BELOW |

Don't include any Council Tax for any property you have told us about in **Part 3**.

| HOW MUCH DO YOU HAVE TO PAY THIS YEAR? *Tell us the amount after you have taken off all discounts and Council Tax Benefit. Don't include arrears and in Scotland don't include water rates.* | £ |
| | GO TO QUESTION 5 |

| **5** | Do you or your partner pay ground rent? | NO | ✓ | GO TO QUESTION 6 |
| | *In Scotland this is called feu duty.* | YES | | GIVE DETAILS BELOW |

HOW MUCH GROUND RENT DO YOU PAY? *Don't include arrears.*	£
	EVERY
	GO TO QUESTION 6

Figure 7.2: Page 4 of the HCI form

The participants were all male students between 18 and 23 years old, so I did not have to consider gender and age as factors affecting my findings. Because I wanted them to be relaxed and honest in their form-filling exercises I chose people with whom I was well acquainted. Three participants had completed the HC1 form previously and three were planning to do so soon. Table 7.1 summarises the participants' details:[2]

Name	Age	University Year	Experience of filling in the HC1
Carl	18	1	No
Jay	19	1	No
Gary	20	1	No
Doug	21	2	Yes
Matt	22	4	Yes
Lee	23	4	Yes

Table 7.1: A summary of the participants' details, indicating their number of years at university and their HC1 experience

The data collection and analysis

My evidence on the participants' form-filling behaviour is based mainly on their 'concurrent verbalisation' of the form-filling activity, i.e. when given the form to complete they verbalised things that they read, wrote and thought throughout the activity.[3] I also collected other supplementary data: pre- and post-form-filling questionnaires; the completed form itself; and observational notes made during the form-filling process. All this was conducted on a one-to-one basis, with only myself and the individual participant in the room. The combination of data provided me with a small but diverse range of evidence from which to make claims about these six students' form behaviours.

The audio-tapes of the six 'concurrent verbalisations' were transcribed and then coded. The strategies which arose from the form-filling activity, seeing, for example, whether the participants tended to read or ignore section headings, whether they read all the routing instructions, whether they actually followed these routing instructions, whether they read the information and instructions, were identified. This process led me to focus on the places where the participants were experiencing a clash between their own sense of self and the identities made available by the form, and where they were submitting to or challenging the power exercised by the form.

Table 7.2 shows the range of form-filling practices identified.

- Scan the form/instructions before starting it.
- Answer relevant questions and use routing instructions to guide them away from irrelevant ones.
- Proceed linearly, only digressing at points of conflict.
- Omit questions they cannot answer immediately then return when they have the necessary details.
- Check details before sending form off.

Table 7.2: The form–filling practices of the students

Form–filling is not just a process which people do automatically and similarly, but one which is unique to the person and the particular form. People take their life practices and experiences to the text (Barton, 1994). The participants in my study each approached the form differently. Some read virtually everything there was available to read, while others rushed through it, only paying attention to the things they considered applicable to themselves. Even the simplest instructions are variable and dependent on the user for how they are interpreted and tackled. For example Carl, who is known for being a perfectionist, commented on the difficulty of pulling off the form's cover sheet, whereas Doug, who is very laid-back, just yanked it off, tearing it as he did so. These things are interesting to study because they reveal details about the individuals as well as the form, and thus link up with the focus on identity – such material aspects of form-filling were not addressed in previous studies.

What conflicts with the form did the participants experience?

I use the term 'conflict' not just to mean struggle and disagreement, but to refer to any part of the form which caused the users difficulties in answering. Table 7.3 summarises the conflicts which occurred for one or more of the participants, and their strategies for resolving them.

An example of a term which caused problems was 'maintenance grant'. Matt struggled because he had applied for a maintenance grant but had been rejected. He decided to tick the box saying that he had one, but when asked whether it was for 'fees' or 'maintenance' he did not know the difference and gave the wrong answer, thus accidentally giving false information and representing himself wrongly. Doug didn't know what this was, so he left the question asking if he had one, continuing down the page until he read another question which made him realise he did have a grant, and then returned to answer the earlier question. This is what Frohlich described under his 'principle of question review'.

Conflicts occurred:
- at points asking for details not stored in participants' short-term memories.
- through unknown terms or terms with definitions differing from the norm.
- through irrelevant topics/questions.
- by not knowing where to go and what to answer.
- largely in same places for all users, though some problems were unique to individuals.

Conflicts solved by:
- returning to questions when details are known.
- re-reading questions/instructions.
- using own interpretation.
- reading other local questions to aid understanding of troublesome question.

Table 7.3: Conflicts the students experienced while filling in the form

Other terms were problematic because the users had to fit them to their personal circumstances. In Part 4 of the form, question 3, they were asked if their rent included 'heating, lighting, cooking or hot water': they had to decide what the term 'cooking' was actually referring to. Figure 7.3 is an example of a reader going beyond the text to arrive at an interpretation of this, and using his life experiences to do so (as described by Wright , 1980; Cochran-Smith, 1984; Barton, 1994).

er it does include heating . lighting (2) cooking equipment but not cooking (1.5) erm (3) well I suppose . yeah that would be cooking equipment wouldn't it . and hot water (1)

Figure 7.3: Jay interpreting the meaning of 'cooking': words underlined were read from the form

Another main cause of confusion occurred when the questions appeared irrelevant to the users (as found by Waller (1984) and Wright (1981a:160)). The participants responded by re-reading questions and/or instructions, and scanning the local area. This behaviour is captured succinctly by Frohlich's principles of 'question omission', 'question preview' and 'topic scan' (see Figure 7.1). Wright also discovered that some readers 'seem to consult the instructions only when they have a query in mind' (1986: 132).

These few examples indicate how problems arise and are resolved differently by each individual. They also signal how difficult a form can be to fill in, largely because it asks questions and gives instructions in over-complex ways, and it asks for information which is not relevant to all form users, sometimes causing the users to miss the questions out completely as a consequence.

What errors do the participants make in the form-filling process?

The six students made many errors while they were filling in the form. Table 7.4 summarises the causes and repercussions of these errors.

Errors made by:
- using their own definitions (e.g. of 'savings').
- the form-designer's assumptions (e.g. student loan).
- putting details in wrong sections.
- being confused about how they should categorise themselves.
- answering irrelevant questions.
- not following instructions.
- being forced to provide an answer to questions they could not answer adequately.

Possible repercussions:
- not getting the amount of benefit deserved.
- legal action, for giving incorrect and incomplete information.

Table 7.4: Causes of errors, and possible repercussions

Form designers have several assumptions about members of the community, many of which are incorrect or do not apply wholly. Because of these assumptions, you have to categorise yourself in ways which may not be correct, often causing you to give incomplete information. Yet, despite this, you have to sign a declaration at the end of the form to say that all the details you have given are correct and complete. This situation leaves the form-fillers with the dilemma of adjusting themselves to the fixed boxes, or using additional notes to make their situation clearer. There is a huge gap between what the form-handlers want to know and what the form users want to tell them, and unless the form users conform to the prescribed categories their application will not be processed smoothly (if at all). The repercussions are not just because they have done something incorrectly, but because they have been made to sign a legally-binding declaration, pre-written by the form-designers, which states that all information within the form is accurate and complete. The problem is that errors, by nature, are mistakes, not purposeful intentions to deceive, but there is no way of proving this, and so the mistaken form–filler is then open to legal action being taken against him/her.

Discussion: how forms like the HC1 constrain people's identities

According to Charney:

> In order for ... [a] form to be successful ... the clients must be able to fit their wishes to the options provided and encode the required information on the form. (1984: 131)

This is clearly not the case with the HC1 form which places users in a position where they have to accept prescribed versions of self in order to obtain the benefits claimed. The issue of identity manifests itself in various ways.

• By placing a tick on the form the participant was identifying himself as a particular person.

Unless directed otherwise, the participants had to provide an answer for every question, often in the form of a tick. Each time this tick was placed, so he was accepting the subject position established for him.

• The 'you' in questions was taken by all participants to be a reference to themselves.

As Foucault (1972) pointed out, the subject in texts 'is a particular, vacant place that may in fact be filled by different individuals' (cited in Smith, 1990: 214), but the readers did not challenge this. Rather, they went so far as to indicate their allegiance to it (when the content was relevant), with Matt and Jay often verbally changing the 'you' in questions to 'I', and with the other participants treating columns entitled 'you' as 'their' place. Although all participants accepted this without much thought or awareness, they became aware of the potential incursion on their identity when the 'you' seemed to be less applicable to them. The participants said things like 'that's not applicable' and 'that's not relevant', signalling a breakdown between the subject position prescribed by the form and the subject position the participant is prepared to accept. This breakdown arose because the form is addressed to a general audience so has questions which are relevant to some readers and not others.

• The participants' identities were restricted by the nature of the questions and definitions on the form.

In answering the questions, the participants usually had to decide between a 'yes' and 'no' response. There was no category which allowed for responses other than these, so the users had to shape their identities to fit into one of the boxes, but in doing so they were representing themselves in ways which did not match their circumstances entirely. For example, for the 'savings' question, Matt had to say how much money he had in bank accounts, and since he had just received a bank loan for £7,500 he included this. However, on the form there is no box where he can indicate that this is not his own money, so on paper it appears that he has lots of savings but in reality he owes money to the bank.

- Throughout the form the participants had to present a view of themselves on paper.

The 'personal details' section on page 1 forced readers to represent themselves not only through their name, age and address, but through their National Insurance Number too – and the participants revealed their unique code, without even wondering why. This intrusive questioning is an institutional practice connected to bureaucracy which has become so naturalised that people are not aware of its penetrative nature – they just accept it as part of the form-filling process (Fairclough, 1998). Nobody even commented about having to provide confidential financial details, again accepting this as a necessary practice.

All the participants identified themselves as belonging to the social category of 'students' (see Tajfel, 1982, for the concept of social categorisation). The instructions on page 10, however, said to tick 'no' to the question asking if you are in full-time education, if your course has finished. Since Matt and Lee were soon to finish they had to decide whether this applied to them. Matt chose to represent himself as a student still, but Lee decided to follow the instructions rigidly. By being forced to fit into this box he is composing a paper image of himself which does not match his concept of his real self as a student, but he has to compromise his identity in order to complete the form correctly. This example of Matt and Lee highlights how reading is based on individual interpretations. It shows how the subject-positioning imposed by a text does not always have to be accepted but can be challenged to suit your own purposes, as Fairclough (1998) discussed. However, as Ivanič (1998) and Rose (1981) pointed out, there exists a tension here because you can only choose from the categories already determined for you.

From the questions asked about students it is evident that the form-designers have fixed notions about this social group. They believe that students fit only into the areas specified for them, since many other questions are difficult for students to accommodate their situation to. Page 8 asks, 'Do you have a job?', but this question cannot be addressing students because there is only a 'yes/no' option. There is no box to tick if you do vacation work, which caused difficulties for Gary and Jay who both have holiday employment. The form-writers view people either as 'workers' or as 'unemployed', pushing users into being one thing and not the other. These categories stripped the participants of their identities, with Jay, Doug and Gary being occasional workers and Matt and Lee starting jobs soon but none of them being able to represent this.

Form-filling as self-surveillance

Filling in a form is like conducting a self-analysis in terms of bureaucratically imposed categories. The questions constrain what we recall about our 'self'; we then compare these already limited details of our lives to the items presented on paper, seeing whether they match, and producing a 'form-self': a regimented version of who we are, made official and concrete by being committed to paper. However, as this research has demonstrated, this 'form-self' is usually an inadequate depiction of a person's sense of their 'true self', showing how our identity changes according to situation and according to the socially constructed identities which are made available to us. This practice of defining ourselves through a system of prescribed categories constitutes a type of self-surveillance: a characteristic of post-modern forms of regulation and discipline as discussed by Foucault (1979). It is perhaps an even more powerful form of control than that exercised by those who fill in forms on or for us, since we are submitting ourselves to regulation through our own actions. On the other hand, it opens up the possibility of resistance, as we discuss further below.

Relations of power in form-filling

Bureaucracies are important sites where power is located, and one of the ways in which they wield power is by suffocating people with forms in every domain of their lives. Forms come to represent the abstract but pervasive presence and authority of bureaucracies, and to carry out their disciplinary role.

The apparent purpose of the HC1 form is an empowering one: to help people to apply for financial benefits. Yet its actual effect is often the opposite: regimenting, disempowering, and even leading people to forfeit benefits by producing incorrect details. The form exercises power over its users through unnecessarily complex language, terms with definitions contrary to their everyday meanings, and topics selected by form-designers to which users have to accommodate themselves.

There is an apparent difference in power relations between forms used by people wanting a service they will pay for (form-filling from a relatively powerful position), and forms like the HC1 which are used by people wanting financial help. The first form places users in the superior position because the company's success relies upon the customer. The latter form places users in an inferior position because they are dependent on the help of the organisation to which they are applying, thus leaving them vulnerable to the demands of the form. Depending on the purpose of the form, the power relations shift. However, irrespective of whether you are completing a form from a relatively powerful or powerless position, you are still under the obligation to fill it in, and are therefore subjected to the 'technologies of power, which determine the conduct of individuals and submit them to certain regimes of domination, an objectivising of the subject' (Foucault, 1988: 18).

Foucault (1979) drew attention to the shift in power between pre-modern and modern societies, suggesting that today's bureaucratic discourses are a distinctive feature of power. For instance, the practice of form-filling is embedded into so many social institutions that it has become a mundane, unquestioned activity that only causes comment when problems arise. Rarely do we question the requirement to fill in the form at all. As Fairclough points out, 'Certain key institutional genres [such as form-filling] ... are among the most salient characteristics of modern societal orders of discourse' (1995: 136), and it is their sense of normalcy that sustains the administrative relations of power. By completing the forms we are allowing ourselves to be dominated by the discourse and we are legitimising the social attitudes and practices which they sustain.

It is precisely because the bureaucratic demands made by forms have become naturalised that people do not usually attempt to challenge them. We take it for granted that we have to fit into inadequate categories, even though we are compromising our identities by doing this. We tend not to acknowledge the fact that we are being positioned in this way, designing a paper character of ourselves to be typed into a computer. We represent ourselves as people we are not, and we leave ourselves open to attack on the grounds that we have given details that are 'incorrect and incomplete'. By not subverting the regime of the form we are suggesting that it is sufficient in representing our circumstances – so how is a change going to be made if there is no apparent need for it?

Reclaiming our identities

This is where we can make a stand. If we want to receive help we have to enter into a dialogue with the institution which has the power to provide it, but we don't have to conform to the positioning and accept the constraints imposed on us by the questions. We need to put ourselves in charge of the form rather than just fitting ourselves to it: to manipulate rather than maintain the power relations and assumptions. Doing this needs awareness of the ways in which administrations use form-filling as a means of regulation, and of the positioning effects of forms themselves. Being 'form literate' means being critically aware and confident in the literacy and social practices surrounding forms. It includes such things as knowing when to say, assertively, 'This does not apply to me', and write 'N/A' on the form. It includes exercising the power to adapt the form to suit your own circumstances, and even to resist the regulatory demands of some forms altogether by refusing to fill them in. Critical awareness-raising of these issues could replace lessons in 'obedient' form-filling in Basic Education classrooms and could be taught in schools and community centres across the country.

Form-filling is a complex social practice perceived by many with dread, and a 'critical' approach to form-filling might help to transform this fear into positive critique and resistance. But form designers also have a responsibility to make forms more user-friendly, as The Plain English Campaign have argued for many years. More thought could be given to ways in which users of forms can have an impact on their composition (Duffy, 1981). If forms were genuinely designed to serve the needs of users, rather than to regulate them and the benefits they can claim, the forms might be very different. Sam, a homeless person in the United States, when asked what questions he would include in a form, replied:

> I'd get the basics, Social Security, stuff like that … then I'd ask, What's going on? What seems to be your problem? I wouldn't ask them anything else. Just how they've been surviving. I'd find out what they want for help, and go from there. I mean you don't need tons of paperwork to find out something. (cited in Taylor, 1996: 151)

Such an approach to form design would reduce the gap in power relations and would allow users to be on a more equal footing with the form.

Concluding comments

We have argued that form-filling is not a matter of individual skill, but a social practice located in the technologies of power wielded by bureaucracies in an ever more pervasive information society. The research has shown that university students can have considerable difficulties with forms, even though they are considered to be highly literate on the evidence of their educational achievement. Everybody experiences some literacy difficulties (as argued by Street, 1990), especially with complex literacy practices such as form-filling which are imbued with issues of power and identity. Being aware of these issues and taking a critical approach may put power into the hands of even those with the greatest fear and hatred of forms.

Notes

1. For further details see Fawns (1999).
2. The names given are pseudonyms.
3. 'Concurrent verbalisation' is when you say aloud everything you are thinking and doing at the time of doing it. This simultaneous behaviour is difficult because it is something we are not used to doing and thus seems unnatural. Since the form-filling session relied on this

method of data collection to reveal the participants' inner thoughts about the form, it was necessary to 'train' the participants in this activity by giving them a practice period before the main data collection.

References

Barton, D. (1994) *Literacy: An Introduction to the Ecology of Written Language*, Oxford: Blackwell.

Barton, D. and Hamilton, M. (1998) *Local Literacies: Reading and Writing in One Community*, London: Routledge.

Charney, D. (1984) 'Redesigning and testing a work order form', *Information Design Journal*, 4, pp. 131–46.

Cochran-Smith, M. (1984) *The Making of a Reader*, Norwood, NJ: Ablex.

Davies P. (1994) 'Long term unemployment and literacy: a case study of the Restart interview' in Hamilton, M., Barton, D. and Ivanič, R. (eds), *Worlds of Literacy*, Cleveland: Multilingual Matters.

Duffy, T.M. (1981) 'Organising and utilising document design options', *Information Design Journal*, 2, pp. 256–66.

Fawns, M. (1999) '*Form Focus: An investigation into the HC1 form*', unpublished MA Dissertation: Department of Linguistics and Modern English Language, Lancaster University.

Fairclough, N. (1998) *Discourse and Social Change*, Cambridge: Polity Press.

Fairclough, N. (1995) *Critical Discourse Analysis: The Critical Study of Language*, London: Longman.

Foucault, M. (1972) *The Archaeology of Knowledge*, New York: Harper Colophon.

Foucault, M. (1979) *Discipline and Punish: The Birth of the Prison*, trans. A. Sheridan, Harmondsworth: Penguin.

Foucault, M. (1988) 'Technologies of the self' in Martin, L.H., Gutman, H. and Hutton, P.H. (eds), *Technologies of the Self: A Seminar with Michel Foucault*, London: Tavistock Publications.

Frohlich, D.M. (1986) 'On the organisation of form-filling behaviour', *Information Design Journal*, 5, pp. 43–59.

Ivanič, R. (1998) *Writing and Identity: The Discoursal Construction of Identity in Academic Writing*, Amsterdam: John Benjamins Publishing Co.

Rose, A.M. (1981) 'Problems in public documents', *Information Design Journal*, 2, pp. 179–96.

Smith, D.E. (1990) *Texts, Facts and Femininity: Exploring the Relations of Ruling*, London: Routledge.

Street, B.V. (1984) *Literacy in Theory and Practice*, Cambridge, UK: Cambridge University Press.

Street, B.V. (1990) 'Putting literacies on the political agenda', *RaPAL Bulletin*, 13, Autumn.

Tajfel, H. (ed.) (1982) *Social Identity and Intergroup Relations*, Cambridge, UK: Cambridge University Press.

Taylor, D. (1996) *Toxic Literacies: Exploring the Injustice of Bureaucratic Texts*, Portsmouth, NH: Heinemann.

Waller, R. (1984) 'Designing a government form: a case study', *Information Design Journal*, 4, pp. 36–57.

Wright, P. (1979) *Communicating with the Public*, London: Central Office of Information.

Wright, P. (1980) 'Textual literacy: an outline sketch of psychological research on reading and writing' in Kolers, P. *et al* (eds), *Processing of Visible Language II*, New York: Plenum Press, pp. 517–35.

Wright, P. (1981a) 'Informed design for forms', *Information Design Journal*, 2, pp. 151–78.

Wright, P. (1981b) '"The instructions clearly state …" Can't people read?', *Applied Ergonomics*, 12, pp. 131–41.

8 Literacy, literacies and ABET in South Africa: on the knife-edge, new cutting edge or thin end of the wedge?

Catherine Kell

Introduction

At the time of the *RaPAL* conference in June 1999 I remember that as I spoke I noticed that my thumb still had the ink mark on it which had allowed me to vote in South Africa's second national democratic election. As in the first election, the images of peaceful queues of people lining up in the darkness of the early morning, or waiting patiently until way after sunset, had again shown the world what a remarkable transition our traumatised society had been through. Thabo Mbeki, our new President, had been inaugurated, and one of his first, inspiring moves was to appoint Kader Asmal as Minister of Education. Since then, Asmal has made 'the eradication of illiteracy' one of his priorities.

In this chapter I sketch an overview of the key developments in policy and provision in adult literacy in South Africa. Many millions of adults in South Africa either did not attend school or attended only for a few years; they are therefore seen as functionally illiterate, and increasing their literacy capacity is seen as fundamental to their further participation in 'lifelong learning'. However, the difficulties of increasing the literacy capacity of unschooled adults are legendary and in this chapter I suggest that despite the noblest of intentions the form of the new developments in policy and provision may end up undermining their spirit. I hope to show that this contradiction in which South Africa is caught, however, results from global shifts in technologies of learning, which may be having similar effects worldwide. In this analysis I draw on the theories of Basil Bernstein (1996), in particular his charting of what he calls different pedagogic modalities over the past few decades, as well as his concept of 'recontextualisation' and 'recontextualising fields'. Finally I indicate that at the time of writing (October 2000) there seems to be a serious rethinking of the overall approach to policy and provision, and I point to some possibilities for addressing current contradictions, which I hope will have relevance beyond the South African situation.

Restructuring Adult Basic Education post-apartheid

Adult literacy work in South Africa in the period of change and transition of the past 10 to 15 years has been characterised by a general move from non-formal and informal modes of provision to formalisation and standardisation. In this process literacy has been subsumed into what, by 1994, had became known as Adult Basic Education and Training (ABET).[1]

Prior to 1994, there were as many definitions of ABET as there were sites in which it was practised. There was no overall state regulation in the field, no canon, no professional structures and no agreed-upon measures of success. Adult literacy teaching did take place in roughly three different sites of practice: within industry; within the state night schools (where the school syllabus of 'Bantu education' was followed) and within a wide range of non-governmental organisations (NGOs) many of which were influenced by and committed to the Freirean approach. Adult literacy work, particularly in the third site of practice, commanded tremendous moral authority, and the dominant discourse around literacy was deeply embedded in the narrative of the struggle against apartheid, with the concepts of empowerment, learner-centredness and relevance placed in the centre.

By the early 1990s a number of the literacy activists working particularly within NGOs and the trade unions initiated various policy development processes, with the view that as South Africa achieved the long-struggled-for democratic government, adult education would receive priority treatment. The main effort of this policy work was to develop an overarching framework that could regulate literacy provision and pedagogy within all of the three main sites of practice. The key influence in this phase was the wholesale adoption of 'outcomes-based education' (OBE) – seen as the key to educational reform in South Africa, borrowed largely from Australia. Since then, work within the policy arena has been characterised by intensive and costly national processes of formalisation and standardisation. After 1994, in the atmosphere of national reconciliation and consensus-building, 'stakeholder forums' (in which representatives of big business, trade unions, NGOs and other organisations thrashed out their proposals and attempted to reach consensus) played a prominent role in policy development.[2]

Our National Qualifications Framework (NQF), now almost in place, is seen to open up the possibilities for lifelong learning for human resources development in order to build a 'clever country' and increase economic competitiveness. ABET levels on the NQF correspond with the levels that children go through in formal schooling, and the outcomes-based approach for literacy learning for adults has been harmonised with the approach for children (this approach was enshrined in the development and adoption of 'Curriculum 2005' for formal schooling from Grades 1 to 12). Literacy is seen as a 'fundamental' category, acquired in staged and sequenced ways along with other areas of learning called 'core' and 'specialisation' categories. It stands firmly at the bottom rung of those well-known ladders, grids and matrices which have become so much part of the semiotic vocabulary of educational reform. Every aspect of life in South Africa now belongs in 12 recently-defined 'Organising Fields', governed by a 'Sectoral Education and Training Authority', and the race is on to define unit standards in already-specified 'Learning Areas' and get them registered with the NQF. The unit standards, however, do not specify the content of learning, but rather the outcomes of learning. The way in which content is brought into learning programmes in ABET is through published packages, which for literacy learning, include workbooks, calendars, often pens and so on.

Another important development in the field during the 1990s was the establishment of a national examination board for the ABET levels, the Independent Examination Board. This Board currently offers a range of exams, which according to French (1997) constitutes a two-sided project: 'they provide real certificates with national street credibility, and at the same time they are experimental and developmental in nature' (with):

> an innovative system of assessment using outcomes, explicit assessment criteria and requirements, and annotated exemplars. The aims and outcomes attempted to accommodate different perspectives: major trends in curriculum development, cherished adult education values (which are sometimes difficult to reconcile with a certification system) and the demands of professional educational assessment.

Each of these developments has had effects felt at the level of the literacy class itself, over the past few years.

Firstly, the balance between the different sectors of provision of ABET has shifted. Most long-standing NGOs have had to close down as a result of funding crises. These crises arose when overseas funders went into bilateral agreements with the new government rather than continuing to fund organisations in civil society. A crucial stratum of educators, teacher-trainers and materials-developers with long years of experience has thus been lost to the field. Increased funding through government structures has led to some strengthening of the state sector (particularly in correctional services and public works programmes); however, it is in this form of provision that the inadequacies of teacher-training are most keenly felt.

Observations of ABET classes showed that very poorly trained literacy teachers with minimal resources at their disposal were unable to bring content into their lessons in order for meaningful learning and progression to occur (Kell, 1996). Standards became the curriculum, and there was a general evacuation of content. The vacuum thus created was then easily filled by substituting procedures for content. The way the outcomes had been written provided just such a recipe.[3] This seems to be backed up within the structuring of teacher training, which is also subject to the unit standards, which at a quick glance seem to be concerned with 'how to' (achieve a specific output) rather than the 'inputs' related to the content of learning.

The only point at which the content of teaching and learning has been seriously considered has been by the educational publishers, who have produced materials to address this gap. The term 'teacher-proof' materials entered the discourse, as the inadequacies of teacher training became apparent. The result of this is expensive step-by-step packages with high development costs, which have been passed on to providers, causing further crises in the system. These packages are now seen as essential to the work of any provider worth its salt.

The exams system has also had a dramatic effect in the field over the past few years. The Joint Education Trust, the most powerful funder in the field, made the registration of learners for the exams a condition for project funding (Harley *et al*, 1996). A number of studies showed that the published lists of outcomes and the 'mock' exam papers had penetrated into the most remote rural areas. The lists of outcomes were being used as a syllabus and the exam papers were being used to teach to the test. Harley *et al* (1996) note that:

> materials writers and publishers immediately began slotting existing material into levels dictated by the Independent Examinations Board exams and made efforts to start writing materials for apparent gaps. People involved in ABE teaching scrutinised the exams for items their learners would have struggled with and changed the content and structure of their courses accordingly. Designers of teacher training courses are similarly adjusting their courses to equip teachers to get their learners through the examinations. Although the ... lists of competencies (outcomes) that will be tested are supposedly a way of avoiding being tied to particular courses, course constructors are beginning to use these lists of competencies as a kind of syllabus. The general impact of this 'backwash effect' will undoubtedly be great over the next few years.

At the same time a new urgency has been created in public discourse about the need for ABET, that plans for economic growth and for the 'African Renaissance' would be stymied by the problem of 'illiteracy'. The slogan adopted for 1999 was 'No ABET, No Renaissance!', accompanied by images of how the masses need ABET in order to make the transition from darkness into light, from backwardness into modernity. ABET was portrayed as the technology for making this great leap forward – the evolutionary conception of literacy hard at work!

Over the past year (1999 to 2000) and under the leadership of the Minister of Education, Kader Asmal, there has been a recent review of the implementation of Curriculum 2005 in the formal schooling sector, and the recommendation has been accepted that it be radically restructured. 'Curriculum 21' will now replace Curriculum 2005, and this has implications for the implementation of ABET.[4] It appears that there has been a rethink of the NQF-based approach to basic literacy and a national literacy campaign has been announced. The details are still under discussion but it appears that there is agreement that teaching will be done by volunteers, using a standard primer with additional reading materials and supplemented by TV and radio broadcasting. The implications of this departure from the work of the past 10 years are still to be felt.

Shifting pedagogic models

Bernstein (1996: 54–80) provides us with a useful means of analysing changes such as these with his discussion of changing pedagogic models, in particular the shift from competence modes to performance modes.[5] He explains that in the 1960s, a remarkable convergence in the human sciences occurred around the concept of competence. Drawing from specialist fields within the social and psychological sciences, this convergence embraced linguistic competence, cognitive competence, cultural competence and communicative competence:

> Where some writers have stressed its biological, some its acquisitional, provenance, and some an interaction between the two, all agree that competence refers to a tacitly possessed capacity capable of generating creative variety ... Competence announces a universal democracy of acquisition.

Bernstein details the pedagogic consequences of this convergence, showing how the concept of competence gave rise to specialised pedagogic modes which constructed specialised identities for teachers and learners, taking a number of forms which Bernstein has termed the 'liberal/progressive; populist and radical'.

Performance models, however, place the emphasis on the specific and specified output of the acquirer, are considered instrumental, and stress economic goals. Muller (1996) presents the differences between competence and performance as shown in Table 8.1.

Bernstein shows how these modes achieve dominance in different historical periods through an analysis of the relative autonomy of what he calls recontextualising fields. He argues that 'pedagogic discourse is constructed by a recontextualising principle which selectively appropriates, relocates, refocuses and relates other discourses to constitute its own order'. The recontextualising principle creates recontextualising fields; the official recontextualising field (ORF) 'created and dominated by the state and its selected agencies and ministries' and the pedagogic recontextualising field

Pedagogic Models

	Competence (acquisition-competence)	Performance (transmission-performance)
Learner	Control over selection, sequence and pace of learning	Little control over selection, sequence and pace of learning
Teacher	Personal control	Positional control
Pedagogic text	Ungraded and unstratified performance	Graded and stratified performance
	Competence read through the performance	The performance itself
Assessment	General competence criteria	Specific competence criteria
	Presences in terms of difference	Absences in terms of deficit
Learning sites	Anywhere	Clearly marked
Role of the state	Increased	Decreased
Class sponsors	Professional educational middle class	Economic sector and entrepreneurial middle class
Costs	High teacher training cost	Lower teacher training costs
	Hidden time-based costs	Economies of external control
	Less efficient with large classes	Can deal with large numbers

**Table 8.1 The differences between competences and performance
Source: Muller (1996)**

(PRF). 'The latter consists of pedagogues in schools and colleges, and departments of education, specialized journals, private research foundations.'

Table 8.1 helps to show that much of the progressive and oppositional literacy work in South Africa prior to 1990 operated within a competence model as described by Bernstein. This period was characterised by a complete absence of an ORF (no state regulation, standards, curriculum guidelines, and so on), but there was quite a strong and autonomous PRF (active teachers, producing and testing materials, attempting to share experiences and so on). Learner-centredness was seen as crucial. Teachers were defined by their 'dedication' and 'commitment' to the field rather than their class positions as professionals. They relied on less visible forms of pedagogy, preferring to let learners control the direction and pace of their learning. Learner achievements were neither graded nor stratified. Learning sites were not clearly defined, and so on.[6]

The period from 1995 to 1999 seemed to represent the ascendance of the performance model. With the decline of the NGOs many of the university-trained activists moved out of the field and the autonomy of the PRF declined. State regulation took hold of the entire field from top to bottom. Performance became monitored through the specification of outcomes and the adherence to unit standards. Unlike the competence model, the view has taken root that learners are not assumed to have knowledge and self-direction 'within' but are to achieve externally defined goals. Teachers therefore play a more visible role in prescribing and evaluating achievement of these goals. National standards for teacher training have been introduced, and these will be linked to pay scales. The deficit model pervades the approach – as in the slogan 'No ABET, no Renaissance!'.

Bernstein suggests that the competence model is sponsored by the professional educational middle class, while the performance model is sponsored by the economic sector and entrepreneurial middle class. This became evident during the proceedings of the stakeholder forums as described above, and many of the NGO participants became very disillusioned as the voice of big business drowned out other voices.

In these processes of contestation, a coalition of NGOs (the National Literacy Co-operation, now defunct) drew on the assistance of Professor Bhola, a well-known figure in literacy work internationally, who argued that 'the conceptualisation of ABET in South Africa was well-structured in its formal logic, but ideologically and theoretically flawed'. According to him, ABET represented 'an ideological retreat from earlier proclamations of the liberation struggle, for it now excludes by benign neglect, the populations in greatest need of assistance: the rural poor, urban and peri-urban settlements, and the constituencies of women, youth, the unemployed and under-employed, and farm labour' (quoted by Hamilton, in Kell, 1996). Bhola thereby implied that really the only constituency that was to be served was the industrial sector. This echoed much of the general response from NGOs who claimed that big business was driving the process, and that all that they had fought for over the past few years, i.e. the earlier version of competence, was being lost.

Autonomous or ideological models of literacy

The policy and provision issues described above can be conceptualised as one discursive domain (Domain One). In this domain 'literacy' becomes a kind of virtual image (created through the standardising processes of fixing levels, writing unit standards and setting performance criteria) which is projected onto the framework of the NQF and where it lives as a uni-dimensional, autonomous phenomenon (Freebody, 1997; Kell, 1998), accredited with the power to effect change in people's lives. People who have had little schooling often buy into this notion of literacy. In one part of their identity they see themselves as lacking something, as deficient, as unschooled, as stupid.

Drawing on Street's ideological model of literacy, the Social Uses of Literacy project in South Africa (Prinsloo and Breier, 1996; Prinsloo and Kell, 1998) showed that unschooled people did not necessarily see themselves as being in a state of deficit at all. They had achieved a sense of identity through other valued cultural attributes. They had established important social networks to sustain themselves and their families, sometimes involving reciprocal relationships in which the need for literacy assistance would be traded for other valuable skills, like mechanical skills or child support. In some cases they had apprenticed themselves to others to acquire literacy skills in adulthood, but mainly they drew on the assistance of literacy mediators to decode important texts in their lives.

It becomes possible then, to describe another discursive domain (Domain Two) where people are embedded in literacy practices, where powerful distributive networks operate to counteract literacy problems, and where people achieve important goals in their lives.

The interesting question from a pedagogical point of view is what are the points of connection between these two domains? In which domain does the 'literacy class' exist? During the time that the competence mode was dominant (i.e. prior to 1994), and in the absence of an Official Recontextualising Field (ORF), the 'literacy class' generally belonged in Domain Two. Learner-centredness and relevance were the catch-words. However, with the ascendence of the performance mode (between 1994 and 1999) it has largely shifted up into Domain One. My own research has shown that, in South Africa, there are few points of connection, in fact the two domains almost seem to miss each other. Recent research on letter writing practices (Kell, in Barton and Hall, 2000) showed that in Domain One, personal letter writing was seen as a practice regulated by standards which specified 'elements' of letters, including even the type of affect expressed in what were called 'greetings', 'opening sentences' and 'acknowledgements'. Additional 'elements' necessary for the sending of letters through the postal service were prescribed. However, when I studied the letter writing practices of unschooled migrant workers, a completely different picture emerged which bore minimal resemblance to that portrayed in the publisher-produced packages and government-prescribed lists of outcomes. None of the elements from Domain One was relevant in Domain Two. Even the notion of using the postal service was laughed at by the workers, who said that they never used it, they had worked out an effective and efficient system of sending letters (even those including substantial amounts of money) by the buses which travelled the thousand or so kilometres between Cape Town and their homes in the rural areas.

Literacy in the third space, or literacy as sign?

Wilson, in her work on literacy amongst prisoners (in Barton *et al*, 2000), develops what she calls third-space theory, drawing on post-colonial theorist Homi Bhabha (1994). Wilson claims that in between literacy and prison, and literacy practices and particular prisons, there exists a third space which, according to Bhabha, is the 'precondition for the articulation of cultural difference'. This space could potentially lie between, or overlap, the two discursive domains described above, providing a context for literacy learners and teachers to appropriate from each, as the prisoners in Wilson's study did (see Figure 8.1). Clearly this is the potential pedagogic space in which the capacity for critical literacy (Lankshear, 1997) or meta-learning (Gee, 1992) or 'reflection literacy' (Hasan, 1992) could develop. And maybe people will appropriate from each domain.

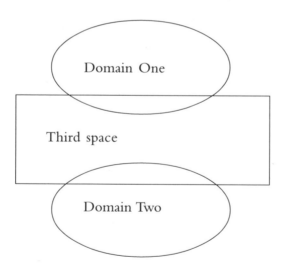

Figure 8.1 A third space, needed for the 'articulation of cultural difference' (see Wilson, in Barton et al, 2000)

But what seems to be happening in the meantime is that a phenomenon which I call 'literacy as sign' (or perhaps 'simulacrum') interposes between the two domains, creating a barrier to the emergence of the 'third space'. This could perhaps be conceptualised as 'virtual literacy', or perhaps as a version of Bernstein's performance model: the 'generic mode'.

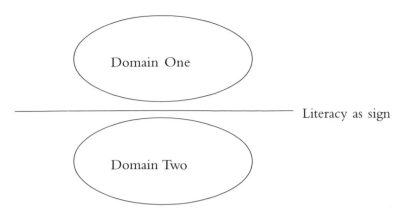

Figure 8.2 Literacy as sign creates a barrier to the emergence of the third space

Bernstein claims that 'generic modes' are constructed and distributed outside of pedagogic recontextualising fields, for example through manpower commissions, departments of labour and training agencies. These involve the identification of a set of generic skills which underlie a range of specific performances which occur outside of schooling (i.e. work and life), and are directly linked to the instrumentalities of the market, to the construction of what are considered to be flexible performances. 'The extension of generic modes from their base in manual practices to a range of practices and areas of work, institutionalises the concept of trainability as the fundamental pedagogic objective'[7] (1996: 73). Furthermore, Bernstein suggests that the identity constructed by generic modes is socially 'empty', and emptied of the 'possibility for critical thought':

> The specialized recontextualising field produces and reproduces imaginary concepts of work and life which abstract such experiences from the power relations of their lived conditions and negate the possibilities of understanding and criticism.

Coming back to Domain One in Figure 8.2, because literacy is presented as generic skill in the outcomes (there is no content automatically attached to it) teachers end up presenting learners with emptied outcomes which become hyper-pedagogised. Unfortunate learners try to learn this hyper-pedagogised literacy, but it bears little resemblance to what goes on in their everyday lives. It seems that they engage with it for the purposes of exchange value (certification purposes) rather than use value, and this is characterised by the fetishisation of procedures above content, which I touched on above. The form that this generic mode takes seems to involve a technologisation of language, which turns knowledge of language into procedures to accumulate credits. Indeed, it has been suggested that learners' credits could be registered on a smart-card.[8]

The new National Qualifications Framework has been conceptualised as a huge virtual jungle gym (Kell, 1996) hovering over South Africa, with supposedly vertical and horizontal learning pathways. To traverse the vertical or horizontal bars, literacy and language teaching is creating new discursive products with new currencies of exchange. This seems to be leading to the commodification of language for the purposes of learning, which may well exclude from such processes of learning those who can least afford it.

In the meantime, in Domain Two, new communicative modalities are being thrown up through South Africa's re-incorporation into global markets: oral, gestural, visual channels of communication jostle with the printed word, and the cell-phone; the Internet; on-the-spot marketing through dance and music seem to show up staged and sequenced literacy pedagogies as outdated. At the same time, in the world of training, in the workplaces of the new capitalism, as Gee has pointed out:

> Newcomers (apprentices) are 'trained' by being scaffolded in 'joint practice' with those already adept at the practice, not (just) through overt instruction which cannot carry the full load of 'tacit knowledge in practice' and goes out of date. Everyone in the community of practice gains knowledge through immersion in the collaborative practice; knowledge that they may not be able to explicate in words, but which they can pass on through the socialisation of new members. (in Barton *et al*, 2000:186)

The worry is, might the literacy pedagogies (and the subsequent commodification) in Domain One be further disadvantaging potential learners, or excluding them?

As indicated above, this worry may have been heard by the Education Ministry, with the idea of a volunteer-driven national literacy campaign now taking shape. A new call has been made for the recognition of another paradigm to the ABET/NQF one – called ALBED (Adult Literacy and Basic Education for Development). There is a growing interest amongst trainers and teachers in the REFLECT approach (Regenerated Freirean Literacy Through Empowering Community Techniques). These all seem to suggest something of a return to the competence model discussed above.

The big question is, could we be doing it differently? To expand: could we avoid the evolutionary step backwards (getting adults into ABET classes at Level 1) in order to go forwards (to the 'clever country')? What means can we find to short-circuit that step backwards? Can we avoid the raised expectations, pitfalls and failures of literacy campaigns worldwide? There are no easy answers to these questions. The events of the first half of 2000 seem to indicate that approaches to literacy work are poised on a knife-edge.

In my view, what would be important steps would be to play down the schooling and standardising of literacy for unschooled adults. At the same time it would be useful to play up a view of literacies as connected into flows of information, people and knowledge within broader social relations and processes. This would imply a located view of literacies, and a growing awareness of the acquisition and transmission processes embedded within communities of practice (Wenger, 2000). Furthermore, we have dynamic and intelligent national language policies and telecommunications policies, which may enable our diversity of languages to be seen as a resource rather than a problem, and which may be able to bring communications technologies within reach of the majority of South Africans. Such possibilities, while needing a great deal of research, are not incompatible with the rhetoric around lifelong learning, the building of learning organisations and a learning society. These may yet prove to be the cutting edge for literacy work compatible with the demands and processes of the twenty-first century, less disabling and somehow happier and healthier than the stale 'bringing light into the darkness' metaphors provided by the tired, old, evolutionary conception of literacy embodied in the ABET levels and standards – the thin edge of the wedge.

Notes

1. There has been a recent move (2000) to challenge formalisation and this is touched on further below.
2. 'Stakeholder politics', as it came to be called, has both advantages and disadvantages which have been hotly debated in South Africa. The participatory and anti-elitist ethic of this form of politics held enormous appeal initially (early 90s). However, it soon became evident that this very ethic could conceal deeply unequal power relations, as well as mask the question of the source of 'educational authority'.
3. This problem has also been noted as a key problem in the adoption of the outcomes-based approach in formal schooling.
4. The Curriculum Review can be interpreted as saying that there is a need for a 'Back to Basics' approach to schooling. The Review, however, did not address itself to the implications of such an approach in the ABET sector and the Further Education and Training sector.
5. The terminology used in South Africa prior to 'outcomes-based' approaches was 'competency-based education and training (CBET)' which arose in vocational training contexts. CBET is more compatible with Bernstein's performance model. Bernstein's competence model arises from an analysis of developments in the fields of cognitive psychology, anthropology, linguistics and so on which he feels were allied to the liberal, progressive and radical ideologies of the late 1960s, and which were taken up in the educational arena by figures like Paulo Freire.
6. It must be stressed, however, that Bernstein's models are constructed as ideal types for the purposes of analysis. In reality, curricula are usually hybrids of performance and competence elements. This was certainly true in the earlier period of literacy work in South Africa, where the 'competence' model was promoted by university-trained, often left-wing activists, deeply committed to the Freirean approach. In practice, however, literacy facilitators were often unable to implement the approach because of a lack of inputs and training. There were also literacy activists who were starting to realise the limits of implementing the competence model on a large scale in conditions of lack of training, expertise and resources.

7.   The importance of this should not be underestimated in the context of general educational reform in South Africa. It should be remembered that some the earliest discussions around outcomes-based education originated in the industrial training boards and the trade unions. These drew firmly on the Mayer lists of competencies which were developed in Australia to define what competent workers across industries could do (Mayer *et al*, 1992; Lyster, 1997).They assumed a strong foundation of general education and were aimed at preparing young people for the world of work.When implemented in the context of basic education and at the earliest levels of schooling (as was attempted with the introduction of Curriculum 2005) there is little wonder in the fact that they could not provide the content for learning and the mechanisms for sequencing learning.These inadequacies have now been shown up by the very recent Review of Curriculum 2005.

8.   This was suggested by the person who is now the Director of the South African Qualifications Authority at a seminar held by the World University Services in Pretoria in 1996.

References

Aitcheson, J., Harley, A., Land, S. and Lyster, E. (1996) *Survey of Adult Basic Education South Africa in the 1990s*, Cape Town: SACHED Books.

African National Congress, Education Department (1994) *A Policy Framework for Education and Training*.

Barton, D. Hall, N. (2000) *Letter Writing as a Social Practice*, Amsterdam: John Benjamins.

Barton, D. and Hamilton, M. (2000) *Situated Literacies: Reading and Writing in Context*, London: Routledge.

Barton, D., Hamilton, and Hamilton, M. (1998) *Local Literacies*, London and New York: Routledge.

Bernstein, B. (1996) *Pedagogy, Symbolic control and Identity: Theory, Research, Critique*, London: Taylor and Francis.

Bhabha, H. (1994) *The Location of Culture*, London: Routledge.

Department of Education Directorate: Adult Basic, Community Education and Training (1995) *A National Adult Basic Education and Training Framework: Interim Guidelines*, Cape Town: SACHED Books.

Department of Education Directorate: Adult Basic Community Education and Training (undated) *A National Multi-Year Implementation Plan for Adult Education and Training: Provision and Acreditation*, Cape Town: SACHED Books:

Freebody, P. (1997) 'Assessment as communal versus punitive practice', *Literacy and Numeracy Studies*, 7 (2), pp 5–17.

French, E. (1997) 'Learning from the IEB's ABET exams: A Selective Reflection on Data from IEB's Year-end ABET Examinations', in *ABET Journal*, Vol 1, No 1.

Gee, J. (1992) *Social Linguistics and Literacies: Ideologies in Discourse*, London: Taylor and Francis.

Harley, A., Aitcheson, J., Lyster, E. and Land, S. (1996) *A Survey of Adult Basic Education in South Africa in the 90s*, Johannesburg: SACHED Books.

Hasan, R. (1992) *Literacy in Society*, London: Longmans.

Kell, C. (1998) 'Living with the literacy line: a response to Peter Freebody', *Literacy and Numeracy Studies*, 8 (2), pp. 79–90.

Kell, C. (1996) 'Getting the 15 million onto the NQF jungle gym: towards a critique of current policy and practice in Adult Basic Education and Training' in Robertson, S.A. (ed.), *In Pursuit of (E)quality*, Kenton 1995, Cape Town: Juta, pp. 169–87.

Lankshear, C. (1997) *Changing Literacies*, Buckingham and Philadelphia: Open University Press.

Lyster, E. (1997) 'ABE practitioner development in South Africa: the gap between theory, policy and practice', paper presented at the *Australian Council for Adult Literacy Conference*, Sydney, Australia, 9–11 October 1997.

Mayer, E. *et al* (1992) *Key Competencies* (Draft Report), Canberra: Commonwealth Government.

Muller, J. (1998) 'The Well-Tempered Learner: Self-Regulation, Pedagogical Models and Teacher Education Policy' in *Comparative Education*, Vol 34, No 1.

Prinsloo, M. and Breier, M. (eds) (1996) *The Social Uses of literacy*, Cape Town: SACHED Books and Amsterdam and Philadelphia: Benjamin Publishers.

Prinsloo, M. and Kell, C. (1998) 'Literacy on the ground: a located perspective on literacy policy in South Africa', *in Literacy and Numeracy Studies*, 7 (2), pp. 83–101.

Street, B. (1998) 'New Literacies in theory and practice: what are the implications for language in education?', *Inaugural Address*, University of London, October.

Street, B. (1995) *Social Literacies: Critical Perspectives on Literacy in Development, Ethnography, Education*, London: Longman.

Wenger, E. (2000) *Communities of Practice*, London: Routledge.

9 Democracy as a way of life: literacy for citizenship

Jim Crowther and Lyn Tett

> *Of a group who were tried in connection with a Chartist outbreak in the manufacturing districts, a large proportion could scarcely read or write. But the human material was different from what it had been half a century earlier. Intelligence, 'in a degree which was formerly thought impossible', had spread to 'the lower and down to the lowest rank'; and with intelligence went the faculty of disciplined action and adherence to principle. (Dobbs, 1919: 213)*

In this chapter we ask, what can literacy work do to contribute to democracy as a *way of life*? The skills of reading and writing are important for an active and informed citizenry. However, the practice of democracy involves much more than reading names on a form and marking a ballot paper with a cross. Whilst not demeaning the important choice this literacy skill involves, one of the central themes of democratic life is the extent to which people can participate in the processes of decision making in all aspects of communal and public life. It's quite obvious that formal equality of voting rights does not translate into equal levels of influence. Inequalities of wealth and power generate inequalities of political influence in all spheres of life (Phillips, 1994). Literacy work, we suggest, must be part of a broad education that provides opportunities for adults to take greater individual and collective control over their lives.

Literacy, access to information, and effective communication skills must be considered as part of the way inequalities of power are systematically reproduced. In a democracy, political representatives, public institutions and services, the activities of those who work for them (e.g. doctors, teachers, welfare workers), community organisations and groups, have to be accountable to the people they represent or work for if democracy is to become a way of life. Literacy education should, therefore, contribute towards enabling people to interrogate the claims and activities done on their behalf and, in turn, encourage them to develop the skill, analysis and confidence to make their own voice heard.

In relation to writing and understanding text we live in times where there is a widening gap between the information 'rich' and the information 'poor': a phenomenon affecting relations between different countries as well as relations within society (Lankshear, 1998). The volume of textual and non-textual information is increasing whilst our ability and time to make sense of it seems to decrease. What hope have people struggling to read and write to make of this? How can they effectively participate and gain back some control over their lives? We should not, of course, assume that because some adult students lack techniques of reading and writing they are incapable of critical inquiry. The equation that 'illiteracy' implies a deficit person has to be strongly resisted. Instead, we subscribe to Jackson's (1995) view that 'adults bring something which derives both from their experience of adult life and from their status as citizens to the educational process' which in turn has implications for the literacy curriculum and what it seeks to achieve. Moreover, the current policy interest in citizenship, we argue, presents an opportunity to go beyond the limited – and limiting – functional way of thinking about literacy and a deficit model of literacy students.

Discourses of citizenship

Citizenship, as Carr (1991) makes clear, is a 'contested concept' in that the 'criteria governing its proper use are constantly challenged and disputed'. They are contingent in character depending on changes in society and how a proper relationship between the individual and the wider community are understood. Where the balance between the rights and duties of individuals is struck is an obvious source of tension. Marshall (1950), in his seminal analysis, makes the distinction between three types of rights essential for understanding citizenship. The first, civil rights, involves individual freedom of the person, of speech and so on. The second, political rights, concerns the extension of the franchise to enable people to share political power. Finally, social rights indicates the right to economic welfare, social security, health and education as a context in which other rights are exercised. There is also an important difference between citizenship as an *ascribed status* and citizenship as an *asserted practice* (Lister, 1998). The former refers to the legal rights people possess as members of a society whereas the latter recognises that rights have often to be realised by actively claiming them through a political process. The question then, is about *how people learn to claim their rights of citizenship* as distinct from *being taught how to be citizens*.

Martin (1999) makes an important distinction between the *rhetoric* of the current policy context on citizenship and the *discourses* that inform them. The rhetoric has been seductive (e.g. promoting active citizenship and social inclusion) and seems to offer the opportunity to engage in a critically informed education. What more could the socially purposeful educator want? However, the discourses that are having an important influence on how policy is inscribed in experience are more limiting than the rhetoric suggests. He identifies two dominant economistic discourses of citizenship that position the adult learner as either a worker/producer or as a customer/consumer. In the first, education is equated with training for work. In the second, education is understood as a demand-side commodity to be bought and sold. Both are reductionist in that adult learning is seen only in economic terms. As Martin goes on to say:

It is not, of course, that these economistic discourses do not matter –
self-evidently, they do. Rather, it is that they simply do not account for
enough of what adult education, let alone lifelong learning, should be
about. We are not just servicers of the economy or traders in the
educational marketplace. On the contrary, our interests lies in enabling
people to develop to their full potential as 'whole persons' or rounded
human beings. This suggests that adult education should help people
to engage in a wide range of political roles and social relationships that
occur outside both the workplace and the marketplace. We are more
than simply creatures of the cash nexus. (1999: 17)

There are various examples of both types of this discourse in adult literacy. In
relation to the adult learner as a producer/worker the basis of much current
policy is aimed at providing young adults and others with basic skills in reading,
writing and numeracy as pre-requisites for entering the job market. For
example, the Green Paper, *Opportunity Scotland* (Scottish Office, 1998), identifies
literacy as an essential pre-vocational competence or a component of workplace
learning. Unemployment, particularly for young adults, is assumed to be caused
by the absence of functional literacy skills. Public policy generally provides
funding to support literacy provision that is linked with economic
improvement for both society and the individual. For example, a Scottish Office
consultative document argued that: 'Scotland's future competitiveness demands
a more highly skilled and adaptable work force' (SOEID, 1997: 5). The
assumption made from this economistic perspective is that literacy is the same
thing for everyone since it is regarded only as the skill to employ the
technology of print. Literacy is therefore seen as completely independent of
specific social contexts and the uses to which it is put in daily life. 'It is neutral
in that it is detached from the concerns, values, attitudes, trends, tastes, practices
and patterns of power or influence to be found within social settings'
(Lankshear and Lawler, 1989: 40). However, what is regarded as 'functional'
cannot be understood outside of the processes that define it, and differentially
distribute it, to different groups. Decoding words and texts cannot simply be
understood as a neutral skill. For example, what is functional rarely includes
the ability to control or influence the decisions that affect people's lives – but
surely these are essential too for everyday life? What could be more basic for
an adult? How more adult-like can basic education be?

The other discourse of the adult learner as a consumer has been present
in adult literacy work but the learner has been seen as a reluctant participant.
For example, the Scottish Office has suggested that 'we must convince
individuals of the relevance of continuing learning' (SOEID, 1997: 5). Adult
literacy provision has not been fostered as a consumers' market because the
literacy student has been seen as a reluctant consumer to be encouraged to
shake off the stigma of literacy and participate in a learning programme.

However, competition between providers has been encouraged, particularly in relation to training for employment initiatives. This has led to some adult literacy learners being put in the position of 'quasi-consumers' choosing between different providers offering different packages of training.

Instead, of seeing the adult learner as a worker or consumer we want to argue for an 'adult education of engagement' (Jackson, 1995) in which adult students are located as active (and, if necessary, dissenting) citizens in a democratic society. Martin (1999) goes on to argue that we need to open the critical and creative space between the politics of the state and its concern with citizenship as an individually ascribed legal status and the cultural politics of civil society where citizenship is learnt through a collectively asserted social practice. However, we need also to address the way in which policy is also informed by a moral discourse too. The vision informing New Labour policy is one of an ethical community in which individuals are essentially co-operative (Bhaskar, 1994). Not only is it the duty of citizens to actively seek work, but they should also give their time and effort for the wider benefit of the community. In terms of citizenship this becomes translated into urging people to undertake voluntary 'good deeds' where these become substitutes for political action. The current Scottish policy context is a case in point. Adult and community educators are urged to address active citizenship but are discouraged from seeing this as a political process: 'achieving education of our citizens, as opposed to politicisation of our citizens, is perhaps the most difficult balance to achieve' (Osler, 1999: 10).

Adult literacy in Scotland is largely carried out through the provision of Community Education Services and the development of policy in this area is critically significant. Osler, the author of the influential policy statement for community education, proposes that community educators should be educating the 'good citizen' and this would include:

- *Political participation*: providing individuals with the capacity, confidence and interest to engage with the political decision making processes at all levels;
- *Economic participation*: through functional preparation for, and enhancement of, work which includes literacy, numeracy, ICT and other core skills;
- *Social participation*: empowering the individual to engage effectively with others in society and in their communities. (1999: 8)

Whilst people should be encouraged to participate in various aspects of social, economic, political and educational life, the ideology informing this is a liberal-pluralist one. Participation in politics, for example, is seen to involve regular voting and making use of established political processes, rather than activity in the 'new politics' of social movements or collectivities in struggle. Individual 'good deeds' are to be encouraged, e.g. volunteering is acceptable, but not collective social action. Literacy skills are assigned to a vocational role as a core skill. The contribution it may have to offer, for those seeking to become actively involved in community struggles, and who are learning to assert and extend their rights as citizens, is not on the curriculum.

The moral dimension of the above discourse on citizenship is not in itself the problem: the assumption that we concur with its claims and that such claims are outwith a political process of debate and dialogue is where the problem lies. The meaning of citizenship will always be open to conflicting interpretations. All formulations of citizenship involve moral considerations; however, this itself is not sufficient unless it includes a political dimension too. As Carr and Hartnett (1996) point out:

> The only kind of civic education which can prepare people as citizens for life in a fully democratic society is one which acknowledges both that the meaning of citizenship is perennially the subject of contestation, and that it is through this process of contestation that the relationship between the citizen and the state is being continuously redefined (1996: 82).

Without a broad political analysis included in our understanding of citizenship a number of important questions are evaded. The first is that it deflects attention away from the context in which moral duties are to be exercised. We need to ask why those who benefit least from society should be expected to offer the same as those who benefit most. The second is that it is historical. Where did our existing rights come from? Who fought and struggled for them? Where did these struggles take place? Can we assume that governments will always look after our rights? Or do rights have to be continually argued and struggled for? Assuming we have not reached the end of history, where will the forces for new rights come from?

An education that does not alert people to the forces that infringe their rights and examine ways in which they can be protected and extended will sell them short. The location of adult literacy in policy mainly as a contributor to economic participation effectively excludes it from issues relevant to full citizenship. This is a discourse of deficiency. Moreover, the distinction between acceptable education for citizenship and an unacceptable form of collective community or social action assumes a particular way of thinking about the public arena of politics as self-evidently correct. Challenges to existing representative institutions and procedures by social movements would constitute an infringement of democracy, from this perspective, rather than an arena in which a legitimate politics is carried out. This is an asserted politics and not a justified one.

The problem that is implicitly the focus of community education policy in Scotland is that of 'under-active' and 'over-active' citizens: too much active citizenry can lead to a more politicised populace whereas too little can result in an apathetic and unemployed one. Either way the legitimacy of democratic institutions of the state and society may be called into question. The space that exists between these two terms and how they are regulated may provide the ground for a socially purposeful adult literacy. The terms of the relationship between the private interests and activities of individuals and the public sphere of power and politics cannot be prescribed in policy. The terms of this relationship must be the outcome of a democratic process and is always subject to contestation. As Oliver (1996) remarks, 'when the relationship between the state and its population is in crisis, citizenship becomes the device whereby such a crisis is talked about and mediated'. This is the process that has to be opened up rather than closed down – and this is an educational as well as a political task and one that connects education, citizenship and democracy.

Democratic intellectualism: literacy for citizenship

Building a literacy curriculum has to recognise that many people want to acquire literacy for a variety of purposes – most likely the dominant one will be an instrumental purpose related to an everyday life problem. On the other hand, people often desire to get involved in community life but are hampered by low self-confidence and low self-esteem. To address this requires not only literacy but also a much broader education (see Coleman, 2000). Moreover, adults' expectations of literacy have been shaped by previous experience that treats literacy as a neutral skill. Developing literacy in the context of a rich and broad curriculum will, therefore, have to work with, as well as against the grain of cultural expectations.

In the Scottish context there is a tradition of educational philosophy that links the aspiration to connect education with wider issues of a democratic way of life. The tradition of 'democratic intellectualism' was part of a debate related to a claimed meritocratic form of university education that was specific to the curriculum of these institutions. It was not seen as a project *outside* of these institutions, nor was it, in all likelihood, seen as a feasible project for the mass of people. Nonetheless, we would argue the principles that inform it do connect with the aspiration for a critical and questioning citizenry that can be adapted for literacy work in communities.

Alexander and Martin (1995) argue that this tradition '... provides the basis for a distinctive vision of a rich and humane civic culture that is worth working for and requires the commitment of all democratic adult educators'. Briefly, democratic intellectualism dates back to the Scottish Enlightenment and refers to the role of higher education to engage all students in the study of first principles in a commonly understood way through the study of subjects such as philosophy. The problem this sought to address was that of over-specialism and a narrow technical rationality of how to get things done rather than why they should be done in the first place. The case for a 'common sense' approach pointed to the need to get to the root issues, in a democratically informed way, before questions of detail were addressed.

Writing about the influence of George Davie as an exponent of this tradition, Murdoch (1999) points out that

> The key notion to take from Davie's ideas is that the expert's knowledge is inherently incomplete. In short, the narrow focus of the specialised expert creates blind spots. The point about a generalist approach such as democratic intellectualism is not that non-experts have a right to scrutinise the work of the expert, but that the work of the expert is only complete in the light of such scrutiny ... Thus, others in the community, by virtue of their lack of expertise (which gives them a different perspective from that of the expert), have a responsibility to comment on these blind spots. (1999: 85)

Davie's argument for a democratic intellect where non-specialists are encouraged to interrogate specialists is seen as a vital part of a healthy society. An educated community of specialists are unfit to govern without the process of scrutiny argued for. They become, in effect, intellects without democracy. Whilst this argument was used within universities, there is no reason why it cannot be applied to other areas of adult education and adult literacy. Simply because some adult students lack techniques of reading and writing does not make them incapable of critical inquiry.

The issue for the adult literacy worker is how to develop a curriculum that can facilitate the mutual illumination of blind spots in the sense referred to above. This would necessitate a dialogue between tutor and student to scrutinise the claims of specialists based on the premise that all have a valid contribution to make. What is essential is to engage the critical intellect of people in a way that motivates, stretches them and enables people to engage with public issues. If people are to gain a voice – to question and speak back to power – they will need the confidence and authority that comes out of experience reinforced and tempered by study. Notions of literacy that focus purely on the skills of reading, writing and numbers provide little opportunity for people to read the meaning beyond – or between the lines – and the interests behind the meaning.

We would agree with Green's claim (cited by Lankshear, 1998) that literacy involves three levels. The first, an operational level, involves the competence in reading and writing; the second, cultural literacy, involves understanding the meaning embodied in communications and texts; the third, critical literacy, involves understands how some meanings are selected and legitimated whilst others are not. The difficulty, of course, is working these levels together in practice. For example, during the era of the poll tax, Lothian Region's Adult Basic Education Unit commissioned the production of a resource pack to deal with the literacy issues associated with it (see Small,

1989). The poll tax opened up a number of important issues of literacy and citizenship. It involved complex forms for registration, payment and voucher books and rebates that everyone had a duty to complete, not to mention summary warrant forms for non-payers. Refusal to register meant that individuals lost their formal political right to vote – hence its popular name as a poll tax and not the community charge that was its official name. In these respects, form filling and the poll tax involved *operational* literacy and numeracy skills that were essential to citizenship. Indeed, the choice to fill in the form incorrectly was used as an important political tactic by opponents of the scheme.

The rationale for the poll tax also involved a vocabulary loaded with meanings. It involved a definition of 'fairness', for example, that was deeply problematic because it treated everyone the same despite their level of income and the property they owned. Moreover, there was a debate about whether or not local government services would be better off, or worse off, because of it. In short, the meaning of the poll tax involved *cultural* literacy skills in working out the vocabulary and its implications. The interesting point about the resource pack, referred to above, was that it dealt with these two levels of literacy in a creative way. It also included information from anti-poll tax organisations about the consequences of non-payment and where individuals could go for support if they decided not to pay. It included a *critical* dimension to the learning process that was designed to help people, if they opposed paying the poll tax, to explore why and how this could happen. The resource pack embodied all three dimensions of literacy Green refers to. That is, the operational literacy associated with filling in the poll tax forms was extended to a debate about what citizenship means and how individuals and groups could act as active citizens in resisting government policy, i.e. the development of cultural and critical literacy skills.

Example from practice: Platform

If literacy is to be more than learning techniques of reading, writing and numeracy – yet still address these because they are important – it has to locate them within a rich curriculum and one that enables literacy learners to take a full and active role as citizens in society. The view taken here is that work with individuals and groups in communities, based around their interests, provides an opportunity to generate a literacy curriculum for critical intelligence. The work of Platform exemplifies this concern.

Platform is based in a 1960s high-rise housing estate in an outer-city area of Edinburgh that is characterised by poor amenities, poverty and other related problems. Whilst the project recognises the central issues of language and literacy in Adult Basic Education provision, it adopts a broad definition of their work that includes, '... the pursuit of those fundamental critical, communication, computational and life skills without which people cannot gain access to society's resources, and without which they cannot contribute to the development and shaping of society' (Platform: Information Booklet).

A key aim of the project is to engage the critical intellect of people in a way that motivates and stretches them. There are three main strands to their curriculum: traditional literacy work, e.g. literacy groups, study clubs and one-to-one provision; certificated courses, e.g. Communication courses, Philosophy, Social History, Environmental Studies; issue- and interest-based work, e.g. Politics, the Scottish Parliament, Football. Students are encouraged to enter the curriculum where it is most suitable to their interests and purposes and to then go on to participate in a broader, richer educational experience (Heywood *et al*, 1995). Guidance and progression into other community-based activities or institutions of education are built into a course of study in order to encourage students to consider future options and links. The project has been concerned to ensure that local experience and interests provide the basis for developing a curriculum. The Football Course is a case in point. The course was aimed at hard-to-reach young men who typically come into little contact with educational agencies after (and probably during) the statutory educational years. These young men were enticed to participate by the offer of free tickets to a Scottish international match. The 10-week curriculum that culminated in going to see a game involved studying the history of Scottish football, violence, racism, commercialisation of football and the 'macho' culture surrounding the game. Embedded in the curriculum were skills of literacy, listening and discussion, presentation of argument and confidence building. When the course finished, members of the group were then encouraged to take part in other aspects of the curriculum Platform offer and more than half the group of 10 young men did so. What was particularly notable about the course was the groups' willingness to discuss, and their interest in, issues which, if presented via another more traditional vehicle, they would have been much less likely to attend.

The project is acutely sensitive to the low levels of confidence and low levels of basic skills that many students coming to Platform have. The language and style of the tutors, therefore, has to embody openness and a willingness to engage with the expressed interests of participants whilst not emasculating their own purposes and authority as educators. This is always a difficult and delicate balance to achieve. However, if literacy is to be part of broad and critical educational experience it cannot be avoided. As they argue, tutors '... should also strive to ensure that the curriculum on offer challenges, as far as possible, the hegemonic structures implicit in solely functional "lifeskills" courses which, at their most obvious, can be seen as ways of "educating" students into accepting their given place in society' (Heywood *et al*, 1995: 22).

Conclusion

The task of building a literacy curriculum that enables people to make some real choices about what being a citizen means and how they can contribute to democratic processes is by no means easy. We must act nevertheless, as Giroux (1993) urges, 'as if' we live in a democracy even if this seems difficult and at times not to be the case. To do so will require enthusiasm and determination, as expressed by the following worker:

> Many of the people in the groups that I teach say that concepts like 'citizenship' and 'democracy' seem to be 'on another planet' – just big words which have nothing to do with the daily mesh of job-seeking, cut-price shopping, family dynamics and media escapism. Sometimes they laugh cynically when I say that these can all be linked and, what's more, that our understanding can be used to take action for change. A surprising amount of professionals also tell me that 'big is bad', that life for the majority should be about learning to manage in small ways: computer skills ... part-time jobs ... 'good' parenting ... crosses in boxes ... Challenged, I work to stimulate passion for 'BIG' knowledge and a curiosity about how to reclaim that which seems extraordinary for everyday use. (Hunter, 1998: 24)

What needs to be avoided is both cynicism and apathy that literacy can make little contribution to the issue of citizenship in people's lives. We must not impose our own 'limit situations' on the potential in people. Adult literacy workers with an interest in social purpose have to contest the meaning of citizenship. Democracy and citizenship is too important to be left to the policy makers and politicians. If we do, what kind of democracy are we living in? We need to develop a space for critical and creative work that imparts genuine skills and understanding whilst developing the confidence of people to play an active and informed role in the issues that are important to them. We need to become resources for individuals and collectivities to take some control over their lives by building a broad and rich curriculum that firmly embraces education for democracy. Hirshman (1970) showed how people could either take the 'voice' or the 'exit' option if they wanted to bring about change. The suggestions that we have made here are aimed to maximise the 'voice' option because to 'exit' from democratic participation means that alternative experiences of what it means to be a citizen are excluded.

References

Alexander, D. and Martin, I. (1995) 'Competence, curriculum and democracy' in Mayo, M. and Thompson, J. (eds), *Adult Learning, Critical Intelligence and Social Change*, Leicester: NIACE, pp. 82–96.

Bhaskar, R. (1994) 'Democracy and the market', *Red Pepper*, October, pp. 28–31.

Carr, W. (1991) 'Education for citizenship', *British Journal of Educational Studies*, 39, pp. 373–85.

Carr, W. and Hartnett, A. (1996) 'Civic education, democracy and the English political tradition' in Demaine, J. and Entwhistle, H. (eds.), *Beyond Communitarianism*, London: Macmillan Press, pp. 64–82.

Coleman, U. (2000) 'Making connections' in Thompson, J. Shaw, M. and Bane, L. (eds), *Reclaiming Common Purpose*, Leicester: NIACE, pp. 15–19.

Dobbs, A.E. (1919) *Education and Social Movement, 1700–1850*, London: Longman, Green and Co.

Giroux, H. (1993) *Border Crossings*, London: Routledge.

Heyward, J. Wilkinson, M. and Sinclair, A. (1995) ''Platform's approach to curriculum in ABE', *Concept*, 5 (2), pp. 19–22.

Hirshman, A. (1970) *Exit, Voice and Loyalty*, Cambridge, MA: Harvard University Press.

Hunter, A. (1998) 'Inspirations on a shoe-string', *Concept*, 8 (2).

Jackson, K. (1995) 'Popular education and the state: a new look at the community debate' in Mayo, M. and Thompson, J. (eds), *Adult Learning, Critical Intelligence and Social Change*, Leicester: NIACE, pp. 82–96.

Lankshear, C (1998) 'The educational challenge of the new work order: globalisation and the meanings of literacy', *Concept*, 8 (2), pp. 12–15.

Lankshear, C. and Lawler, M. (1989) *Literacy, Schooling and Revolution*, London: Falmer Press.

Lister, R. (1998) 'In from the margins: citizenship, inclusion and exclusion' in Barry, M. and Hallet, C. (eds), *Social Exclusion and Social Work: Issues of Theory, Policy and Practice*, Dorset: Russell House Publishing, pp. 26–38.

Marshall, T. (1950) *Citizenship and Social Class*, Chicago: Chicago University Press.

Martin, I. (1999) 'Adult education, lifelong learning and active citizenship', *Adults Learning*, 11 (2), pp. 16–18.

Murdoch, M. (1999) 'The significance of the Scottish generalist tradition' in Crowther, J. Martin, I. and Shaw, M. (eds), *Popular Education and Social Movements in Scotland Today*, Leicester: NIACE, pp. 83–94.

Oliver, M. (1996) *Disability: From Theory to Practice*, London: Macmillan.

Osler, D. (1999) *Education for Citizenship*, paper presented at conference, Edinburgh: Community Learning Scotland.

Phillips, A. (1994) *Local Democracy: the Terms of the Debate*, Commission for Local Democracy research report No 2.

Platform: Information Booklet (undated), Platform, Wester Hailes, Edinburgh.

Small, R. (1989) *The Poll Tax: An ABE Resource Pack*, Lothian Regional Council.

SOEID (1998) *Opportunity Scotland*, Green Paper, Edinburgh: HMSO.

SOEID (1997) *Lifelong Learning: The Way Forward*, Edinburgh: The Scottish Office.

Section Three
Repositioning learners and teachers

10 The politics of really useful literacy: six lessons from Bangladesh

Ian Martin and Habibur Rahman

'To make some difference': learning to move society

> Adult literacy is not a panacea for all social problems. But it can bring about a movement in society. Some members of literacy courses may inspire others to break the chain of subjugation and poverty. Programmes of adult literacy can act against deeply entrenched systems of inequality and injustice. (Habibur Rahman, *Bangladesh Daily Star*, 8 September 1994)

When we in the rich North see pictures from Bangladesh on our television screens, what we tend to see is images of natural disaster and human misery: floods, famine and destitution. What we do not see is anything of the history and culture of an ancient civilisation or the daily struggle of millions of ordinary Bangladeshi people for dignity, justice and respect (as well as the material conditions in which these can be attained and sustained). No wonder, then, that we know little about how local, community-based literacy programmes are being used by the people of Bangladesh in their struggle not simply for survival but also for the extension of their democratic rights as citizens. Nevertheless, in much of the so-called 'developed' world there is now increasing interest in family literacy and the link between political literacy and citizenship. So the question is: what can we learn from Bangladesh about how literacy work can help people to 'move society'? What does this mean? How does it happen?

Perhaps the first thing to say is that grassroots people's organisations in Bangladesh know only too well the distinction between what the radical tradition in British adult education calls 'useful knowledge' and 'really useful knowledge' (see Johnson, 1979). This is not really about what kind of knowledge counts, e.g. technical/instrumental versus theoretical/analytical. Rather, it is about who decides what kind of knowledge counts – and why, and what they want to do with it:

> Really useful knowledge ... encompassed all that was required to 'enlighten' learners, i.e. for them to understand the world in terms of their own experience of it and to recognise their potential power to act effectively and collectively to change it. In this sense, it epitomised a truly emancipatory form of 'counter-education' and was the antithesis of 'provided education'. (Martin, 1994: 4)

In Bangladesh really useful literacy is what the rural and urban poor, with little or no access to formal education, need – and demand – in order to take more control over their own lives as both workers and citizens. This means acquiring practical knowledge and skills (e.g. in reading, writing, numeracy and income generation), which can help them to act on their world, and, at the same time, develop the civic and political competence – and thus the confidence – to begin to change that world for the better, i.e. in their own interests. Such a process of *using education to act on the world in order to change it* continues throughout people's lives because once they start doing this, they cannot and will not stop. Harnessed to a social purpose, this is precisely what 'lifelong learning' should be about. Maybe the difference is that while we seem to talk a lot about it, they get on and actually do it.

Lesson 1: 'Theory' cannot be separated from 'practice'. In the end, we must be able to make sense of the world in order to change it for the better.

Proshika: 'splicing the people into sustainable development'

Habibur Rahman is now the Senior Programme Co-ordinator (Materials Development) of a large indigenous NGO (non-governmental organisation) called Proshika which is currently working in more than half the rural villages in Bangladesh. 'Proshika' is an acronym of the Bangla (Bengali) for *training*, education and *action*. In describing itself as a 'centre for human development', Proshika is arguing, in effect, that development (as distinct from disaster relief) must be people-driven if it is to be people-centred. It must also be sustainable in the sense that it is the kind of development that ordinary people want and can sustain for themselves and for future generations (see Eade, 1997). It is worth emphasising that this kind of people-centredness is about enabling ordinary people to take for themselves some degree of power in order to change the objective conditions of their social, cultural and material reality in ways which serve their own collective interests. This is quite different from the introspective and self-preoccupied 'person-centredness' that is characteristic of certain 'soft' variations of the humanistic tradition in Western adult and community education. In this sense, there is a distinction to be made between the politicised and collective notion of 'the people' and the sanitised and individualised notion of 'the person'.

It is these ordinary people, most of whom live in poor villages or urban slums and shanty towns, who must be the key resources for change if they are to be the beneficiaries of change. They must learn to rely on themselves and their own capacity for collective learning and social action to make the sort of changes that are in their interests. No one else will do this for them. In other words, people-centredness is a philosophy which embodies simultaneously the vision of a better world and a strategy for changing the world. Thus, Proshika defines the basic goal of all its educational work as:

> To eliminate illiteracy by ensuring children's schooling at primary level and by enhancing adult education to splice the new literates into the process of sustainable development and thus to engage them in a continuous process of learning.

Literacy must therefore be functional in the proper, non-reductionist sense if it is to be 'empowering', i.e. by enabling ordinary people to take more control over their lives in the day–to–day world as it really is. For example, Proshika defines what it calls 'actual literacy' as 'one's proven capability to make use of one's education consciously for social, economic and human development '. In other words, literacy must be made 'meaningful' to people in terms of their enhanced capacity to make their lives better in an objective way. This can only happen if education helps people to act together by learning to understand the linkage between the micro and the macro, the personal and the political. This linkage is demonstrated in the way in which Proshika makes quite explicit the connections between the literacy process, social consciousness, political organisation and material change: 'literacy → awareness → independence → organisation → sustainable development'. Throughout all the accounts of Proshika's work there is, then, a conscious and consistent attempt to relate practical skills development to political emancipation, to connect literacy to what Paulo Freire calls 'conscientization', and to turn learning into social action.

This kind of approach to literacy can help people escape both the material reality of poverty and what Freire describes as the 'culture of silence', i.e. the political and cultural exclusion and powerlessness:

> Literacy will make the people ... conscious and self-reliant; and help them to consolidate themselves within organisations and proceed steadily and firmly towards development and empowerment and towards realising their fundamental rights.

Official government figures indicate steady progress, with the literacy rate for the adult population rising from 46 per cent in 1997 to 51 per cent in 1998 and 56 per cent in 1999 (personal communication between authors). But the harsh reality is that Bangladesh's population is still growing. What this means, in effect, is that although the national literacy rate is increasing, so is the total number of illiterate people. The struggle against illiteracy must therefore go on. This is the background to Proshika's Universal Education Programme, which is based on the following propositions:

- Education is the prerequisite for any development;
- Only education can make development sustainable;

- Education is the tool for the all-out emancipation of the poor;
- Learning is an endless process, coterminous only with an individual's life.

Proshika puts this programme into action by carrying its work into four different educational sites: formal schooling (supporting children in primary school), non-formal primary education (providing alternative community-based education for the 60 per cent of children who have either dropped out of school or never got into it), adult literacy and post-literacy work (developing literacy programmes geared specifically to the interests of the poor and the goal of sustainable development) and, finally, village study circles (making available and accessible at the village level the educational resources needed to acquire 'really useful knowledge' in its widest sense).

Lesson 2: Education can only 'empower' people if it enables them to act collectively on their own reality in order to change it.

Democratising the curriculum: making experiential learning educational

In many of the 'over-developed' societies of the rich world, one of the costs of the development of public welfare systems is that much of the vitality and autonomy of civil society has been absorbed into and incorporated within the institutions of the state. In contrast, in poorer societies the state services tend to be minimal whereas social movements in civil society remain strong and vibrant (e.g. see Kane, 1999). In this respect, it is important to emphasise that Proshika's work is built on a 'bottom-up' process. It is, in effect, more of a popular social movement than a professional educational and development agency. It derives both its legitimacy and its dynamism from the grassroots people's organisations (POs) it has helped to establish and consolidate in poor communities throughout Bangladesh.

The thinking behind this strategy of building education on popular movements is made explicit in the Proshika Activity Report for 1995–96 *Strengthening People's Endeavour.*

> Proshika pioneered the concept of the people's organisation in Bangladesh. Understandably, the most important step towards empowerment of the people is to forge their unity for collective action in the social, cultural and economic areas. Individually, it is simply impossible for the poor to work their way up against the forces of underdevelopment which are much more organised and firmly seated in the prevalent system. But the numerical strength of the poor, when they are organised in larger scales, does make a difference in making their voices heard. Two decades of Proshika's experience is testimony to this reality.

> Forming people's organisation is built into the core strategy of Proshika upon which is founded all the other activities of the organisation. The poor people living in the rural areas and urban slums are encouraged to form 'primary groups', popularly known as *samitees*. The landless and marginal farmers, occupational working folks like fishing communities, weavers, small traders and poor women ... are the eligible members of these *samitees*. According to Proshika's philosophy of alternative development, these *samitees* are the primary units for all kinds of development interventions. (Proshika, 1996: 1).

This means two things. First, Proshika's primary concern is to develop education and social action programmes that grow directly out of and respond directly to the day-to-day social reality of its members/learners. Given this priority, it chooses to use whatever methods and materials work. Nothing is privileged in pedagogical, espistemological or ideological terms. Proshika describes this as an 'eclectic' approach, i.e. taking, mixing and using whatever happens to work best in a given situation. In this way, for example, the 'discussion component' which is at the heart of the curriculum is supported by 'a combination of group interaction, simulation exercises, individual expression, observation of the surroundings and the analysis of the learners' real life situation [in order to] respond to the complexity of reality' (Habibur Rahman, *Bangladesh Daily Independent,* 3 March 1998). This may sound like pragmatism, but it is a principled pragmatism harnessed to a clear social purpose. Second, there is a strong element of democratic control over the curriculum and the development of literacy materials. The people's organisations have recently, for instance, demanded that in future there should be more emphasis in the curriculum on gender relations and the power differentials between women and men, environmental issues and the goal of sustainability, communal harmony between different religious and ethnic groups, and poverty alleviation and human rights.

Perhaps the point to emphasise is that in this version of 'experiential learning' people learn to use their collective experience and common social interests as a resource for understanding their world and acting upon it. Consequently, learning is a process of political struggle, and education is an instrument to be used in this struggle – rather than the source of individual intellectual capital or the ornament of a more nuanced and reflexive ego. The task is not to celebrate the authenticity of personal experience, but to test and confirm its social and political significance. The rich world, of course, contains lots of poor people who could do well to learn this lesson for themselves.

Lesson 3: If literacy is to give people power, the learning process must enable them to take power. In this sense, learning from experience is quite different from simply experiencing learning.

Joining the wider political struggle: changing the political culture

One of the problems in much community-based education is that it has an in-built tendency to become disablingly parochial, narrowly conceived and self-referential. Proshika sets out quite deliberately to avoid this by locating itself firmly within the wider popular struggle for active and inclusive citizenship in a democratic society. What this means, in effect, is that the struggle to reform the state must start outside the state in the social movements of civil society. The cultural politics of communities is the seed-bed for growing a new political culture (see Crowther *et al*, 1999). In this respect, the record speaks for itself:

> In 1996 Proshika along with other NGOs and in alliance with civil society and grassroots people's organisations conducted a number of mass mobilisation campaigns which contributed in a major way to the successful resolution of a two year long political conflict which was threatening to tear the country apart in a civil war, famine and military takeover. The dark days of extreme conflict and insecurity ended with the setting up of a neutral caretaker government and its successful conduct of a free and fair election. In the run-up to the election, Proshika along with 500 other NGOs conducted the largest ever voter education campaign. This reached about 10 million people in the grassroots through village-based training programmes, popular theatre, posters, leaflets, stickers, and audio and visual communication materials. Voter education messages were also prepared for TV and radio. Voter education sought to motivate people to participate in the election and exercise their rights of franchise in a responsible way. This was the first important step towards the establishment of an accountable democracy and a poverty-free country. The voter education programme contributed to the largest voter turn-out ever (73%) in this country. The turn-out of women voters was particularly impressive. But what was most impressive was the responsible choice made by the people: the most corrupt, anti-democratic and anti-women elements were rejected at the polls. (Proshika, 1996: 82)

The task is to renew rather than abandon politics. Again, community-based educators in more affluent countries would do well to learn from this as the poor (however apparently quiescent and invisible) are, indeed, always with us. But – and perhaps this is the crucial point – changing the macro political culture of the state in this way presupposes a micro cultural politics in communities which frees ordinary people to act as autonomous citizens:

> Anwara and fourteen other women, who used to work in rich men's houses, joined a functional literacy class. When they discussed their

wages in the class, they found that they were unjust. Soon after the completion of the course, they were offered jobs in a newly established biscuit factory. All of them took the jobs. For the first time they were earning cash for their work. One day the village headman, as a representative of the rich men, called all of them together. The *iman* (priest) of the mosque was also present. The *iman* declared that it was against their religion for the women to work outside their village and the headman ordered them to stop going to the factory. But Anwara and the other women did not stop their work. When they were declared isolated from their society, the fifteen women created a new society in the village. Ten years after this incident, their new society is dominating the life of the entire village. Many of the village women are doing different kinds of jobs, and there is nobody to order them to stop. (Rahman, 1994, citing the work of another NGO, *Bangladesh Daily Star*, 8 September 1994)

There are certainly different kinds of power in any society, but, when they remain unchallenged, they all serve to confirm and consolidate systematic patterns of poverty and inequality. In effect, therefore, the 'empowerment' of the poor must, to some extent, mean the disempowerment of the rich, privileged and respectable. It is as well not to be confused – or coy – about this reality. Literacy is always political – either implicitly or explicitly, propping up the status quo or challenging it.

Lesson 4: Popular education explodes the (often convenient) myth of apathy, and it is a vital weapon in the political struggle to defend and extend the democratic rights of ordinary people.

Gender and power: shifting the balance

In Bangladeshi society (as in many others) the most pervasive and deeply entrenched division of power is that between men and women. Proshika has always seen it as a priority to address this and to do what it can to change the gendered distribution of power in what remains, essentially, a deeply traditional Islamic society. It is worth noting that about three-quarters of Proshika's teachers and adult learners are women and that the drop-out rate in its programmes is much lower for women than it is for men. In terms of the cultural and material status of women in Bangladeshi village society, it is also significant that the dowry system (by means of which women become, in effect, part of the goods and chattels of men) is declining much faster in the areas where Proshika is at work than elsewhere. As all feminist educators know, 'learning liberation' must be both a social and an educational process if it is to be a political one. As Rahman has argued:

Rural women get the opportunity to be organised and discuss their own problems in the literacy groups. Usually this is the first time they attend a socio-political gathering for them. The classroom situation is very much participatory which inspires them to be vocal about their own problems. The facilitators come from the same socio-economic background as the learners. The discussion sessions are lively and interesting to the learners. Thus solidarity grows among the groups. After a six month course, more than 60% of the women learners achieve the following skills:

a) They realise and pin point the causes of and the connections between their problems. They feel that problems cannot be solved by solitary steps. Building organisations is very important for collective development.

b) They can read simple books and the newsletters designed for neo-literates.

c) They can keep accounts, both individually and for the group.

d) Many of them have the confidence to stand against social injustices. (Habibur Rahman, *Bangladesh Daily Star*, 8 September 1994)

But, as Habibur Rahman goes on to show by giving a series of practical examples, 'women's empowerment' grows out of changes not only in their critical consciousness but also in their material conditions. Literacy cannot be truly functional – or 'really useful' – unless it addresses both these aspects of women's reality by enabling them to act differently and decisively in the real world of their everyday lives:

Twenty women in a group of villages used to borrow money individually and at a high rate of interest from private money lenders to buy bamboo and cane from which to make baskets and mats to sell. They never thought about working as a co-operative. When an adult literacy centre was set up in the area, ten of them joined it. During their literacy course, they formed a co-operative. Other local women became members of the group. They applied for credit from the public sector and were successful. The literate portion of a big group saved everybody from the exploitation of the money lenders. (Habibur Rahman, *Bangladesh Daily Star*, 8 September 1994)

Cultural power is reinforced through material power. As Gramsci always reminds us, culture is rooted in and routed through structure. In most societies today, patriarchy (whatever form it takes) needs to be related to capitalism (whatever form it takes). It is precisely these connections – and the dialectical engagement they imply – that must constitute the logic and the texture of any curriculum and pedagogy that claim to be emancipatory. The movement for the liberation of women all over the world confirms this essential and uncomfortable truth, but perhaps we learn the lesson most clearly where we see it demonstrated most simply.

Lesson 5: Women's self-education shows us how the struggle for agency and identity has to be conducted within (as well as against) the real constraints of structure.

Constructing the future: learning to trust the people

When asked what he had learnt from his lifetime commitment to popular, community-based education with the rural and urban poor in Bangladesh, Habibur Rahman's answer was simple: 'I have learnt to respect the people' (Martin and Rahman, 1993). Perhaps the final lesson from Proshika's work is one that we, as educators, have to learn about ourselves. We must learn to respect but also to trust the people. Their interests, abilities and aspirations must become the template for defining the values, purposes and efficacy of our work. If we can learn to do this, we will also endorse Proshika's basic tenet that:

> the abilities of poor people [are] the best tool of development. It helps them to organise under the umbrella of their own institutions ... giving the emphasis to empowering the poor through education and training so that they can think critically about their problems and take the necessary steps for their own development. (Habibur Rahman, *Bangladesh Observer*, 9 August 1996)

So, in the end, the politics of 'really useful literacy' is about how a social and political vision can be expressed and demonstrated in a collective educational experience:

> In spite of a tremendous potential in human resources, Bangladesh suffers a major setback because of, among other things, widespread illiteracy. Proshika's vision of a just, egalitarian and democratic society will remain unrealisable if [so many] of the people remain, as they are now, illiterate. Indeed, literacy is the first building block toward social development. Lack of education is both a cause and a consequence of privation, unemployment and the uneven distribution of social resources. It is obvious that people's well-being is directly related with their level of education. Education widens the vista of people's lives and secondary experiences, expands the range of their livelihood opportunities, promotes self-esteem and their ability to control their own destiny. (Proshika, 1996: 8)

Lesson 6: In the rich world, we have something important to learn from the poor people of Bangladesh about how popular community-based literacy programmes can help to turn our own rhetoric about both lifelong learning and democratic renewal into a reality.

Conclusion

In the end, one of the political lessons of globalisation is that the local and specific struggles of ordinary people all over the world can become part of the wider, international struggle for democracy, social justice and equality. As we all, in our different ways, live out the meaning of 'globalisation from above', the question is: how can we make our work part of an alternative – and deeply subversive – process of 'globalisation from below' (Walters, 1997)? This, of course, is a very big question, but we can begin to answer it in our work – albeit modestly and incrementally – if we can begin to learn more from each other. To do so, perhaps the most important lesson we, as educators, have to learn is, in Habibur Rahman's words, that:

> The people can express themselves in a better way than we can tell them.

'Useful literacy' can teach people to read and write, but we can only learn what 'really useful literacy' means from our students.

References

Crowther, J., Martin. I. and Shaw, M. (eds) (1999) *Popular Education and Social Movements in Scotland Today*, Leicester: National Institute of Adult Continuing Education.

Eade, D. (ed.) (1997) *Development and Patronage*, London: Oxfam.

Freire, P. (1972) *Pedagogy of the Oppressed*, Harmondsworth: Penguin.

Johnson, R. (1979) 'Really useful knowledge': radical education and working-class culture' in Clarke, J., Crichter, C. and Johnson, R. (eds), *Working Class Culture*, London: Hutchinson, pp. 75–102.

Kane, L. (1999) 'Learning from experience in Latin America' in Crowther, J., Martin, I. and Shaw, M. (eds), *Popular Education and Social Movements in Scotland Today*, Leicester: National Institute of Adult Continuing Education, pp. 54–69.

Martin, I. (1994) *'Community' and the Control of Schooling*, London: YMCA National College.

Martin, I. and Rahman, H. (1993) 'Literacy for empowerment in Bangladesh', *Concept*, 3 (1), pp. 11–14.

Proshika (1996), Strengthening People's Endeavour: Proshika Process of Sustainable Development (Proshika Activity Report 1995–96).

Rahman, A.N.S. Habibur (1994) 'The impact of adult literacy among rural women in Bangladesh', Paper presented to the 1994 World Assembly of Adult Education, Cairo, and subsequently published in *Bangladesh Daily Star*, 8 September.

Rahman, A.N.S. Habibur (1996) 'Non-formal primary education: Proshika approach', *Bangladesh Observer*, 9 August.

Rahman, A.N.S. Habibur (1998) 'Changing the character of functional literacy materials', *Bangladesh Daily Independent*, 3 March.

Walters, S. (ed.) (1997) *Globalisation, Adult Education and Training: Impacts and Issues*, London: Zed Books.

11 Speaking as equals to professionals: people with learning disabilities talk back

Catherine Jamieson

Introduction

This chapter looks at a small-scale practical attempt to equalise power relationships by working in partnership with service users to develop literacies that value difference. In order to begin this, it was necessary to acknowledge that a narrow interpretation of literacy can exclude or marginalise people with learning disabilities who will always be less than competent in these terms. The contribution of Adult Basic Education (ABE) was to help provide an opportunity where adults with learning disabilities would speak about their experiences with their own voice, develop confidence, assertiveness and be the experts on their lives.

It is an interesting point in the history of education for disadvantaged groups in our society. The lot of people with learning disabilities has turned around over the past few decades. Local authority human services now work with the generation who were born between total exclusion from most social interactions (often through placement in residential institutions) and the current social and political drive towards care in the community and social inclusion.

With the Education (Handicapped Children) Act 1970, children termed as severely mentally handicapped, previously deemed ineducable, were brought into the education system for the first time. The Mental Health Act (1983) removed most people with learning difficulties from the mental health legislation and allowed many the right to vote. These changes combined with the social and political movement away from the large, long-stay hospitals provided the seeds for this group to begin to articulate aspirations of their own. Armstrong (1982) argues that current services, influenced by Wolfensberger's 'normalisation principles' (1972) and O'Brien et al's subsequent adaptation and refinements (1981 and 1989), have begun to encompass planning for change and a shift towards choice and empowerment, thus moving away from the 'caring' model, still remaining as a legacy of the medicalisation of 'mental handicap'. It is clear that people with learning disabilities have been seriously disadvantaged by the systems that have ostensibly sought to serve them. Needs are defined both by bureaucracies and professionals often as a way of rationing services and reinforcing professional ideologies. In this sense, the concept of need disempowers the users of services because it begins from the premise that professionals know best.

The speed of change sometimes creates dissonance between the needs of the bureaucracy and those of professionals working with individuals. Both participants and professionals struggle with the predominant able-bodied/minded perception of the world, and prejudices that make it difficult to embrace a new order. As educators, we need to be sure that what we espouse really serves the needs articulated by the people we work with and that our own beliefs and ideals, political or otherwise, are not being put forward at their expense. The real impetus for change must come from people with learning disabilities themselves. This implies the right to an education that enables choice, literacies which value difference and the corollary of a significant and lasting shift in existing power relationships between professionals and 'clients'. This requires willingness on the part of professionals to challenge their own prejudices and organisational constraints in order to work alongside people with learning disabilities as equal people.

Background to the group

From 1990 until 1997 the ABE team, part of the Community Education Service in Scotland, seconded a senior worker to a Social Work (Resource) day centre. The secondment was intended to develop and extend the educational experience of the ABE team in the field of learning disabilities. The role was seen, in part, as one of creating, developing and implementing opportunities for service users to increase confidence, develop effective literacy, numeracy and communication skills and be active in the community. As part of an overall communications strategy, developing advocacy and in particular self-advocacy for service users in a community context was considered an important part of the work.

Tentative beginnings – how the group began

Part of the ABE role in the day centre was to participate in a multi-agency committee planning the development and implementation of day services for people with learning disabilities (The Edinburgh North East Joint Planning and Coordination Team). It was disturbing that the two people with learning disabilities coopted on to the committee were expected to take part with no explanation or assistance either before, during or after the meeting to make sense of the complex issues and arguments they were hearing. Sometimes the issues they brought to the group seemed to get lost, passed over or talked over by the professionals. On other occasions, one individual would get stuck and embarrassed about making a point and would feel unable to stop, repeating the same point over and over, with all the parties to the meeting feeling powerless and unable to progress. No concessions were made by the senior professionals on the format of committee meetings.

It seemed that the part service users would play in the process would be at best tokenistic, at worst demeaning, humiliating and patronising. These individuals were members of the committee with no power, few opinions and unused to speaking – even in peer groups they could be easily intimidated by professionals. They were being placed in an untenable situation.

Service users who have experience of institutional care are a marginalised section of the community, both isolated and institutionalised. Additional crippling difficulties faced by this group of people often centre around their experiences of education. Most of the people who wanted to take part in the committee had been subjected to a deficit model of educational practices, some having been incarcerated before the legislation began to recognise them as being fully human. Extensive 'occupational training' had commonly been experienced as part of a skills-based functional approach to educational and social needs. All knew failure within the norms of the education system.

Getting together

To begin to address the above issues, a small group of staff and service users came up with the idea of developing a group to support anyone with learning disabilities who might be interested in planning local services and looking at existing day service provision. The meetings were to be held in a socially valued setting, the local Community Centre.

There was an extraordinary response to the offer. Around 20 people with learning disabilities came along to the first meeting and continued to attend weekly over the next few months. Participants came from Social Work day centres, the voluntary sector, further education and the community. A wide range of ability was represented on the group. Several people showed signs of having very poor self-esteem and low confidence. Some used sign systems, some were already members of clients' councils in their day centres, some were supported to attend by staff, one had lived in long-stay hospitals for as long as 40 years, others were not long out of school. All were ready to have a chance to speak about the kind of things that mattered to them.

Professional roles

The support group sessions were developed initially by negotiation with the group, who agreed to base the discussions on an existing Social Work report on day service provision. In addition to this, issues the service users identified formed the agenda. The group rejected a 'committee style'; one objection to this way of working was that 'it is not fair and that some people do not get a chance to speak' while 'others dominate the meetings, especially office bearers'. It was established through discussion that staff would help to provide structure, minute the meetings and set up graphic recording systems for non-readers. Also, staff should not express views or opinions and would give advice only when asked. This was sometimes hard, as in some instances the views of the participants were diametrically opposed to those of the facilitating staff. For example, while discussing the issues surrounding day centre provision, almost all the group wanted provision to continue and even expand while the professional staff regarded day centres as potential blocks for people attempting to access the community. Opportunities for debate were created in small groups and in other settings as well as through clients' councils in day centres.

The participants developed ground rules through discussion and went on to set down aims. The meetings were clearly minuted, initially by the staff, and typed up so that everything discussed could be reported to clients'/members' councils and discussed by other day centre users. The group soon enjoyed having the power to establish what was talked about. They decided, by thinking up various options and then by democratic process, to call themselves the Sticking Up For Your Rights Group (SUFYRG).

Speaking as equals to professionals

The participants worked out a number of strategies to bypass the need for reading and writing skills; for example, the group formulated letters by getting together in small groups and referring to the larger group before sending them out. The facilitators put what was being said on to paper and were available to read the replies for group members when required. One of the important areas that the group needed to address quickly was how to communicate effectively with professionals in face-to-face situations. The group worked hard over several sessions to discuss various strategies. It was essential to find a way to feed back to the Joint Planning Group which would allow people to express their opinions without getting confused or tongue-tied. Also there was a need to create a culture in the planning group where other participants would really listen to what was being said by the adults with learning disabilities. Through discussion, the group came up with the idea of deciding what to say from the issues on their own weekly agenda, then making a tape of the main points to play to the professionals at the monthly meeting. A transcript was made of the contents. A 30-minute slot for the tape and the subsequent discussions was negotiated for and gained.

A small group from SUFYRG attended the planning group on a monthly basis and answered questions about the issues on the tape. This small group changed every month so that everyone could have a turn presenting their ideas and the ideas of the group to a professional committee.

SUFYRG: speaking up and campaigning against the cuts

Edinburgh local services were hit by lack of available funds as a legacy of local government cuts in the early 1990s. This affected the services that the participants were receiving. The work of the group became focused on campaigning as various services were threatened with cuts. The SUFYRG chose to play a major campaigning role and helped to save one of the day centres from being shut down. They organised and ran a seminar in February 1997 enabling 100 service users to 'Get A Voice'. These are now being held on a yearly basis and have increased in size. SUFYRG have:

- produced their own first report in the summer of 1997, and launched it in a seminar with workshops to discuss the findings;
- presented delegations and individual delegates to the City Council;
- met representatives of the Scottish Executive;
- become part of a new Social Work Strategic Development Group for people with learning disabilities in the City;
- produced reports in 1998 and 1999;
- been instrumental in the setting up of a City Advocacy Facilitators Group;
- produced a consultation document in collaboration with the above group;
- have been instrumental in the setting up of a second group for service users in the south of the city (named by participants as the SURGING AHEAD group).

(Adapted from Jamieson, 1999)

Adult status and real educational opportunities: a lifelong learning approach

The principles underpinning the setting up and implementation of the SUFYRG group had been developed in the wider context of ABE work and embraced the notion that learners should be equals in the learning process. Teale and Ballantyne (1990) use the work of Jarvis (1985) to differentiate between 'education from above and the education of equals'. The former, they suggest, is when the teacher imparts knowledge and transmits the values and attitudes of the dominant ideology in society and is 'in control of the learning outcomes'. Using examples from the education of equals model they state:

> ... the emphasis is placed on the individual's ability to achieve his or her potential: the curriculum is selected by the learners in collaboration with the teacher according to interest and relevance; the outcomes are the responsibility of the learner. The education of equals model implies empowerment, the taking of control of learning and the learner accepting responsibility with the tutor for the learning. (1990: 4)

It was hoped that working alongside the participants would enable them to feel more equal and empowered. Staff perceptions of literacy had to broaden to encompass a wider view of literacy and change so that all group members could begin to participate effectively. Sutcliffe (1990) contends that a variety of options should be, but are often not, available to all students and she comments:

> A narrow and exclusive educational focus on literacy and numeracy is common. It is likely to concentrate on the areas where a student has already experienced difficulty. The heavy emphasis often placed on literacy and numeracy for students with learning difficulties may accentuate rather than overcome past failure. (1990: 14)

In the context of working with the SUFYRG it was agreed that ABE would not be seen narrowly or traditionally in terms of encouraging people simply to attempt to improve reading and writing skills. The ABE role would be one of providing educational opportunities that allowed people to become more competent, more independent, more able to speak up for themselves, and willing to speak about, participate in and plan for areas relevant to their own lives. It was clear that without the confidence to develop new skills and a sense of self-worth, work in the group isolated from real life experiences would simply be a poor reflection of what is commonly achieved by the majority of people (Jamieson, 1999).

The staff, in order to facilitate these factors would need to:

> ... learn to confirm student experiences and voices so that students are legitimised and supported as people who matter, as people who can participate in the production and acquisition of their own learning, and as people who in doing so can speak with a voice that is rooted in their sense of history and place. (Giroux 1992: 245)

Literacies that would fairly represent this group had to value and articulate differences and extend the boundaries of what is commonly accepted and unconstrained by existing hierarchical structures which serve only to maintain the status quo. The problem for people with learning disabilities is that they are often regarded as being less than equal and are thus prevented from taking power and control of anything, or indeed gaining valued adult status by the restraints of 'economic and cultural realities'. Corbett and Barton

(1992) take the view that being given responsibility is vital to the process of gaining adult status; also, they warn that staff need to be aware of their power in this process. They state:

> The issue of adulthood is inextricably linked to the ability to act responsibly. Decision making is a key act of those who are deemed responsible. It thus assumes a privileged status. Within the rhetoric of empowerment, decision making is a central component. Yet the realisation of an effective outcome can begin to be accomplished only if existing professional expectations and practices are open to question. (1992: 33)

The kinds of impoverished educational opportunities offered to adults with learning disabilities serve to highlight and reflect the actual status accorded them. This group is routinely kept in a marginalised position by their experiences within society. There has been some evidence of movement towards greater participation, especially through the spirit of the legislation since the 1980s; however, these intentions have often been undermined by vague wording in the legislation and by inadequate funding. Some aspects have taken a long time to be even partially implemented. The Disabled Persons (Services, Consultation and Representation) Act 1986 is such an example. The Act, arising from a Private Member's Bill, has not yet been fully implemented. The main themes arising from this legislation suggest that curriculum development for adults should encompass person-centred models as well as the development of self- and citizen-advocacy. Collaborative working between social work and education departments was highlighted as a means by which this might be accomplished.

For this kind of legislation to become operational and influence effective change, existing paradigms have to be challenged in a political context. This is often dependent on staff in a situation where the client group is consistently viewed as being powerless. Unfortunately both social work and educational staff who work with this group are regarded as having low status both in day centres and in colleges. In colleges, staff are also subject to performance targets which can restrict creative development of curricula. A concentration on skills-based individual programmes allows services to ignore the broader political issues in order to provide remedial work. Staff are rarely in a position where they can develop effective means to promote real social justice or empowerment, although the client councils set up in social work day centres purport to offer real choices and a say in services.

There is evidence that service users are given few opportunities for realistic involvement on key decisions either at centre or local level. It would seem that any adult status conferred by belonging to groups such as the clients' councils is arbitrary and conditional. Barnes (1990), as well as Corbett and Barton (1992), argues that:

> Education is political and takes place in a political context. Working with such groups, therefore, requires more than the teaching of 'appropriately adult' skills and attitudes. It necessitates an involvement in the difficult struggle of achieving something greater than what is essentially a spurious form of adulthood. (1990: 26)

It is important to consider whether current educational opportunities may be a factor that prevents people with learning disabilities from gaining adult status and acceptance in society. The lack of available quality services for this group says much about how they are viewed by the policy makers.

Petrie and Shaw (1999) argue for disabled people to provide their own 'narratives' and histories, and for those narratives and histories to be recognised as illustrating the 'active social and political discrimination' endured by this group. New educational strategies and practices will have to be based on partnership in order to begin to influence the progression of social inclusion for this group. It is evident that a broader view of society must be embraced, with opportunities to build shared social purpose and political awareness in all parties concerned.

In setting up the SUFYRG group it was hoped to create an environment where the confidence and personality of all participants would be emphasised. The narratives and histories of the individuals were seen as valued knowledge and central to the learning experience. It was believed that a behavioural remedial approach would undermine the work and give little useful information about the needs of the individual. It was considered vital to avoid any approach that reinforces disempowerment of individuals by focusing on standards defined and decided by professionals. Standards which contribute: 'both directly and indirectly to the maintenance of the status quo, as part of the cultural hegemony' (Armstrong, 1982: 24).

Many of the people attending the Joint Planning group from the SUFYRG wanted to share personal histories, their stories. For some this was the only way they had of bringing their experiences and opinions to the perceived power holders. Unfortunately, both then and now, committees are not designed to cope with this kind of difference and 'otherness' in communications. Additionally, some professionals suggested (usually outwith meetings) that the views expressed by the SUFYRG members were being influenced by the support staff and were not theirs. The participants demonstrated increasingly that this was not the case by being clear and confident of their own views. The responsibility for the content of the tapes lay entirely with the group, who took this very seriously. As the participants began to take control of their own learning and develop their own literacies, through the issues from the group, there was a real motivation to learn and develop. The medium of non-directive, participative group work gave opportunities for shared interactions. This enabled the participants to decide their own curriculum, within which they could assess themselves, the facilitators and the running of the group. Even where language and communication skills were restricted, the responsive learning context helped to promote confidence, expertise and enjoyment. The methods used to communicate demonstrated active shared control over learning situations in contexts that had genuine shared meanings for all parties. This was clearly evidenced by the group working together to fight for services under threat of cuts.

Negotiation

Crucial to any partnership is the means to negotiate the base from which the relationship will take place and central to this is the notion of power.

> Negotiation involves a commitment to sharing power with the student in order to maximise the learning potential of the student. Whilst it is understood that the teacher or student are unlikely to be equal in terms of status, knowledge or power, there is an inherent commitment to the acknowledgement of power to both parties which can be invoked, by a refusal to negotiate if necessary, since inter-dependence is necessary, to the process [of] negotiation. (Bee, 1992: 12)

It is extremely difficult for an individual who has been systematically treated unequally to begin to accept power (Tomlinson, 1982). Certainly, students should be supported in coming to terms with this. A common view of disability often includes a perception of lack of independence, implying an inability to make decisions or be competent in all or some areas. In many cases this leads to people with disabilities having things done for them. Consequently it may be difficult to convince some students that they are able. Others demonstrate their frustrations by claiming unrealistic abilities or powers. For a significant number, lack of motivation may prove to be the limiting factor. This has important implications for staff beginning to redress the balance in learning situations, especially where the learner has little experience in making decisions and may offer resistance to new methods of learning. Staff may also have to confront their own prejudices in the process. Corbett and Barton (1992) state that:

> True empowerment involves the redefining of social values, extending the boundaries of what constitutes 'appropriate' behaviour and accepting a wide range of cultural differences. (1992: 44)

Initially, several of the SUFYRG participants found it difficult to value themselves and believed the staff should be telling them what to do and what to learn. Some interacted only with the staff, or other perceived authority figures, and did not always fully acknowledge or value the contributions of other members of the group. This difficulty improved over time, as every contribution in the group setting was valued equally by the facilitators, and discussion between all the group members encouraged. The sessions were carried out in a structured and directive way, especially in the early weeks, as many of the participants had little or no experience of the kind of interactive discussions that would encourage democratic decisions to be made. Directive influences were relaxed as people began to interact more, and took more control of the learning situation. Confidence increased as the students saw that their contributions and ideas were influencing their peers, the group and the role of the facilitators. They were becoming partners rather than passive recipients. This made it possible for the facilitators to 'stand back' from the process and 'give back' the power to the students. It was essential from the start to attempt to enable students to begin to set objectives that had meaning for them. The process in which this occurred provided the main vehicle for learning. The students were actively involved in the sequencing and structure of the sessions and this was achieved through negotiation.

Participants were encouraged to choose options, and were also asked to decide what these options should be. Issues such as the control of information, money, power and major decisions affecting lives were brought up to be considered and discussed. The topics sometimes challenged commonly held precepts and attitudes deeply inculcated in both the professionals and the users of the day services. However, interaction in the group provided a forum that helped to allay some common fears on the part of the students. For example, that being able to read and write is the only key or that education is a fixed body of knowledge and that both must be accessed in order to be included as an autonomous adult. The SUFYRG provided a forum where people could learn to change, and develop their own powerful ways of communicating in a changing world, as opposed to merely learning to cope in a world full of unattainable, fixed or ideal knowledge.

Conclusion

It is vital that the curriculum includes opportunities for students to learn an approach that can be made to work for them. The Adult Literacies in Scotland Project identified deficit models of provision in ABE as those most commonly in use in Scotland. A preferred option, described by their study, is a Lifelong Learning Approach designed for: 'adults whose needs and aspirations relate to any area of working, private, public or educational life' (Macrae, 2000).

The way in which the SUFYRG has evolved clearly shows the beginnings of such a lifelong learning approach. The group and its one-year-old sister group, SURGING AHEAD, are demonstrating that community education, in partnership with other organisations, can begin to provide models for new projects. Exciting initiatives such as this may prove to be the kind of catalyst described by Baron, Riddell and Wilkinson, that is instrumental in:

> ... the development of people with learning difficulties as a self-conscious political and social movement within the wider disability movement. (1997: 41)

The literacies embraced by the SUFYRG must be publicly endorsed as a means through which people with learning disabilities can cross the divide from 'other' to work in tandem with professionals, teach us their histories and knowledge, to extend the boundaries of rights, freedom, justice and equality. Giroux puts it this way:

> At its best, critical literacy provides students and audiences with the competencies needed to develop and experience a pluralistic conception of citizenship and community that dignifies democracy as a forum for creating unity without denying specificity. (1992: 245)

The literacies developed by the SUFYRG, as with many innovations, have attracted controversy. Some people have expressed the view that these literacies are not genuine and have not been generated by adults with learning disabilities. Difficulties can also arise where in order to make the messages from the participants clear, the facilitators have helped the group to translate their discussions into language commonly used in professional and bureaucratic settings. The reality is that people need a lot of support and confidence to be able to develop thinking and extend their own literacies. The role of the facilitators can undoubtedly carry a great deal of power. The group used the mediation of the boundaries agreed for the staff role in SUFYRG to avoid skewing the power differential in the group as well as for sorting out any conflict of view occurring between the participants and the professional facilitators. Difficulties were sometimes experienced when the facilitators were perceived as being a bridge between various sets of other professionals and the SUFYRG. Conflict and dissonance with professional bodies and power holders arose where ground rules to fit new situations have not been considered or formulated. Another difficulty for organisations is to have service users (supported by the organisation's staff) challenging their cultural norms, especially where there are implications for scarce, contested, resources.

An important further paradox is that without social work day centre provision there is no obvious existing locus through which day centre users with learning disabilities can come together to have a voice. The main function of social work in this context is care. Powerful literacies can challenge both the caring base of social work and traditional notions and curricula in education, because asserting previously unheard voices can make unexpected and challenging demands. People with learning disabilities need to be encouraged to value their own history and background in order to develop the literacies that ground education for this group in the realities enabling choice and participation. In their study, Baron, Riddell and Wilkinson state:

> None of our informants talked of people with learning difficulties as a group having a distinct history or distinct social interests which could provide the basis for 'the education of desire'. There appeared to be no engagement with existing organisations of people with learning difficulties and little with advocacy type organisations. The role of the adult with learning difficulties in structuring educational provision was largely limited to informal discussions with individual tutors, with users' groups commenting on provision and plans in one area being the limiting case. (1997: 39–40)

However, despite the successes gained by the SURYRG and SURGING AHEAD, there are enormous challenges still to overcome. Lack of professional support for these groups at this stage certainly means that they will be unable to continue. An insistence on the mechanics of reading and writing at the expense of meaning and community participation reinforces the power of professionals and perpetuates the cycle of oppression. People with learning disabilities are still closely tied in to social and health services and have few links with adult or community education. Local authorities espouse the principles of social inclusion and suggest that monies will be available to support communities of interest. The reality is that were social work day centres to close, service users would have few opportunities to access the kind of resources that can enable them to develop their own voice, within the communities of interest that day centres somewhat unwittingly provide.

Community education through both adult education and ABE, working alongside adults with learning disabilities and in collaboration with other agencies, is well placed to help people develop their own powerful literacies, especially in that their ideological background is rooted in an ethos committed to both personal and political development. The value of educational opportunities for any group needs to be reinforced by a climate in which different literacies are valued and have political currency. In order to achieve this it will be necessary to take a broader view of literacy than many orthodox forms of thinking currently allow. Professionals purporting to serve the needs and interests of people with learning disabilities have to extend their views of acceptable forms of literacy to include the simple eloquence, strength and immediacy of these emergent voices.

References

Armstrong, P.F. (1982) 'The myth of meeting needs in adult education and community development', *Critical Social Policy*, 2 (2), pp. 24–37.

Baron, S., Riddell, S. and Wilkinson, H. (1997) 'After karaoke: adult education, learning difficulties and social renewal', *Scottish Journal of Adult and Continuing Education*, 4 (2), pp. 19–44.

Barnes, C. (1990) *Cabbage Syndrome: The Social Construction of Dependence*, Lewes: Falmer Press.

Barton, L. (ed.) (1988) *The Politics of Special Educational Needs*, London: Falmer Press.

Bee, E. (1992) 'The principle of negotiation: some considerations and delineations', Paper given at the BERA conference: Stirling University, unpublished, August.

Corbett, J. and Barton, L. (1992) *A Struggle for Choice: Students with Special Needs in Transition to Adulthood*, London: Routledge.

Disabled Persons (Services, Consultation and Representation) Act (1986), London: HMSO.

Education (Handicapped Children) Act (1970), London: HMSO.

Education (Scotland) Act (1981), London: HMSO.

Giroux, H.A. (1992) *Border Crossings*, Routledge.

Jamieson, C. (1994) *The Role of Adult Basic Education in a Social Work Day Centre for Adults with Learning Disabilities*, M.Ed. Dissertation: Stirling University, unpublished.

Jamieson, C. (1999) 'Developing literacies within ABE to promote self-advocacy work alongside adults with learning disabilities', *Research and Practice in Adult Literacy*, 38, Spring, pp. 11–13.

Jarvis, P. (1985) *The Sociology of Adult and Continuing Education*, Croom Helm.

Macrae, C.A. (2000) 'Project paper 3; a good practice framework for literacy and numeracy programmes', *Adult Literacies in Scotland Project*, Edinburgh: Scottish Executive, Enterprise and Lifelong Learning.

O'Brien, J. and Tyne, A. (1981) *The Principle of Normalisation: a Foundation for Effective Services*, London: The Campaign for Mentally Handicapped People.

O'Brien, J. and Lyle, C. (1989) *Framework for Accomplishments*, Georgia, USA: Responsive Systems Associates.

Petrie, M. and Shaw, M. (1999) 'The disability movement and the struggle for inclusion' in Crowther, J., Martin, I. and Shaw, M. (eds), *Popular Education and Social Movements in Scotland Today*, Leicester: NIACE, pp. 159–74.

Sutcliffe, J. (1990) *Adults with Learning Difficulties: Education for Choice and Empowerment*, Leicester: NIACE/The Open University Press.

Teale, M. and Ballantyne, M. (1990) 'Learn to learn in adult basic education', in *ALBSU*, Summer, 38.

Tomlinson, S. (1982) *A Sociology of Special Education*, London: Routledge and Kegan Paul.

Wolfensburger, W. (1972) *The Principle of Normalisation in Human Services*, Toronto: National Institute on Mental Retardation.

12 Empowering literacy learners and teachers: the challenge of information and communication technology (ICT)

Fiona Frank

Introduction

In April 1999, a group of employees from four workplaces in the North West of England came together for a 'computing for the terrified' residential weekend course at Alston Hall, a former manor house now used for all kinds of adult learning opportunities. Some of the participants had literacy difficulties, and some of those had taken part in basic skills courses at their workplaces. Some used computers in their work, others didn't. All were taking part in the course in their own time, and the fees of all the learners were being paid by their employers as part of the 'Employee Development schemes' that all four companies were running.[1]

During the weekend, the learners were interviewed individually, and they also took part in discussion sessions about the role of computers in their lives. The themes from these discussions form the main substance of this chapter.

The conversations and discussions at Alston Hall were tape recorded and later transcribed by an experienced transcriber. Although the transcriber hadn't been at the sessions, the transcripts sent back were accurate and thorough: the equipment had been working well and all the discussions had been clear, calm and easy to follow. The only place in the discussions where there was no chance that the transcriber could record what was said was where there was a near-riot among the 12 participants (this came back on the first draft of the transcripts as 'confusion'). This was when one of the participants had suggested that a handyman/cleaner in his organisation shouldn't be entitled to computing courses paid for by their employer, as he was never likely to need it in his job.

The participants from the other organisations felt that this was an untenable attitude. Some of the comments that were decipherable amid the general outcries included these:

> You never know at what point in his life or which circumstances where he may be required to access a computer. If he hasn't got the faintest idea how to go about it, he's lost.

It shouldn't matter whether you work in stores or whether you're the managing director. Everyone should be entitled.

Most of the participants on the course had talked about the importance of learning to use the computer outside of their workplace. They talked about using the computer with their children and grandchildren – to play games, to do project work, and to find information. They felt that their children already knew about computers and they didn't want to be left behind. Although only two participants owned a computer at the time of the course, one participant had grown-up children who used computers daily as part of their work; and one participant's father sold computers. And at least three of the participants were planning to buy a computer as a result of the course.

They talked about computers being part of daily life – both now and particularly in the future:

> You can't turn round and say 'well, I'm not going to do anything with computers' because that's just burying your head in the sand, because they're here, and they're here to stay: I've got to learn something about them because they do affect everybody's life, from the bill through your door to the newspapers, to your work. It affects all parts of life.

> Everybody will have a PC. Everybody will be using e-mail, everybody will be surfing the net – that's how I see the future. It's inevitable, because everything's getting automated, everything's getting computerised, it's just a matter of time before everybody's got one.

They talked about using the Internet for all kinds of reasons to do with their home lives and their community – to find out about health problems, to communicate with other people with interests in similar issues, to buy a car or to find a particular wallpaper sample. Even those who didn't currently use a computer as part of their work could see how ICT could benefit their workplace – the cook, for example, could see that she could use the computer to store menus, keep records of regular attenders' special dietary needs, and co-ordinate ordering of ingredients. The carer working with people with learning disabilities talked about how she would be able to find out information about little-known syndromes from the Internet. They talked about needing to understand computers to get a better job, to get promotion:

> Of course it's very hard to get a job when you've not been working with computers all along: they'll choose somebody who's been doing it more often.

Even the participant who felt that the handyman/cleaner shouldn't get access to computing lessons paid for by his workplace admitted that he himself was gaining as much from the computing course to keep up with his children, as he was for his workplace.

> The older girl ... she's got special needs ... writing and reading are very, very, difficult to her, and I think that's why we got [the computer] ... she did a project which was absolutely fantastic and she did it all on the computer, which to her credit is very, very, big, because it took her hours and hours and hours. ... If it had been written, she wouldn't have done it, she wouldn't have been capable. And another thing that was nice about it as well, she had a skill that I ... that her parents didn't have, which makes your ego go 'whoo'!

These learners' discussions of ICT as a day-to-day part of their daily life resonates well with the 'social practice' view of literacy. In research by Merrifield *et al* (1997) and by Barton and Hamilton (1998), for example, interviews were carried out with people with literacy difficulties. The interviews took place over a number of visits and participants talked about all aspects of their lives and about how they used literacy, what it meant for them and how it (and increasingly, technology) impacted on their whole lives. Barton and Hamilton, in particular, talk about individuals, often with apparently low levels of literacy, using text to become 'experts' by necessity in matters, for example, of health or the law.

Power of the purse strings: who can learn about ICT?

The discussion on access to learning – about who has the right to learn about computers, and at whose expense – was the first indication in the discussions that the participants were very aware that power is very much involved in access to learning. It led to a good deal of emotion, anger and strong feeling, as people talked about the injustice of being denied access to something which they all saw as being the key to the future, the route to promotion, something entirely essential which they realised their children were going to understand and which they therefore saw as an urgent training need.

For workers on variable shift patterns (which affected 11 out of the 12 participants on the Alston Hall course), even with the best motivation in the world it's very difficult to attend courses outside work. If you do sign up, you miss half the sessions and lose the thread of the course. The employee development schemes that the participants' companies had signed up to at the time of the course went some way towards solving this. Each company was committed to contributing towards the cost of their employees' undertaking all kinds of learning in their own time – and to facilitate this by organising shift patterns for the courses. Each company had a different attitude towards the kind of course that could be covered by the scheme. The public service organisation (where the unlucky handyman/cleaner mentioned above worked) was particularly concerned about not wanting to be seen spending public money on 'unnecessary' training.

Power is associated with ICT in other very solid ways, both literally and figuratively. Power is associated with the actual text produced by a computer. The course participant quoted above, who had a daughter with special needs, used the power of the computer to type a document as part of his appeal to try to get his other daughter into a particular school.

> I felt it was a little bit more professional. It showed that we were trying as much as we could rather than just writing the note ... I got to think of it as a little bit of a game, because it was something new.

Brian Street (1995) refers to this same issue saying '... the status associations of written forms can lend added power to documents and letters over oral communications ...' and goes on to say:

> Such significance cannot, in fact, be detached from the supposed intrinsic 'meanings' of words communicated: the whole social practice, including the form of literacy, serves to constitute meaning. (1995, 90)

Our learner was very aware of this when he chose to word process his letter to the school appeal board, rather than hand-write it. He felt able to gain some measure of power by being able to communicate with the board in their own medium and he was very aware that it was a kind of game that he was playing.

In the most literal way of all, you need a power supply to gain access to information technology. There is an economic cost in the acquisition of reading and writing in that someone has to teach you to do it. However, once you've learned the technology of writing you could scratch your letters in the ground, or on a stone, for another individual to read: and you don't need to be plugged into technology to read a book (at least during the day, in natural light!). To use the literacy of the information society, however, your community needs to have access to electrical power – through the national grid, through generators, or through conventionally or solar charged batteries. If you have mobile technology you can access solar tracking devices via a laptop and a phone deep in the rain forest, as a TV advertisement in the UK in 1999 demonstrated. However, there's an issue about exclusion here. In the same way that not every community has access to literacy, not every community has access to electrical power and to telephone lines (come back from the rain forest, for a moment, and think about the UK traveller community). Not everyone has the economic power to access mobile phones and computers. And not every community, not every individual, has access to the training they need to use this technology.

ICT and the workplace basic skills learner

The context of my own research is the basic skills learner and ICT in the UK workplace. In this area, at first glance, there is no problem about access to computers, electricity, or power. However, even in what looks like a privileged sector of society – people in work, in a context of quite high unemployment levels, at the beginning of the twenty-first century – there is a visible emergence of another underclass: those who will continue to be excluded from access to ICT despite all the best efforts of policy makers and of training providers.

The Moser Committee, the Working Group on Post-Sixteen Basic Skills, was commissioned in 1998 by the new Labour government to look at adult basic skills and make recommendations to how they should be addressed. The UK government's National Adult Literacy Strategy, announced as a response to the Moser Report (1999), has set a target of reaching 3.5 million learners by 2010 and includes a commitment to provision of free courses in literacy and numeracy for those who need them.

One of the Moser Report's recommendations was that all workplace basic skills courses should be funded publicly. It includes a key section on new technology as an underpinning tool to improve basic skills. It includes the fact that ICT

> provides a powerful motivation for adults with poor basic skills. It does not therefore evoke the memories of struggle and failure that paper, pencil and books often recall. A computer can also enable a learner to be a more successful writer, more quickly: to produce letters and other writing that looks good, without crossings out, poor handwriting or a number of paper drafts. (paragraph 9.27)

The Report also mentions the fact that there is still discussion about whether ICT should be treated as a basic skill in itself.

> As for Information Technology as a basic skill in itself, we welcome the intention of the National Skills Task Force to examine the question of IT literacy in its work on key skills and employability. (paragraph 9.41).

This paragraph is of paramount importance for basic skills and ICT providers throughout the UK. There is a commitment to (continue to) provide free basic skills courses for all, as part of the national adult literacy strategy. Including ICT as a basic skill would mean that there would be no problem in offering free ICT courses as part of the basic skills curriculum in and out of the workplace.

From workplace-based Training Needs Analyses (TNAs) carried out nationwide by members of the Workplace Basic Skills Network it is very apparent that there is a consistent demand within workplaces for computing courses. Taking the figures from one North West company interviewed by Lancaster Employee Development Consortium (Frank 1997):

- 11% of those interviewed were interested in reading, writing, and handwriting training,

- 24% were interested in brush–up grammar training,
- 21% were interested in brushing up their spelling,
- 33% were interested in report writing,
- 39% were interested in presentation skills, and
- 74% of those interviewed were interested in computing training, mainly at introductory level – and many of these potential ICT learners were people with an interest in basic skills training at different levels.

The above pattern has been reflected in every workplace where TNAs have been carried out (see also, for example, Holland and McHugh, 2000), showing that, as Moser says, there is consistent motivation among workplace learners for training in computing.

The National Adult Literacy strategy includes a huge commitment to ICT as a mechanism for delivery and for assessment of the basic skills curriculum, including, rather worryingly, a commitment to tests as an underpinning strategy for assessing progress. (For a comment on the use of tests, see Frank, 1999.) Much of this work will take place within the framework of the UfI (the University for Industry, now operating as learndirect). The UfI was officially launched in September 2000. At the time of writing it is commissioning a large amount of ICT-based materials for basic skills delivery, and plans to co-ordinate a number of 'learning hubs' run by existing training providers, both in workplaces and in community settings in order to reach the maximum number of learners. The UfI is also consulting with adult literacy tutors and others on ways in which ICT materials have been used successfully with adult basic skills students, and on what combination of print materials and ICT materials is most effective. It is also setting up training packages for its learning centre managers including awareness raising on the learning needs of basic skills students, and the issues around workplace basic skills programmes.

Although the UfI is likely to have a huge effect on access to ICT for disadvantaged groups – particularly that of access to equipment – it is essential that basic skills tutors join in this debate in an informed way.

The basic skills tutor and the tutor–student relationship

All the 11-year-old children at the exhibition could show me how to design a Web page, whereas their teachers couldn't. (Ian Taylor, former Minister for Science and Technology, in Walker, 2000)

Another power issue, which the learners at Alston Hall touched on in the discussion quoted above, is that of the shifting balance of power. With the advent of new technology, the parent/teacher/older person no longer holds the power of knowledge and of how to use the essential tools, to be passed on to the child/pupil/younger person. With ICT, it is all too often the child, the person who would traditionally be in the role of the apprentice, who holds more of the keys, who is in control of the knowledge and therefore a good deal of the power in the relationship. The learner quoted above who says 'I'd like to stay ahead of them, I'd like to know what they're doing' is probably fighting a losing battle with his first wish, 'I'd like to stay ahead of them'. His second wish, 'I'd like to know what they're doing', is probably the best that he (and any of us) can do.

The Moser Report stresses the need for basic skills tutors to be trained in the use of ICT with basic skills learners. It is doubly important that they have an understanding of ICT: first, so that they do not themselves form another barrier to their students' access to the power and potential of ICT in their lives; second, so that they begin to feel comfortable with the shifting power balance mentioned above. It is possible that student and tutor will become more equal partners, both learning about a new development, in a context where it's conceivable that the 'teacher' is not the quicker learner.

Papert's (1993) comments on dealing with the issue of changing teacher–student relations in the secondary classroom are interesting and pertinent for adult educators:

> The first few times I noticed that the students had problems I couldn't even understand, let alone solve, I struggled to avoid facing the fact that I could not keep up my stance of knowing more than they did. I was afraid that giving it up would undermine my authority as a teacher. But the situation became worse. Eventually I broke down and said I didn't understand the problem – go discuss it with some of the others in the class who might be able to help. (1993: 65–66)

Papert's students do 'go and discuss it' with their peers and work out a solution together. In the course of discovering that it was possible as a teacher to tell his students that he didn't know everything, Papert found an amazing kind of liberation:

> ... I no longer had to fear being exposed. ... I no longer had to pretend. ... What a relief! It has changed my relationship with the children and with myself. My class has become much more of a collaborative community where we are all learning together. (1993: 65–66)

And Ian Taylor, the former Minister for Science and Technology, quoted at the beginning of this section, is very aware that a group of 11-year-olds is going to be more 'savvy' than their teacher on ICT issues. He notes that this is a training issue for the school teacher. For the purpose of developing learners in the basic skills 'classroom' we need to note that it is as important to be aware of these shifting relationships as it is to be aware of how to use the technology.

Tutor training in ICT – the constraints

It is not only the workplace literacy learner who has a problem with gaining access to training in ICT. The adult literacy tutor – who is very likely to be on a part-time contract – may well also have a problem gaining access. Although the Moser Report recommends training in ICT for adult basic skills tutors, and in addition acknowledges that career paths and professional development pathways for adult basic skills tutors need to be improved, the experience up to now is that part-time tutors are not given very much. Neither do they have much access to ICT equipment on which to undertake training.

Comments made in their post-course evaluation forms by basic skills tutors participating in a pilot training course on 'Using the Internet in Workplace Literacy' are worth including here. Although the course content and support was viewed favourably, many of the participants mentioned technical constraints:

> I did most of the course at home – no facilities nor time at work. The Internet is only available at certain centres and I was teaching when the computers were not being used.

> Access to Internet limited to one site at start of course.

> Internet connections at college were decidedly 'iffy'.

> Fortunately, I was able to buy a new PC for home use until more reliable access to [the] Net.

Twenty-two people who had registered on this course were interviewed as part of a follow-up evaluation exercise (Helsby, 2000). Four had been unable to access the course because of late delivery of equipment and seven more had only followed a small part of the course. Five of those seven had encountered technical or practical difficulties, including lack of time. Of 11 tutors who did complete all or most of the course, a high proportion (7 out of the 11) said that they 'had encountered technical difficulties during the course, including poor equipment, limited availability of machines, problems in accessing the Internet and the lack of a proper browser. One interviewee had not been able to obtain an e-mail address through her college.

There has been a steady improvement in ICT resources in Further Education, Adult and Community Education colleges over the past year since those tutors undertook that training, and this is likely to improve further. However, it is essential that colleges address the problem of the power they hold in allowing access to time and equipment for professional development.

It is only when tutors have knowledge of the technology that they become confident enough to work with their own students to develop this knowledge together. And developing ways in which the tutors can work with students to use the Internet, or even to use ICT-based basic skills learning materials, takes time and commitment on the side of the employer/college as well as the tutor.

Literacy through the Internet – a new model

Bigum and Green (1992) talk about four ways in which the terms 'technology' and 'literacy' might be combined: they talk about 'technology *for* literacy' (meaning using ICT materials to teach literacy); 'literacy *for* technology' (meaning the literacy you have to read in order to access technology – e.g. an instruction manual); 'literacy *as technology*' (remembering that writing itself is a technology – both the practice of writing and also of 'applying means to ends, tools/techniques to purposes …'); '*technology as* literacy' (the now common phrase 'computer literacy' refers to a whole new literacy in itself). I propose an adaptation of Bigum and Green's model for defining the Internet in its relationship with literacy.

- **The internet *for* literacy**: Some specific exercises for literacy learners have been made available on various Web sites set up by national literacy agencies, software developers, etc.

  You can find all kinds of adult literacy exercises on the Web if you search the adult literacy sites. David Rosen, Director of the Adult Literacy Resource Institute, the Greater Boston Regional Support Center of the Massachusetts System for Adult Basic Education Support, maintains a 'literacy list' which includes a 'webliography' for adult literacy sites, with reviews by adult basic skills tutors, under 'resources' at http://www/alri/org.
- **Literacy *for* the internet**: this is literacy which you need in order to access the Internet – but large print views, graphics, simplified text and real audio voice options mean that this does not have to be a prime consideration.
- **Literacy *on* the internet**

  Many literacy practitioners and projects have included information about ways of working with basic skills students on their Web sites, and these sites can all be accessed to enhance this work (see, for example, the links from the UK Workplace Basic Skills Network Web site http://www.lancs.ac.uk/wbsnet). In addition to being a resource for students, the Web can also be used by students as a way in which their own work can be published for a wider audience. But there are other possibilities, in addition to the publishing of straight 'student writing' on the Web. 'Virtual visits' are 'trips' to various sites where students not only learn about their own world (by, for example, going to see their local political representatives and asking specific questions) but also make a Web site about their visit, with photographs and commentary. The idea of virtual visits was developed by David Rosen and Tom Macdonald. David Rosen and Susan Gaer, an ESOL teacher at Santa Ana College, have developed a variation, the classroom 'virtual visit' where students in one part of the world virtually visit a group or class of students somewhere else using the Web and e-mail. A sample of these 'virtual visits' can be seen on http://www2.wgbh.org/mbcweis/ltc/alri/vv.html and http://www.otan.dni.us/webfarm/emailproject/school.htm

- **The internet *as* literacy**
  Most importantly of all, the Internet provides a vast range of exciting sources of information on all kinds of topics for students as well as for tutors – not just 'literacy exercises'. Tutors should provide the key for their students to be able to use the Web as an enormous and live library: like the 78-year-old woman reported in the *Guardian* (11/2/00) who, after two hours of using a computer for the first time, managed to locate her long-lost brother after 38 years of separation.

The virtual visit type of activity with students Rosen calls 'constructivist' activity (1999) in that it takes account of the literacy student as a whole person and moves away from the notion of ICT-based literacy tasks and tests. Constructivism, Rosen explains, 'is a theory of cognitive growth in which … a learner constructs knowledge by actively connecting and assimilating new information or experience into his or her existing knowledge structure' (1999: 306). A constructivist approach would include project-based participatory work on a topic of high interest to the student, where ICT tools would be used for *research*, *presentations*, *communication* and *publication* rather than as a resource for simply completing literacy tasks. Rosen also stresses the importance of staff development in using technology with adult literacy students.

Such an effort needs to go beyond training in the use of hardware and software to focus on integration of technology in support of curriculum and instruction. It must also enable creative, constructivist uses of technologies in support of student enquiry and student project-based learning, and it must enable teachers to see beyond the classroom, [and] to create new models for learning. (Rosen, 1999: 313)

Conclusion

It is important to see the literacy student as a whole person and to understand the role that literacy – and technology – play in their lives which are themselves structured by relations of inequality. None of the learners described in Barton and Hamilton's (1988) account described themselves as inadequate. All had rich networks within their lives and all had developed competent literacies. The learners at the 'computing for the terrified' course mentioned at the beginning of this chapter, too, had rich networks within their lives and many ideas for accessing the new technology with which they were beginning to interact on a more and more frequent basis.

The basic skills tutor has an important role to play in supporting adult learners in gaining the many different kinds of power they need to access, and to use, this new technology. This does not have to be a solitary practice. The technology itself – e-mail, the Web, and 'chatrooms' – can all be used to find support and encouragement – sometimes from the most unlikely sources – for both tutor and student.

Acknowledgement

1. The Employee Development schemes were co-ordinated by 'Lancaster Employee Development Consortium', a DfEE-funded partnership of Lancaster University and The Adult College Lancaster. The residential weekend was financially supported by LAWTEC.

References

Barton, D. and Hamilton, M. (1998) *Local Literacies: Reading and Writing in One Community*, London: Routledge.

Bigum, C. and Green, B. (1992) 'Technologizing literacy: the dark side of the dream', *Discourse: the Australian Journal of Educational Studies*, 12 (2), pp. 4–28.

Frank, F. (1997) Report on the Training Needs Analysis at *Company B, Chorley*, including recommendations for setting up an Employee Development Scheme. Unpublished report, Lancashire Employee Development Consortium, Lancaster: Department of Continuing Education, Lancaster University.

Frank, F. (1999) 'No more Cinderella? Basic skills in the workplace context – after Moser', *Adults Learning*, April, pp. 6–8.

Helsby, G. (2000) *A Cinderella Service: the view from the coach* (Evaluation of the Workplace Basic Skills Training Network Professional Development Programme), Kendal: GH Evaluations.

Holland, C. and McHugh, G. (2000) 'A study of the aspirations, learning pathways and potential for learning and development of 700 manual workers in Oxfordshire', Lancaster: CSET, Lancaster University.

Lankshear, C. with Gee, J.P. and Searle, C. (1997) *Changing Literacies*, Buckingham and Bristol, USA: Open University Press.

Merrifield, J. *et al* (1997) *Life at the Margins: Literacy, Language and Technology in Everyday Life*, New York: Teachers College Press.

Moser, Sir Claus (1999) *A Fresh Start: Improving Literacy and Numeracy, Report of the Working Group on Post-School Basic Skills*, London: DfEE.

Papert, S. (1993) *The Children's Machine: Rethinking School in the Age of the Computer*, New York: Basic Books.

Rosen, D. (1999) 'Using electronic technology in adult literacy education' in Comings, Garner and Smith (eds), *Annual Review of Adult Learning and Literacy*, Volume One, San Francisco: Jossey-Bass Publishers.

Street, B. (1995) *Social Literacies: Critical approaches to Literacy in Development, Ethnography and Education*, London and New York: Longman.

Walker, D. (2000) 'A tale of a PM and his mouse', *TES*, 11 February.

13 Using Scots[1] literacy in family literacy work

Alan F.P. Addison

Introduction

In Scotland's new democracy the idea of 'voice' is of paramount importance if Scotland's citizens are to break free from the democratic deficit experienced between the life of people in communities and the policies and programmes of the state (see Martin, 1999). Scots literacy can be part of a move to develop a voice which can talk back to the institutions that for so long have used a 'dominant form of literacy at the expense of those from non-mainstream cultures' (Tett and Crowther, 1998: 449). It is an attempt to further a spirit of dialogue between the dominant discourse and silenced voices.

Family literacy work in Edinburgh '... respects, strengthens and extends literacy practices as a powerful force for change' (Auerbach in Heywood, 2000: 6) and this chapter argues for the further acceptance of vernacular literacy practice as a legitimate resource and opportunity for learning. Scots literacy credits the vernacular as a force which stems from people's everyday lives (Barton and Hamilton, 1998: 247), from the world as it actually is, and then seeks to build on the diversity of literacy as a social practice, i.e. literacy as it is embedded and used in everyday living. Its aim is to lead to the destigmatising of local literacy practices and the creation of a democratic culture in which local knowledge and experience are seen as a legitimate tool for learning.

By creating collective opportunities for families to use the vernacular, legitimately, Scots literacy aims to enhance the culture within which these expressions take shape and create a space for vernacular literacy practices to be developed as positive educational resources. Scots literacy makes no attempt at silencing minority voices but celebrates the pluralistic nature of working–class communities, democratising literacy work, so that the idea of dominant is replaced by the idea of *egalité* in a process which encourages the voice of marginalised groups. By so doing, Scots literacy focuses on the 'diversity of thought, language and world-view that reflects the actual lives and experiences of children, families and community members rather than a reproduction of a constructed and imposed ideal' (Tett and Crowther, 1998: 452).

The context

Scots literacy is part of the family literacy work developed by Edinburgh's Community Education Service. The intellectual base of the work is founded on the 'socio-contextual approach' of Auerbach (1989) which is critical of deficit and pathologising views of families that seek to develop literacy through the 'transmission of school practices' into the community. Auerbach argues, instead, that neglected aspects of family literacy practice include the following: parents working independently on reading and writing; using literacy to address family and community problems; parents addressing child-rearing concerns; supporting the development of a community's own language and culture; interacting with the school system (1989: 178). The project discussed here refers particularly to work relating to the issue of home language and culture and its interaction with the school system. As Heywood (2000) points out, the aims of Scots literacy in Edinburgh has been to:

• encourage parents to value their own language and not subsume it to Standard English;
• highlight the importance of oral language in terms of literacy and personal development;
• look at aspects of oral language (e.g. storytelling, nursery rhymes, wordgames) and relate these to learning how to read and write. (2000: 28)

These aspirations have informed our attempts to develop the use of Scots literacy as a learning resource and the following account examines aspects of this work to date. By helping people to compare and contrast their own vernacular literacies with school literacy practices it is hoped that this can lead to a valuing and recognition of the cultural resources embedded in literacy as a social practice.

The work takes place mostly within nine primary schools in an urban, working-class community, designated as an area of disadvantage. The positive aspects of this work were highlighted in an evaluation. 'The project has undertaken a good deal of work to generate a responsive and negotiated curriculum which builds on the literacy practices of parents ...' (Crowther and Tett 1996: 17) but then went on to say that regarding 'Scottish context and culture ... the project has some way to go' in that it failed to recognise the cultural significance of vernacular Scots. However, bearing in mind that the work takes place mostly within primary schools, institutions where the literacies of working-class communities are marginalised, and where most of our adult students learned that their language was an inferior or slang version of Standard English (McClure, 1980: 13–15), how could the project find the space to legitimately value vernacular Scots?

To raise awareness and sensitivity to local literacies, the project began student-led investigations which have focused on identifying literacy practices in the home and community. In an informal piece of research which asked the question: 'Dae ye speak Scots or slang?' to adult students in existing literacy groups, the repeated answer we received was, 'Ah speak slang'. These negative self-images [60–70 per cent of the 70 people questioned] became a major concern for the project. If a community's means of communication and self-expression are perceived by themselves to be inferior, then how does that reflect on their self-image and confidence?

The practice of family literacy in Edinburgh is committed to developing a curriculum which is built through a democratic process, sensitive to the voice of local communities. Nevertheless, we were forced to ask ourselves – if the students' voices taking part in negotiations have suffered years of unconstrained, institutional delegitimisation, how can we be sure that we are negotiating democratically? Surely a voice which has been subjected to constant delegitimisation cannot participate equally, particularly when faced with a common-sense view that their own 'mither tongue' (Kay, 1986) is inherently inferior?

The power of Standard English, as the only legitimate language in Scottish education, has been slowly diminishing in the past decade as part of a general revival and democratisation of Scottish culture. The Scottish Office Education and Industry Department (SOEID) stance has eased and provided a basis for developing Scots in the classroom. The suggestion in the *English Language 5–14* guidelines that 'Children's earliest language is acquired in the home … and schools will build on that foundation' (SOEID, 1991: 3) has encouraged the production of literary devices such as the *Kist*, an anthology of literature in both Scots and Gaelic for use in schools (Robertson, 1996).

However, this acknowledgement of a diverse cultural context for language and literacy is not uniform, and Standard English is still the only means used for measuring ability both orally and textually:

> Language is at the centre of pupils' learning. It is through language that they gain much of their knowledge and many of their skills. High priority is, therefore, given to developing pupils' ability to use *English language* effectively. [their emphasis] (SOEID 1994: 8)

On the one hand, account in policy is taken of community histories and concerns 'fostering a sense of personal and national identity' (SOEID, 1991: 7) and, on the other, this can often mean reducing the actual language of participants to a tartan gesture, to be identified with things past, brought out to celebrate the birthday of the national bard (i.e. Robert Burns), whose eighteenth-century Scots most modern urban dwellers would find all but impossible to understand. Where Scots is acknowledged and accorded legitimacy, it is often in terms of an obsolete tradition, something past rather than present. As one primary school teacher remarked after one of our Scots sessions in her class: 'It's such a pity the real language has died away and all we're left with is slang.' Our aim is to demonstrate the relevance, living and evolving nature of this tradition as a resource *for the present*.

As a living language Scots is mainly absent from the curriculum of most classrooms. There are virtually no children's books for phonetic teaching of Scots in schools. The child has no formal comparisons to make when told the phoneme blend 'oo' in 'hoose' is actually 'ou' as in house. Yet according to Giegerich:

> Scots is a group of dialects (or, has been argued, a language) in its own right, with many lexical, syntactic, morphological and phonological features that distinguish it from Standard English. (Giegerich, 1992: 46)

Scots is a language and a literacy which deserves to be named as such. According to Harris, 'Naming languages explicitly is vital' as [not being specific] automatically excludes and problematises speakers of British urban dialects (Harris, 1995: 140). These non-standard voices are effectively marginalised by the cultural power of Standard English and 'the teaching of literacy can be seen, in Foucault's terms, as a process of disciplinary power in which literacies other than Standard English are delegitimated; they are accorded the status of subjugated knowledges which are partial and inadequate' (Crowther and Tett, 1997: 129).

By rejecting the language and literacy of the home, this disciplinary knowledge delegitimises language acquisition prior to school. Harris (1995: 121) believes that 'these groups of learners are adversely affected by a pedagogy which ignores the linguistic properties of their natural varieties of language'. This in turn leads to what Niven and Jackson (1998: 57) terms the 'Scottish cringe' in that the delegitimisation of the indigenous language has led Scots to wear a 'tartan chador', a veil which acts as a barrier and screen to the outside world. Bearing in mind family literacy's formal links with the dominant curriculum, the dialectic between dominant and vernacular literacies is the context for this work.

Scots literacy and the school

> It can hardly be denied that school literacy embodies the language of power; a language which disadvantages working class and other excluded communities. (Tett and Crowther, 1998: 456)

The Scots literacy programme is co-investigating with parents, family literacy workers and schools, the acceptance of Scots literacy in the school classroom. Our experience is that many classroom teachers, if they use Scots in literary terms, do so in a way which is confined to the past and is unrecognisable for people living in modern urban communities. This reproduction of 'things Scottish', however, ignores the present use of Scots by the school population. There are efforts by some teachers to link their lessons, albeit at famous anniversaries, to issues of culture and identity; however, this can often amount to tokenism unless modern-day usage of Scots is more systematically addressed and valued across the curriculum. Our own attempts to inject discussion of the use of Scots, its value and limitations are outlined below.

The following examples are based on work carried out with adult literacy groups based in the primary schools which the project's remit specifies. This remit is concerned with enabling parents/carers of school pupils to be 'partners' in their child's education. Our means of doing this is to explore the relevance of Scots for both adults and pupils learning literacy.

(i) Play production

Our first major attempt at a project was the writing and production of a school play, *Everyday's a School Day*, by our adult students/parents (Malcolm, Robertson and White, 1997). This production took six months to complete. The title represents the fact that school or learning opportunities do not merely exist within the confines of a school building between Monday and Friday. The purpose was to explore the use of literacy, past and present, in school and its implications.

The structure of the play followed a simple format of a dialogue between teachers and a class of children. The teachers' scripts were written in Standard English, while the pupils in the play spoke Scots. The issue of language difference is the focus of the play.

Act 1 scene 2

pupil 1:	we're daen one oan global warmin'
Horace:	eh?
pupil 1:	we've got tae look efter the earth
Horace:	does it not look efter itsel like?
pupil 1:	naw. It's polluted.
pupil 2:	(speaks from another group) we're daen one aboot the moon.
Horace:	(moving to new group) The moon's made o' cheese. (Class laugh)
teacher:	you must be the new boy?
Horace	(Looking around) Mmmm?

In the 1950s, the teacher tells the pupils, 'Speak English', while in the present the slightly more relaxed approach of the curriculum is reflected in the teacher response, 'Oh I do wish you would speak English'. In both cases, however, the results are the same and the class becomes silent. Horace, a character in the play, turns to the audience at the end and says, 'Aye ... somethings huvnae changed. Ah'm no stayin here any longer.' The idea of a silent class, as an analogy with the silenced voice of the Scottish working class, wasn't missed by the parents involved in the production. During the writing of the play the adult students had to address issues surrounding the use of language, its selection and significance. Vernacular literacy practices were used in the text and a comparison of Scots to Standard English took place, as the parents came to terms with transcribing, for the first time, their own pattern of speaking. Both the head and other teachers of the school agreed that it was a work of some standard and could be used as a literacy learning aid as well as a dramatic entertainment for the whole school, including parents.

The Scots literacy tackled in the play is based more on oral language than on school texts. Most of the learning achieved by the parents stemmed from their own knowledge. The parents had tackled the issue of literacy, comparing and contrasting Standard English with Scots. By contextualising their arguments within the curriculum, the parents had used their knowledge to start a debate between dominant and vernacular literacies.

(ii) Magazine production

I wis brought up an atheist. Neither ma or Dad, sisters or brothers went tae church. So ah went oan tae grow up withoot any faith ither than whit ah saw in front o' me in ma day tae day life. No that many years ago ma family wir involved in a drastic accident an' ma youngest son wis left at death's door in the Sick Kids fir months. I kent what prayers wir then! An' a' these folk wir comin' tae see us. A' these religious folk whae ah'd always thought wir oan anither planet. An' they prayed wie us night an' day ... (Becoming a Christian ... selection from Religion and Culture in *Family Allsorts*).

Following on from the success of the play, parents in another primary school decided to produce an educational magazine for their community. This was an opportunity, not only to highlight their own vernacular knowledge but also to widen the debate surrounding the question of language legitimacy, i.e. should their knowledge be transcribed in Scots or should the medium be Standard English?

Some very complex issues soon arose for the project, however, in that not all of the participants in this group were Scots: Bangladeshi, Punjabi, Chinese and English people were in the group and only two others and myself were Scots speakers. Standard English was the literacy medium shared by us all. The composition of the group meant that vernacular literacy practices were diverse and Scots could not assume a priority in a pluralistic and more open idea of identities. The 'new' Scotland is a multi-cultural one and the magazine would have to reflect that diversity. To reach as many folk as possible, the magazine group chose to draw upon the diverse knowledge of the different members of the group and the wider community. Different languages were used in the text with translations; however, the common denominator of Standard English was also included.

During production of the magazine (*Family Allsorts, the magazine fir aa sorts o' folk*, Ahmed, Cluness, Glancy, Poon and Singh, 1999) all the languages of the group were discussed, compared, recorded and 'named'. The different phonetic symbols, grammatical structures and meaning representations were compared and contrasted, shifting the literacy awareness of all of us to a more global perspective, while the eventual content of *Allsorts* reflected a diversity of knowledge. By choosing *not* to write mainly in Scots, the group had shown a willingness to engage with all expressions of language equally. Dominant value structures, associated with literacy teaching, were overshadowed by that willingness to engage with all forms of knowledge in a meaningful, egalitarian way.

The second edition of *Allsorts* will focus more closely on the diversity of literacy and language existing in the community. More textual space will be given to Scots and other languages, with Standard English used more for translation purposes within the extended glossary. The radical nature of this work, continually engaging with the cultural dialectic between dominant and vernacular literacy, has led to a wish to link with other marginalised cultures to begin a process of sharing experience. For this reason we shall be exploring the possibilities of going 'on-line' with the magazine.

(iii) Poetry recital programme

This programme involves parents and family literacy tutors writing and reciting poetry as part of a dramatic dialogue to primary school children, as part of their curriculum. We have done this in five schools across all age groups of pupils. The main focus of the programme is to legitimise present-day vernacular Scots language amongst school children, or more hopefully, to get them to think and question why their own natural ways of speaking are not overtly addressed in the curriculum. After we have performed the recitals we ask the pupils if they could write for us. They are told, when being asked if they would write in their own way, not to be 'feert tae stick in a bit o' French if they like' as a means of democratising literacy awareness.

Scots in space
Come in Earthling!
we are from the planet Mars,
Travelling from the universe
In search of distant stars
Away an bile yer heid!
Wir too busy fir a blether
Tourin the earth at speed
Tae get away fae wir awfie weather
Our on-board spell check is searching
To decipher your language ... so strange
It keeps coming up NOT KNOWN
This language is not in its range

To open the literacy debate in the classroom the stanzas involve two 'voices' which have characters using vernacular Scots and Standard English. This eventually results in a breakdown of communication. After the readings, the children are questioned as to the cause of the communication problems and what they think should be done. The school classroom has become the centre of a cultural debate, focused on the legitimacy of language dominance and on the problems this creates. Teachers are asked to fill in an evaluation form after the sessions and so far most responses have been positive.

Having directed our programme directly at the school curriculum we then invited the parents of the children to discuss the topic. This is a very delicate situation indeed. Centuries of language oppression have led to a great many people believing their language to be educationally irrelevant, if not barbaric (Beveridge and Turnbull, 1989: 6). Many see Standard English as the only language in which to couch their aspirations.

The parents' sessions are structured into a question and answer format as to whether Scots literacy is legitimate or not. The majority at the start believe it to be irrelevant. What is promising, nonetheless, is that parents do come along to the sessions and are interested in what is going on in the curriculum. After questions and answers, Scots literacy students and tutors give a short session on the history of Scots, using language maps, the *Kist* and the *Glasgow Bible* (Stuart, 1997) as examples of Scots texts. The *Chambers Scots Dictionary* and the *Scoor-oot Dictionary of Scots Words and Phrases in Current Use* (Stevenson, 1989) are on hand to legitimise the language as lexicographical. On completion of this history, we then ask how people feel about the legitimacy of Scots, now that it has been given a context. Many people are genuinely surprised that their language has a history at all: 'Ah thoucht Ah'd find the bit in history where we started turnin English intae slang' , as one parent put it. However, as another ironically stated, 'Whit's the point when we're tryin tae git them tae stoap speakin like that?' As we have discovered through our 'research', the inferiorisms experienced by the community are deep-rooted and must be approached tactfully. More importantly, our programme does not seek 'to advance the position that people be denied access to dominant literacies or that their own vernacular literacy is somehow privileged' (Crowther and Tett, 1997: 456).

The important gain made by the above sessions is not that pupils or parents suddenly feel liberated to use their vernacular Scots more openly, but that more people are becoming involved in thinking critically about literacy and their own educational experiences of learning it. Ideas of bilingualism, i.e. Scots/Standard English, as opposed to Slang/Standard English, have entered the debate and are indicative of a shift in thinking. Participants are willing to compare and contrast their language with that of other cultures. One parent, when asked whether they'd come to another session, replied 'Aye', reflected for a second then retorted, 'It's a'right fir me tae say that eh!'

This is perhaps one of the most important aspect of Scots literacy, in that it can encourage a re-reading of the student's words that, in turn, can contribute towards a re-reading of their world (Freire and Macedo, 1987). Language recently taken as inferior and inadequate may become accepted as a language of learning and an educational resource rather than a cultural embarrassment.

Conclusion

No doubt, Standard English will continue to be the main focus of the curriculum in schools and the language of aspiration for many in Scotland and, no doubt, working-class communities will continually be made to feel inferior. However, because we cannot change everything does not mean that we cannot contribute to changing some things and our aim is to continue to argue for a pedagogy which engages with the powerful values embedded in the dominant form of literacy teaching.

From a perspective of working with the grain of cultural experience rather than against it, as seems to happen in much of schooling, our programme on Scots literacy historicises (realistically) present-day vernacular Scots and seeks to legitimise voices that have been ridiculed and silenced. Scots literacy is one attempt to free student voices from stigma so that more democratic curriculum negotiations can take place between adult students and educators. In Gramsci's terms, it is anti-hegemonic in that it refuses to accept the dominant value system as the only way of making sense of the world (Hoare and Smith, 1998: 12). Using Scots literacy is also part of the new powerful literacies debate which engages with real experiences of literacies in use and which recognises that there are many forms, not just one, that literacy can take. It argues for the use of 'vernacular literacies' and highlights their importance as sources of knowledge – particularly if literacy is to be recognised as more than an ability to decode the alphabet. Scots literacy, from this perspective, serves to initiate, organise, justify and support action from voices normally unheard.

Note on Scots

1. Scotland has two distinctive indigenous languages, Scots and Gaelic. Gaelic (Gaidhlig, pronounced 'Gallic') is the older of the two, a Q Celtic language that came to Scotland with the arrival of the Irish people who set up the Kingdom of Dalriada. From the fifth to the twelfth centuries Gaelic was spoken across the whole of Scotland and only entered decline after the establishment of the Anglo-Norman feudal system.

Scots is a sister language of English that developed alongside the process of 'Normanisation' as it spread across the country as the language of law and court. During the period of independence from England, Scots developed different linguistic traits as the link with English language development was broken, and more European influences developed. 'Rural varieties of modern day Scots are romanticised and often treated as the "real thing". Literary Scots, used in poetry and prose, is often also highly valued, although some linguists would argue its conventions are synthetically generated. The least valued variety of Scots is the language of the urban working class, which is frequently regarded as vulgar Scots ...We use the term Scots throughout ... to refer to all varieties of Scots, so that we avoid lending weight to educationally and socially divisive notions that treat the language of urban, working class Scotland as vulgar Scots or even "corrupt" English' (Heywood, 2000: 5).

There are now some 80,000 native Gaelic speakers in Scotland who have fought hard for the survival of the language. With Gaelic-medium education and broadcasting on the increase there is hope that the language can grow and expand. There is a large percentage of the population that currently speak Scots, but there is continued debate about its validity as a language. New initiatives in schools and in writing have given the Scots language new vigour and the development of the Scots Language Development Centre bodes well for its future.

Acknowledgements

Thanks to:

Ah wid like tae thank aw the folk; parents an carers, whae gie sae much o' their time tae help us tae develop oor praxis [theory and practice thegither]. In particular, Cathy Ahmed fir her idea o' *Allsorts* ; Helen Cluness fir daen sae much o' the hard slog [an her faimily fir pittin up wie it]; Susan Glancy fir keepin me right aboot China an Vicky Poon fir keepin me right aboot anither China; Dalbir Singh fir her comparisons o' Scots wie Punjabi; Michael Sufoux fir bringin aw they leids fae Africa; Cass Malcolm – the 'light' o' *School Days*; Liz Young fir her braw East Lothian Scots an Brian Robertson fir a much needed community activist perspective. Ah wid also like tae thank Jimmy Donald an Michelle Mc Dougall, family literacy tutors *extraordinnaire*.

Ma special thanks goes tae Dr John Mackie fir aw his correspondence oan oor Scots leid.

References

Ahmed, C., Cluness, H., Glancy, S. and Singh, D. (eds) (1999) *Family Allsorts the magazine for all sort o' o' folk*, North Edinburgh: Community Publishing.

Aitken, A.J., Low, J.T. and McClure, J.D. (1980) *The Scots Language, Planning for Modern Usage*, Edinburgh: Ramsay Head Press.

Auerbach, E. (1989) 'Towards a Social Contextual Approach to Family Literacy', *Harvard Educational Review*, 59 (2), pp. 165–87.

Auerbach, E. (1994) *Making Meaning, Making Change*, 'Participatory Curriculum Development in Adult ESL and Family Literacy', unpublished.

Auerbach, E. (1994) *Which way for Family Literacy: Intervention or Empowerment*, Massachusetts: University of Massachusetts, unpublished.

Barton, D. and Hamilton, M. (1998) *Local Literacies*, London: Routledge.

Beveridge, C. and Turnbull, R. (1989) *The Eclipse of Scottish Culture*, Edinburgh: Polygon.

Crowther, J. and Tett, L. (1997) 'Inferiorism in Scotland, the politics of literacy north of the border' in Armstrong, P., Miller, N. and Zukas, M. (eds), *Crossing Borders Breaking Boundaries*, 27th Annual SCUTREA Conference Proceedings, pp. 126–30.

Crowther, J. and Tett, L. (1996) *Family Literacy, Evaluation of the Connect Project*, Edinburgh: Moray House Institute, University of Edinburgh.

Freire, P. and Macedo, D. (1987) *Literacy: Rereading the World and the Word*, London: Routledge.

Giegerich, H.J. (1992) *English Phonology, An Introduction*, Cambridge: Cambridge University Press.

Hannon, P. (1999) 'Rhetoric and research in family literacy', *British Educational Research Journal*, 26 (1), pp. 122–37.

Harris, R. (1995) 'Disappearing language: fragments and fractures between speech and writing' in Mace, J. (ed.), *Literacy Language and Community Publishing, Essays in Adult Education*, Avon: Multilingual Matters, pp. 118–44.

Heywood, J. (ed.) (2000) *Involving Parents in Early Literacy*, Edinburgh: City of Edinburgh, Education Department.

Hoare, Q. and Smith, G.N. (1998) *Antonio Gramsci, Selections from the Prison Notebooks*, London: Lawrence and Wishart.

Kay, B. (1986) *The Mither Tongue*, Edinburgh: Mainstream Publishing.

Malcolm, C., Robertson, B. and White, E. (1997) *Everyday's a School Day*, North Edinburgh: Community Publishing.

Martin, I. (1999) 'Introductory essay: popular education and social movements in Scotland today' in Crowther, J., Martin, I. and Shaw, M. (eds), *Popular Education and Social Movements in Scotland Today*, Leicester: NIACE, pp. 1–28.

Mayo, P. (1999) *Gramsci, Freire & Adult Education, Possibilities for Transformative Action*, London: Zed Books.

Macaulay, R.K.S. (1997) *Standards and Variation in Urban Speech*, Amsterdam: John Benjamin Publishing.

McClure D.J. (1980) *Why Scots Matters*, Edinburgh: Saltire Society.

Niven, L. and Jackson, R. (eds) (1998) *The Scots Language – Its Place in Education*, Dumfries: Watergaw.

Robertson, R. (ed.) (1996) *The Kist, Scottish Consultative Council on the Curriculum*, Surrey: Thomas Nelson and Sons Ltd.

Robinson, M. (ed.) (1985) *The Concise Scots Dictionary*, Aberdeen: Aberdeen University Press.

SOEID (1991) 5–14 English in the Curriculum, Edinburgh: HMSO.

SOEID (1994) Education 5–14, A Guide for Parents, Edinburgh: HMSO.

Stevenson, J.A.C. (1989) *Scoor-oot, A Dictionary of SCOTS Words and Phrases in Current Use*, London: Athalone Press.

Stuart, J. (1997) *A Glasgow Bible*, Edinburgh: St. Andrew Press.

Taylor, D. (1993) 'Family literacy: resisting deficit models', *TESOL* Quarterly, 27 (3), pp. 548–54.

Tett, L. and Crowther, J. (1998) 'Families at a disadvantage: class, culture and literacies', *British Educational Research Journal*, 24 (4), pp. 449–60.

14 Challenges to sharing power in adult literacy programmes

Mary Norton

Introduction

Sharing power among teachers and learners is a basic principle of participatory education. When some students at the Learning Centre decided to organise a conference, I had an opportunity to research whether and how I practise this principle.[1] The Learning Centre is an adult literacy and education centre in Edmonton, Alberta, Canada. Women and men come to the Centre to learn and to teach, to engage in meaningful activity, and to be with others. I have been involved with the Centre for similar reasons since 1981: as a government consultant, as a volunteer and, since 1992, as a paid co-ordinator and learning facilitator.

I was attracted to the Centre because it offered possibilities to engage in participatory education. According to Jurmo, participatory education means that students have 'higher degrees of control, responsibility and reward vis-à-vis programme activities' (1989: 17). Gaber-Katz and Watson (1991) suggest that student participation includes a range of activities, from learner-centred lesson development to becoming active in the community. Auerbach (1993) distinguishes between participatory education and other participatory approaches by recalling participatory education's origins in popular education. As well as encouraging active student participation, popular education engages people in analysing power relations and organising action to change oppressive conditions (Arnold *et al*; 1985; Merrifield, 1999; Ross, 1997).

I believe that participatory approaches can enable people to experience more equitable power relationships within literacy programmes and gain skills and confidence to participate more equally in other settings (Campbell, 1994; Jurmo, 1989). However, in facilitating participatory projects at the Centre and reflecting on endeavours to share power with students, I have found contradictions between my practices and beliefs (Norton, 1996). These realisations prompted my research with the student conference committee.

Students meeting students

Learning Centre students initiated the conference project in January 1998 and formed a conference committee. Nine students and I met weekly from January to May, with one of the students chairing the committee from February on. Our work culminated with *Students Meeting Students*, a residential conference attended by 32 people from six literacy programmes. People talked, laughed and learned, about themselves, about each other, and about what they could do.

> We finally got to do something for ourselves, without the staff doing it for us … . It feels really good that we can actually do something. (Holly)

Why do people feel that they 'can't' do things? If we consider that 'power' comes from the root 'to be able' (Starhawk, 1987), we see how feeling able and feeling powerful are linked. As an educator, I want to help students believe that they 'can' and I try to help them develop skills so they in fact can. But to what extent do I really help and how? When do my actions mirror other experiences that contributed to students' feeling that they can't? How do I use and misuse my power, as a teacher and a person? These and related questions took form as I worked with the conference committee and undertook my research about sharing power.

The research

I collected information with the general focus of sharing power in mind. By the end of the conference project, I had field notes, transcribed tape recordings of committee meetings, scripts from committee presentations about the conference project, and summaries of interviews with four committee members. (A colleague had interviewed these members at my request in order to provide another perspective.)

Analysis of information began as I started to collect it. As I wrote field notes, I included questions and ideas about what I was documenting. Through ongoing reading, I found a framework for understanding power. After the conference, I reviewed notes and transcripts, highlighting and sorting parts that seemed to relate to the framework and my research focus. As I wrote about my learnings, I continued to go back and forth between my information, related reading and my writing. Gradually I built an understanding about my attempts to share power with the conference committee.

I reviewed my research report with committee members and incorporated their elaborations into a revision. Committee members concurred with my interpretations and reiterated their consent for me to include their first names, words and ideas in the report.

A framework for understanding power

Writing by Starhawk (1987) and Cranton (1994) provided an initial framework for me to examine and learn from my efforts to share power. Starhawk writes about three kinds of power: power-over, power-with and power-from-within. Power-over is often thought of in terms of persons, groups or institutions having power over others. Such power is sustained by social, political and economic systems and by policies and assumptions about which groups have a right to power. These assumptions are often reflected in prevailing discourses, which help sustain existing power relations. According to Starhawk, power-with is one's influence in a group. It is 'the power of a strong individual in a group of equals, the power not to command, but to suggest and be listened to ...' (1987: 10). Power-with is based in respect, not for the role or position, but for the person.

Horsman (1990) explains discourse as the complex set of language, meanings and assumptions that shape our understanding and influence our actions. As an example, I use the term student in this paper, because that is the term people use at the Learning Centre. Use of this term reflects dominant understandings that align literacy programmes with schools – in fact many people who come to the Centre refer to it as 'the school'. In alternate discourses, programmes might be writing groups or reading clubs, and those who attend might be named participants or members.

Cranton writes about a particular form of power-over, namely the position power of an educator. In my position as paid co-ordinator and facilitator at the Learning Centre I have certain formal authority and control. As well, because of common discourses about school, teachers and students, I am accorded 'teacher' power. Such factors as my Anglo-Norman heritage and my middle class language, education and income provide access to power in many contexts outside of the Centre. These factors intersect with the position power I have at the Centre.

Cranton distinguishes between position power and the personal power that educator – and students – have in the form of skills, knowledge, personal attributes and attitudes. Personal power shifts into power-with, or sharing power, when others both value and are open to receiving what is being offered. As I interpret them, personal power and power-from-within are related but different concepts. Power-from-within has to do with being able to say 'I can'; it is a belief in ourselves and our capacities that enables us to use and further develop our skills, knowledge and attributes, and to offer them to others.

Learnings

Sharing power with the conference committee required students and me to share and develop our personal power – to draw on the skills and attributes we had and learn new ones. As personal power was offered and accepted, power-from-within also grew, in turn making it easier to share personal power and influence. In order for us to share power, however, we needed to learn alternatives to power-over. In the following sections, I describe my learnings about power-over, about shifting to power-with and about students reclaiming power-from-within.

Learning about power-over

Early in the project I tried to devolve power to the committee. As I met with resistance, I realised that in trying to transfer power, I was still exercising power-over. Later in the project, a particular incident revealed how I used position power to manipulate decision making. Another incident reminded me that at times I do have to exercise the authority and responsibility of my position.

Near the start of the student conference project, I was invited to help facilitate a literacy conference in eastern Canada. I arranged funding for two students to attend with me and suggested that students form a selection committee to choose the delegates. Later, I was told that students were talking about the eastern conference and feeling that I should choose who should go. When the conference committee next met

> ... the notion came out that students felt there would be hard feelings if students made the selection. I asked why it would be different if I did. The reply was that it would be accepted more, I was the boss [implied, not said]. (Field notes)

Committee members who were interviewed had similar recall of the developments:

> I said, it's not going to be fair to anybody else because there's going to be a lot of people who really want to go, right and there's going to be hard feelings ... . Say Mary took [name] and I ... Then the rest of the students would be kind of like, well why do they get to go and we don't? So that was, like no, forget it Mary, we're not going to ... help anybody choose.

I chose the term devolution to capture the meaning of these proceedings. Like governments that pass on power and responsibilities to community agencies, I was trying to pass on power to the conference committee. I had not consulted with them about whether they wanted this power or whether they were prepared to accept and exercise it. Starhawk notes that

> An empowering group does not thrust responsibilities on people without preparation, but creates situations in which information, skills, and the knowledge gained by experience can be passed on. (1987: 272)

I see now, that in asking students to choose delegates, I was merely trying to make a shift in who had power-over, rather than initiate a shift to power-with. Work by Wheeler and Chinn (1991) reminded me that I had been raised, educated and employed in patriarchal contexts where power and authority is distributed hierarchically and power-over is the norm. So, in retrospect, it is not surprising that I was influenced by patriarchal/hierarchical discourses of power.

At the same time, if students on the conference committee had mainly experienced power-over in educational and other settings, it may have been hard for them to conceive of other forms of power. Students on the committee also identified strongly with each other. In the follow-up interviews, one student responded:

> I figured Mary should have made [the decision] herself. Because if us students were in it, there would have been a lot of difficulties … . Because there would have been hard feelings and nobody would have been talking to nobody … . I think anything like that where Mary wants to take students she should pick … because we're too close. It's like living in a family.

If some students accepted the role of choosing conference delegates, they would be seen as having power-over – of being one of 'them' rather than one of 'us'.

Shifting to power-with

Arnold *et al* (1991) note that while educators need to acknowledge differences between them and students, these differences don't necessarily have to get in the way. In order for students and I to share power, we needed opportunities to get to know each other and develop personal relationships. When this happened, bridges across power differences started to form, we began to share influence, and I learned about providing responsive leadership. In the process, I learned about listening and understanding silences.

Following the eastern conference discussion, I suggested the committee could use the travel funds for another purpose. We decided to hold a residential conference so a number of people could get away, rather than just two, and we arranged transportation to visit some potential conference sites. On the drive to and from the sites, there was plenty of time to chat and listen in groups and one-to-one. Later, in preparing for a presentation about the conference project,

> Lil said [to me] 'We feel more comfortable now. You're one of the group. We can joke around.' I asked her why she hadn't felt this way before, she hesitated, then said it was just a gut feeling. (Field notes)

I noted

> Lil's comments were interesting in light of my own inner debates about boundaries and my relationship with people. Maybe as long as I stay aloof I will be the 'teacher'. Maybe there needs to be a certain degree of familiarity before we can interact easily. (Field notes)

Cranton suggests that personal power is increased when educators become real persons to learners and feelings of friendship and loyalty develop. Taking time to 'be' through the site visits was a step in this process.

Campbell (1994) introduces the difference between 'being' and 'doing', based on research about participatory approaches in student groups. While students saw groups as a time to *be* with other students, practitioners were concerned about what student groups would *do*. Opportunities to relax and talk with others may be limited for students and educational programmes can provide one venue for people to meet and talk. My own focus on doing reflects my alliance with a society that is concerned with doing; I also have various occasions to meet and talk with others. The site visit offered opportunities for both students and me to *be* and enabled all of us to become real persons to each other.

Responsive leadership

A shift to power-with had started to occur when Helen, one of the committee members, began to chair the committee meetings. With Helen in the chair, I started to feel like a member of the group. I also noticed that there was ' more interaction among people when Helen is chairing …' (Field notes).

In retrospect, transferring the chair's position to a student was another form of devolution. The concept of chairperson relates to hierarchical models of meetings and decision making and my actions were still influenced by these models. However, Helen was keen to accept the role of chair and to learn skills to carry it out. As well, Helen's chairing was a visible example that a student could have influence:

> Helen is chairing, she has more experience than most of us. It makes us feel good that a student could do that. We supported her, we could understand and help out. (Lil, Presentation)

Helen and I generally prepared meeting agendas together. Helen opened meetings and guided the committee through the agenda, while I sometimes coached her about meeting process. In the first meeting

> I reminded her to review the agenda and to tell the newcomers what we had planned so far … . [When a question came up] I suggested she ask people to give reasons for their answers – I could see Helen becoming more adept at asking people this as she went around the circle. (Field notes)

Field notes and meeting transcripts show that I continued to coach Helen throughout the conference project. Sometimes I facilitated when a topic being discussed was complex or emotionally charged. For instance, in a discussion about a conference social,

> Some people started to talk about whether we could bring friends, where we would have tickets made, etc. I find that when this happens I tend to jump in. I suggested that we needed to decide first of all if we

wanted to have an open event or if we wanted it just for students at the conference. I suggested to Helen that she ask people to suggest reasons for either kind of event and to list them on the board ... . (Field notes)

... sometimes Helen is more of a scribe as I take on the facilitating ... . This has happened a couple of times now ... particularly when there is work to be done. (Field notes)

I sometimes berated myself for jumping in or taking over. However, Starhawk's writing suggests that in coaching and facilitating I was exercising 'responsive leadership'. She uses this term to identify 'power-with or influence used to empower the group and individuals in it' (1987: 270). According to Starhawk, responsive leaders train others by providing models or challenging them to stretch their skills.

Silence and learning to listen

Sharing power in the conference project meant that students had to speak and be heard. However, there were times during the project when students did not speak or were not heard when they did.

When I first attempted to devolve power to the committee, students voiced their responses among themselves rather than raise them in a meeting with me. Given the familiar discourse of school and my position power in relation to the committee, this silence is not surprising. Ellsworth (1989) suggests that differences in people's power will consciously or unconsciously influence their decisions to speak. To speak up at the meeting would have meant publicly disagreeing with me.

Creating safe environments where people can risk speaking in spite of power differences is essential if power is to be shared (Arnold *et al* , 1991; Campbell, 1994). In the devolution incident, I did nothing to invite dialogue or to make it safe and comfortable for people to express their views. Later, I successfully invited responses to the idea of choosing delegates to the eastern conference, but I did not listen to people's concerns. Instead I persisted with my agenda. Yet, listening is also fundamental to participatory education:

To listen is to be on an equal footing: listening means putting yourself into the place of the other. How can educators construct a setting in which there isn't a growing 'we versus them', no matter how genuine our intent to do otherwise? ... the art of listening is an important pillar in building structures that counteract some deeply ingrained, top–down teaching habits. (Arnold *et al* , 1991: 162)

As well as listening to what people did say, I had to learn to listen to other silences in order to understand and address what they meant. When it seemed that students were not interested I learned that 'sometimes they just don't know what to say' (Mary, Field notes). At other times, people did not understand because I was not communicating clearly. Nervousness also silenced people:

> Mary or Lil said ... everyone was starting to feel a little afraid of what was going to happen – what if they said something wrong, etc. (Field notes)

> Holly gave a big sigh and threw her hands in her lap. My first response was 'she's not interested, she doesn't want to do this' ... . Around this time, Linda said, I don't think I want to do this ... . Again I realised that they were both getting scared. (Field notes)

Reclaiming power-from-within

All of these forms of silence had to do with power relations, whether between me and the committee or between committee members and others. In responding to my research report, Holly commented that she was nervous about facilitating because she hadn't realised that the people coming to the conference 'were like us, having trouble learning'. She was silenced by assumptions that conference delegates would have more education and use their position to judge her. To break silences required Holly and the others to draw on power-from-within.

As the committee continued to work together, some students started to feel more able to speak up.

> If I didn't know something, or the other students didn't know something, I asked her to explain it to us, and she wouldn't disappoint us. (Interview)

This student went on to explain that if she wasn't understanding something, she knew that other students weren't. She broke the silence by asking what I was talking about and paved the way for others. Eventually, all the committee members had public opportunities to speak and be heard, especially at the conference. As they were listened to and heard, they experienced sharing power. Later, in responding to my research report, Holly and Mary talked about speaking up in situations where they used to be silent:

> I used to be like that. If you don't speak up, people will walk all over you. (Holly)

Learning more about power-over: manipulation

Arnstein (1969) suggests that manipulation is a form of non-participation that substitutes for genuine participation and enables 'power holders to "educate" participants or engineer their "support"' (1968: 217). I use the term manipulation to describe situations where I had an agenda or idea but did not state it. Rather, I used questions and discussion until people came around to my way of thinking.

In some cases, I asked questions, hoping that participants would give the 'right' answers. As I recognised this habit of asking leading questions, I began to state my views directly. Usually, my ideas were taken up or not, depending on whether people valued them. However, there was at least one incident where people agreed with my view, not because they valued it, but because of my position.

The incident occurred about three months into the conference project. A student who had not been on the committee decided to come to a meeting. Up to this point, the committee had not talked about whether or when people might join the committee, although others had been welcomed to meetings. After the newcomer left the meeting, committee members were clear and strong in stating their views that she not join the committee. While some suggested it would be hard for her to catch up, others focused on interactions they had observed or experienced with her. I summarised discussion and then introduced my view:

> I talked about my own belief that if we expect people to behave well or in good ways, and support them, they will. So we could just say no, or we could see if she responded to being welcomed. (Field notes)

After more discussion, some committee members began to soften, noting, 'It's so hard to say no' and 'I'll help her catch up'. However, one member was clearly opposed: 'My answer is still no … .' I then talked about options, 'We could say no, we could say yes, or we could give it a try and have some expectations. At this point, the person who had expressed strong opposition said, "I think I could go along with this"' (Field notes).

At one point in the meeting, I had actually said that I was hesitant to express my views because I didn't want to influence people. Yet it is quite evident from my notes that I persisted until everyone agreed that the newcomer could join the committee. Committee members who were interviewed were asked to comment on my role in the decision.

> It was actually the rest of the conference committee's decision because … Mary couldn't, I mean Mary could say, 'Yeah, sure [name] you could join' and then the rest of us conference committee people … didn't really want her in there … . So she left it up to us if we wanted her or not. So we chose, we said, 'Okay'.

While its outcome reflected my wishes, this meeting differed from the earlier one in terms of how people participated in discussion. Most committee members seemed able to voice their views, once the newcomer had left. By this time, my relationship with the group had developed and people may have felt safer about speaking out. However, my position power may have silenced some:

> ... when everybody said no, it should have been left there ... But the students, a lot of them wasn't happy. They meant no, but they said yes because they didn't want to say no to Mary. ... I think Mary should have discussed it with the students and she should have let the students make up their own decision.

In reviewing this incident, I am aware that the committee and I were still operating from a power-over perspective. Whether it was the committee as a whole or I who influenced the decision, we were still at some level exercising power-over the newcomer.

Exercising power openly

During the conference a situation arose which prompted me to ask a person to leave. Under other circumstances I may have involved committee members in deciding action. I felt there wasn't time for such discussion during the conference and further, that such discussion would have distracted people from carrying out their conference roles.

When interviewed about this incident, most committee members concurred with the decision and how it was made.

> I think that was good what she did because I think it would have upset us at the [conference] Centre. If she would have said, 'Well, we're going to have a little meeting before we start the workshops', I don't think we would have concentrated so well on our work at the conference.

Clearly, however, I acted hierarchically. Reflecting on this event helped to clarify that I have position power within a hierarchical structure. Looking back, I also became conscious of the contrast between this situation and the event described just before. In one situation, I used my position power to include, in the other it was to exclude. It may seem that the rules keep changing. I realised a need to clarify and publicise the policies and principles that guide the Centre's work.

Applying learning to practice

It is hard to believe that almost two years have passed since the conference committee hosted the Students Meeting Students event. Six of the committee members and I continue to learn, teach and be with others at the Learning Centre. Mary and Lil are now employed at the Centre part-time: Mary as a teaching assistant and Lil as a co-facilitator of the women's group.

In all my work now, I am more conscious and accepting that as a full-time paid co–ordinator, I have different authority, responsibilities and power than the part-time staff, volunteers and learners. As much as I and others at the Centre try to share power within the programme, the Centre operates within a hierarchical system. I am also more aware and accepting of my personal power and capacity to influence. Given this awareness, I now try to ask myself, 'How can I use my power responsibly and responsively – while also sharing power as possible and appropriate?'

Distinguishing between devolving and sharing power was a key learning, as was recognising the influence, on me, of the discourse of patriarchal power. I have continued to devolve position power to Centre participants, but have first asked if they wanted this power and the accompanying responsibilities. I have also tried to provide support as needed and hope that I have encouraged people to use power-with approaches.

I have used Starhawk's (1987) framework to encourage analysis of power relations in my work with participants at the Learning Centre as well as in workshops with other practitioners. I have also started to use the framework to invite discussion about power relations and influence among participants at the Centre. I am sure that people are aware of differences in their personal power and influence, yet the differences are rarely named. Rather, they are hidden behind notions of being 'too close ... like a family'.

Sharing power requires group members to share personal power – abilities, interests, talents and knowledge. I have observed how groups in other settings identify and list what each person can contribute. A process like this would have been helpful at the start of the conference project. As well, I could have encouraged people to list what they wanted to learn. We could have returned to the lists periodically to add newly identified or learned abilities. I plan to introduce such a process in future projects. Processes for sharing power in meetings, such as taking turns as chairperson, could also be introduced (Wheeler and Chinn, 1991).

My learnings with the student conference committee strengthened my beliefs that literacy programmes can be places where learners, volunteers and staff experience more equitable power relations. In doing so, we may see new possibilities for resisting power-over and creating more equitable relations outside programmes. My research would not have happened without the other committee members' desire, courage and tenacity to see the conference project through, and I thank them.

Note

1. The research was completed as part of a Participatory Approaches in Adult Literacy Education/Research in Practice project (Norton and Malicky, 2000). The National Literacy Secretariat, Human Resources Development Canada funded the project in partnership with Alberta Learning and with contributions from the University of Alberta, Faculty of Education.

References

Arnold, R., Barndt, D. and Burke, B. (1985) *A New Weave. Popular Education in Canada and Central America*, Toronto, ON: OISE.

Arnold, R. *et al* (1991) *Educating for A Change*, Toronto, ON: Between the Lines and the Doris Marshall Institute for Education and Action.

Arnstein, S. (1969) 'A ladder of citizenship participation', *AIP Journal*, pp. 216–24.

Auerbach, E. (1993) 'Putting the P back in participatory', *TESOL Quarterly*, 27, pp. 543–45.

Campbell, P.M. (1994), *Participatory Literacy Practices, Having a Voice, Having a Vote*, unpublished doctoral dissertation, University of Toronto, Toronto, ON.

Cranton, P.A. (1994) *Understanding and Promoting Transformative Learning*, San Francisco: Jossey Bass.

Ellsworth, E. (1989) 'Why doesn't this feel empowering? Working through the repressive myths of critical pedagogy', *Harvard Educational Review*, 59 (3), pp. 297–324.

Gaber-Katz, E. and Watson, G.M. (1991) *The Land That We Dream Of. A Participatory Study of Community-Based Literacy*, Toronto, ON: OISE.

Horsman, J. (1990) *Something On My Mind Besides the Everyday*, Toronto, ON: Women's Press.

Jurmo, P. (1989) 'History in the making: The case of participatory literacy education' in Fingeret, A. and Jurmo, P. (eds), *Participatory Literacy Education*, San Francisco: Jossey Bass, pp. 17–28.

Merrifield, J. (1999) 'Literacy, community and citizenship: What do we teach, how do we teach it? Reflections from US experiences', *RaPAL Bulletin*, 38, pp. 3–6.

Norton, M. (1996) *Getting our Own Education. Learning about Participatory Education in an Adult Learning Centre*, Edmonton, AB: The Learning Centre Literacy Association.

Norton, M. and Malicky, G. (eds) (2000) *Learning about Participatory Approaches in Adult Literacy Education. Six Research in Practice Studies*, Edmonton, AB: Learning at the Centre Press.

Ross, J.A. (1997) 'Popular education: An alternative strategy for health promotion with women', *FES Occasional Paper Series*, 3 (5), Toronto, ON: York University.

Starhawk (1987) *Truth or Dare. Encounters with Power, Authority and Mystery*, San Francisco: Harper.

Students meeting students, *Putting a Student Conference Together* (2000), Edmonton, AB: Learning at the Centre Press.

Wheeler, C.E. and Chinn, P.L. (1991) *Peace and Power: a Handbook of Feminist Process* (3rd edn), New York: National League for Nursing.

15 Multiple literacies in practice: bilingual workers in East London

Sue Gardener and Ann Janssen

This chapter will describe the work done by bilingual people who work for public service or voluntary sector employers as language intermediaries between professional staff and bilingual communities. This is a growing field of work, as there are still not as many bilingual professionals as there are people in minority linguistic communities who do not share the working language of UK public services or the underlying ideas on which their interventions are based. This is obviously particularly acute when new linguistic groups seek asylum, such as Kosovan Albanians in 1999: but even for linguistic communities with a longer history of settlement, there is still under-representation in professional occupations. The issue overlaps with that of the difficulty of requalification, for example, overseas qualified and experienced doctors and nurses.

We have been involved with these bilingual workers as tutors and trainers, on short and long courses to assist people who are often informally recruited, and may have no pre-service training, in carrying our their work with skill and awareness. We will show how they are at the same time experts and outsiders in the complex conversations of community interpreting, mediation and advocacy. We will link the difficulties of their work to studies of intercultural communication (especially in therapeutic situations) and of cultural metaphor. We will also link them to discussions of literacy events, which may be contexted in, but not exclusively transacted through, literacy. Out of these explorations we will argue for a broader and deeper training agenda than is often possible now, and argue against the way that bilingual communities are presented in public policy as having (and being) language problems rather than language resources. Working through more skilful intermediaries, in face-to-face encounters as we will illustrate, or in using community and neighbours to deal with bureaucratic literacy demands as Baynham (1993) described, are resourceful solutions to the difficulties the post-modern city presents to its inhabitants.

The public policy contexts include current social inclusion and health policies: for example, *Our Healthier Nation*, the policy document from the Department of Health (1998), identifies differential patterns of service use and of illness in minority ethnic communities, and recognises that mediated access may be necessary to change this pattern. But the main public policy context we wish to address is that set by the most recent survey by the Basic Skills Agency of the language skills of the UK population: *Lost Opportunities:*

the Language Skills of Linguistic Minorities in England and Wales (1996). This is published in two forms: a report giving details of the research methodology and focusing on establishing characteristics of individuals and groups which can be used to predict the need for language teaching in a particular local authority area (Carr-Hill *et al*, 1996), and a separately published summary pamphlet (BSA, 1996). They need to be distinguished from each other.

The research report refers to the history of investigations of linguistic diversity in the UK, including the tradition represented by Linguistic Minorities Project (1985) and Alladina and Edwards (1991). In this tradition of looking at actual practices, it is possible to show abilities as well as needs, and to indicate broader educational agendas than a focus on learning English language and literacy. The Linguistic Minorities Project's Adult Language Use Survey, for example, asked people to assess themselves in the four language skills in English and in the principal other language they used, and also to report on the languages of interaction with household members and work colleagues. It also asked how respondents valued the maintenance of minority languages, including reading and writing, and made reference to the possibility of a new education and training agenda developing with the work of community interpreting.

The full BSA research report also acknowledges the variety of language and literacy used in different languages among the populations being researched, and sets up seven 'strata' on a scale which draws on people's ability to read, preferred language for reading and possession of qualifications from any country. But since the commission is a Basic Skills one, they chose not to interview people in the highest of the 'strata', whose preferred reading language and main spoken language are English; and no information is offered about the uses, either oral or reading/writing, that people in this group make of other languages. So the English language performance of people who may be the most competent bilinguals is excluded, and it is not clear what use was made of the strata in analysing the research results. The researchers turn instead to the establishment of a 'survival level' of competence, which they test through materials derived from real-world situations. They then analyse how the research variables – such as linguistic group, age, gender, years in UK employment, length of schooling in other countries and in the UK – combine to make the test scores (and by extension the educational needs) more or less predictable.

The summary report goes straight for the issue of 'survival'. Broad terms are always useful to put on pressure for policy and investment: but it needs to be pointed out that people whose English speaking, writing and literacy are below 'survival level' do survive, in work and in daily life, and that they do so partly by using the language resources of their own and allied communities, including the structures we will describe in this chapter. The risks of concentrating on deficit and lack of skills are many, and among them are the risks that the training and education agenda will be narrowed and shortened, and that the potentials for higher-level language development, exploration of the spaces between the expressive preferences of particular languages and cultures, and the articulation of cultural concepts which can block or enable mutual understanding will be ignored. For example, the preparation of the Linguistic Minorities Project's Adult Language Use Survey included 'translation workshops' as part of the training of interviewers, so that the renderings of the survey questions in minority languages would be consistent, misunderstandings anticipated and translations worked out by consensus – a learning process which relates closely to community interpreter training.

The context of our work

We both work in East London, in areas where (on a crude average between three boroughs) 37 per cent of the population and nearly 60 per cent of young people in schools have a home language that is not English. The work we have been doing comes under several headings:

- An investigation of how schools and special education services use their bilingual staff to communicate with parents;
- Courses for community interpreters (which are run in many parts of London);
- Courses for advocates in health and social care;
- Commissioned training for groups of people newly appointed as link workers and co-workers in general and mental health;
- Training needs analysis for bilingual staff without UK medical qualifications being used as interpreters in a hospital.

Our insights are drawn from this rather than from being users of interpreting ourselves, or from a formal linguistic or other academic perspective. But we find that some of the research being done in diverse academic settings throws light on what we see working in practice.

We will give two examples of the ways in which bilingual staff are used; one from education and one from the hospital. In our study of interpreting in schools, we found that interpreting was rarely recognised in job descriptions (with the exception of a group of staff whose job title was Bilingual Instructors, who have both interpreting and text translation responsibilities); that it was often a response to an unplanned situation; that almost any bilingual person in the school could be called on to interpret (including, in some schools, children, which is an issue not dealt with here); and that there was a tendency for the least powerful bilingual person to be used because they could be interrupted in their work more easily. The interpreting contexts could include negotiating a parent's wish to take her child to the home country for a family funeral, and communicating with parents about statements of special educational need (see Gardener *et al*, 1995).

The health staff involved in the recent training needs analysis were also carrying out language intermediary work on the side of their main employment. Their formal jobs were: health care support workers (carrying out tests and minor procedures like injections); secretarial work; health promotion; theatre preparation; ward clerking; post room work. Their interpreting tasks covered a wide range: admissions and discharges, interpreting telephone enquiries, explaining pre- and post-operative procedures, dealing with patients' fears and anxieties, supporting and interpreting in psychological therapy, taking patient histories, ensuring understanding of procedures and consent forms, and acting as 'walking valium' (their phrase).

Power relationships

In any interpreting encounter there are three participants, described as a 'triad' by Faust and Drickey (1986), but there are one-to-one relationships between each of the three pairs that make up this triad. This is explored further by Raval (1996) in a positive account of using interpreters in therapy which treats them as assets and contributors. The formal relationships are defined by role: professional, intermediary, client. The relationships in each pair are more variable, and in any case, the formal power of the professional and the formal dependence of the client can be crossed over by other relationships of power, language and education. For example:

- The professional is by definition educated and well (or relatively well) paid, and is the expert in the matter of the communication. But the professional is dependent on the interpreter in language and cultural matters relating to the clients and what they say, think and experience.
- The professional is knowledgeable about the substance of the encounter and may expect the interpreter to be less knowledgeable. But the interpreter may have a similar level of professional education in their country of origin. Or what they know about the field may be what they have picked up from training (if any) and from the practice of interpreting and advocacy.
- The interpreter may be more or less educated than the client. Their social position in relation to the client may be read in terms of the culture of origin as being affected by gender, age, marital status, rural/urban origin, recent arrival as a refugee vs. settled and established, being a mother tongue user of the language of interpretation or a marginal user, and so on. Any of these roles could be occupied by either party, and the resulting mix will affect the communication.

- The interpreter and the client may be assumed to come from a common culture but may be either too close to each other for professionalism and confidentiality to be maintained, or they may have deep premises of difference or even hostility. Not all refugees from one country leave it at the same time and for the same reasons; not all members of the same broad language and/or faith community hold each other in equal esteem. Or they may simply not know enough: an Urdu/Panjabi speaker who has grown up in East Africa may find rural Pakistani manners and mores unfamiliar (let alone rural manners acted out in relative isolation in London).

In discussing how particular discourses are shaped and used, Kress (1989: 12) says: 'All texts are constituted in difference ... . The social/discursive histories of individuals, as well as their present social position, determine their access to the set of discourses in a society'. Without further research we can only look at the present social position. In these situations, the clients only have access to professional discourses in English through an intermediary whose positioning and allegiance is set up in a very complex way, who may or may not have been fully informed about the aims and procedures of the communication, and whose power within the three-way conversation is both very great and very small. The professionals only have access to the discourses of the clients to the extent that the interpreter can communicate what lies behind the words, as well as giving a literal version of what the client has said. The more you describe the situation, the more extraordinary it is that interpretation works at all. It is even more extraordinary that professionals are sometimes willing to rely on, and base their actions on, the work of relatively untrained interpreters; but they have few alternatives. They are particularly reliant on intermediaries in medical practice because of the primacy of patients' accounts of themselves as evidence of their condition. In other powerful exchanges the client's perspective may have less value, but the 'patient's history', however mediated and however well understood, cannot be bypassed. So linguistic and cultural mediation is caught up in professional practices and needs as well as in patients' rights.

Interpreters and texts

Mediated conversations of this kind are generally if not always literacy events, in Barton's (1994: 36) sense of 'occasions in everyday life where the written word has a role'. The interpreter may have to render in speech the contents of written texts: forms to fill in, care plans, ground rules and limitations of liability, and so on; and they may have to communicate the contents of notes, the side-effects of medication, letters, leaflets of guidance on diet or post-operative behaviour. The professional may be following a written pro-forma in conducting the diagnostic or treatment interview, and will almost certainly be producing a written record that will be put in the client's file. But in addition, the professionals are used to encoding their meanings in high status written forms in both academic and professional contexts, and their spoken discourse will be influenced by the power of written discourse. The interpreters' position in relation to written text is almost completely unpredictable, but they usually do not have equal access to professional textual practices in English – not necessarily as readers, and not at all as writers. The clients may have a (different) set of written discourses behind their oral account of themselves, or at the other extreme they may have little or no literacy in any language – or anything in between.

To give an idea of the gaps that have to be bridged, we will give short extracts from two texts that might form part of the interpreting event. The first is from a Statement of Special Educational Needs for a primary school pupil:

> A. has received learning support within the classroom for the past few years both from the Education Support Service and from the school's own resources. His difficulties are of a general nature with specific areas of difficulty in language, literacy, attention and listening. There is evidence of earlier intervention by the Speech and Language Therapy Service. It does appear that he has particular difficulties within the English language as his family feel he expressed himself better in Panjabi. The Speech and Language Therapy report indicates overall delay in language skills.
>
> A major area of difficulty for A. is his short attention span. He finds it very difficult to concentrate on a learning task for any length of time and even in conversation he moves around from one topic to another. He requires a great deal of encouragement and refocusing to keep him on task.

This text is full of embedded knowledge of structures and organisations, and also of constructs specific to education: ' difficulties of a general nature', 'overall delay in language skills', and 'refocusing to keep him on task'. It is in an impersonal scientific/bureaucratic mode, with few sentences structured to identify the human agent. A sensitive interpreter will choose to paraphrase, and to do so will have to be sure that he or she is offering appropriate conceptual equivalents.

The second text is from a hospital leaflet for in-patients: it comes from a section called 'Life on the Ward'.

> *Telephones:* Each ward has a trolley payphone available to patients for outgoing calls only. There are also public phones at various points in the hospital. Most payphones are coin-operated. Each ward has a direct line telephone number, which you will be given when you arrive.

Relatives and friends can use this number to enquire about your condition but please ask them to avoid telephoning at meal times and other busy times. You should nominate a single person to enquire about your condition who can pass information on your progress to other relatives and friends.

Please do not use mobile phones in the hospital as they can interfere with sensitive monitoring equipment and endanger lives. Visitors should switch off mobile phones before entering the hospital

This is a mixture of discourse styles and message contents. Some sentences are impersonal and some personalised; 'you' exist as a person but the institution is represented by 'the ward', not by its staff; you are being addressed, from sentence to sentence, through neutral information about facilities, undertakings (in this section, the only undertaking is to give you the ward phone number), permissions and restrictions or prohibitions. In addition, as you embark on 'life on the ward' you have acquired a responsibility to regulate the behaviour of your family, friends and visitors. Institutional practices are deeply embedded in the text, and there is an underlying model of social life outside the ward, shown in the idea that it is straightforward to channel telephone enquiries through one person. Again it is clear that an interpreter would need to work round the text to communicate its essential messages.

The literacy demands that accompany the interpreting role are, then, not simple: interpreters need to understand the context of texts as well as of the face-to-face conversation. Working with text gives them more responsibility but not more power.

Cultural metaphors

The expertise that the interpreter is supposed to have is in both language and culture. But if you are asked to explain and interpret aspects of your culture which you have not consciously examined, you may flounder. Part of the training is to encourage people to examine the basis for what clients say and what it expresses, and how a discipline founded on Western scientific assumptions can engage with beliefs and practices formed differently. Discussion by health professionals makes it clear both that the cognitive assumptions of Western medicine are beginning to be identified as culturally specific, and also that it is not an easy matter to recognise and take into account the different cognitive assumptions and linguistic expressions of people from different cultural formations. Fernando (1991) examines in detail, in the context of mental health practices, the difficulties of positioning the client's cognitive assumptions as 'other', and how this risks reinforcing a racist version of difference; but even in discussing different 'idioms of expression' for mental and emotional distress, he does not comment on the possibility that the material being evaluated as different will only be available to the professional through a linguistic and cultural mediator.

We have found the concept of cultural metaphors useful in raising awareness of the need to interpret beyond the literal in such contexts. The concept is drawn from Lakoff and Johnson (1980), who investigate, using the skills of a linguist and a philosopher, the conceptual metaphors which become part of our reality and on which we base actions as well as utterances. Two examples relevant to this context are *good is up* – contrast ' high spirits' and ' depression' – and *the mind is a brittle object*, which gives us 'cracking up'. This is derived from the basic ontological metaphor *the mind is an entity*, which may be as culturally specific as identifying the heart as the location of emotion, which will be discussed below. Another relevant metaphor is *problems are puzzles*, which entails that they typically have solutions. Lakoff and Johnson argue that such expressions are deeply embedded into our constructions of reality, and that they therefore steer our actions and interpretations of events more than we realise. We see the concept of cultural metaphor as having profound implications for our understanding of language and cognition, and in particular for cross-cultural communication. It is often a new concept for participants in such training courses and there is little chance of doing more than introducing it. Participants in the link workers course gave high value to the chance to experiment with linguistic expressions for mental distress in their evaluations of the course.

Examples of cultural metaphors relevant to mental health can be drawn from research into the statistical relationships between ethnicity and health in the UK population. Nazroo's (1997) concern is with the possibility of under-counting of mental illness and mental distress in some ethnically defined communities, because concepts and expressions for emotional and mental distress take different forms and may not fit the categories of the interviewer in a large population study. He cites expressions like 'sinking heart' and 'thinking too much in my heart', and refers to the concept of somatisation – experiencing and describing psychological distress in physical terms. It is arguable that in all cultures the mind–body relationship is discussed in terms that are, by Lakoff and Johnson's (1980) definition, metaphorical, and may transfer mind or emotional experience into the language of the body or to an external agency. Somatisation is discussed extensively in Rack (1982: 101–5). He refers to a discourse about symptoms and sensations of the heart in a context where, to the European doctor, emotional distress is at issue, and identifies it as part of a metaphoric system: he cites another writer as suggesting that the heart in Muslim cultures is 'an idiom for expressing emotion' – as it has been in our culture for a different range of emotions. He gives an example from Western psychiatric culture, without marking that he is doing so, when he says of people whose culture emphasises a social, rather than an individual, basis for concepts of self: 'They are less accustomed to visualise themselves in terms of what is happening in their own heads' (1982: 108). Locating mental and emotional states in the head surely goes beyond the identification of brain chemistry.

In working with the link workers we encountered expressions which illustrated the metaphorical range: for example, by varying the up/down polarity in terms of heavy/light. Metaphors for illness, 'My body feels heavy', or 'Someone is sitting on me', were contrasted with 'feeling light' as a term for recovery. Link workers also discussed concepts of ghost possession, and of illness as spiritual punishment. We were able to offer examples of metaphorical constructs which can be part of the conviction of a Western patient about what is distressing them: that bad thoughts are being transmitted through television, or that DSS officers are conducting intimate surveillance of their lives. We are not proposing any crude equivalence between these expressions, merely indicating that there is a complex field of language and ideas within which interpreters and mediators have to work. Its complexity is not well recognised in training and qualifications.

The job of the linguistic and cultural mediator includes, then, being aware of different conceptual metaphors in order to interpret in context, and possibly to offer the professionals the insight they need. Even in a research situation, without the load of illness or distress and the search for healing, Nazroo (1997: 84) gives some indication of the difficulties for interpreters:

> Interviewers reported difficulties with the translations they were given, that they themselves had difficulty translating concepts appropriately into South Asian languages and that interviews with those who were not fluent in English took much longer than those with respondents who were fluent.

No interpreter or mediator will be surprised at this finding: the advantage they may have is that they work in the field over time, and have a chance to develop familiarity and a repertoire of concepts to work with. Our job as trainers can only be to start this process.

Holding the message

We have set out above a preliminary description of the relative power of the participants in the interpreting/mediation triad. Here we wish to shift the key term from 'power' to 'responsibility'. What is unique about the person at the centre of the triad is that they hold a degree of responsibility for all the communications and utterances in the interview. The professional *holds* their own utterance, both from the point of view of its professional quality and of its clarity. But in receiving communication, they are restricted to facial expression, body language and other non-verbal communication. The client *holds* the agenda they came in with, which may be to communicate their sense of their own experience and/or situation, and to achieve some desired outcomes (for example to be set on the path to healing, to understand why a child is being problematised, to know what is in the power of this particular professional). They also *hold* the clarity and completeness of their answers to questions, or their decision to withhold; their efforts to seek clarification; the goodwill and hope they invest in co-operation with the professionals. Clients will also read the non-verbal messages of the professional, of which their being a professional is of course one powerful set, reinforced by the setting (often) and by the power to control the interview and its outcomes. The interpreter or mediator *holds* all of these, to the extent that they shape utterances, and sometimes even as they shape silences. They may have come to the interview with questions of their own, based on prior knowledge of the client and the case, and may choose (as they are encouraged to do in training) to intervene and act assertively when they think communication is not complete or that something has been left unsaid or unclear. This produces an extraordinarily complex mix of genre elements – more complex even than a significant conversation in a single language, exactly because of the sliding plates of cultural miscommunication that are present in the encounter. If one of the participants is a therapist they will have access to professional support to deal with and discharge some of the weight of what they hold. Generally speaking, the interpreter or mediator does not have this resource.

This description goes beyond the essential discussions in interpreter training of the difference between first person and third person interpreting. The recommendation to use first person interpreting is based on the proposition that the professional must communicate with and receive the communications of the client, and not deflect or avoid them by using the triangulation of the interpreter. But the interpreter is in all three places, and also has to deal with the difficulty of not being directly addressed in their own person. Clients will address their words to the interpreter, but training steers interpreters to re-route the address from themselves to the professional. Yet by being the carrier of the words the interpreter or mediator is also identified as a cultural ally and cannot easily reject that positioning.

This drama is acted out daily in thousands of settings. It is built into a multicultural and multilingual society, and the jobs that are being created or evolved or adapted to allow interlingual and cross-cultural communication to happen are now vital to social functioning. But the status of community interpreting is not as high as that of, for example, conference interpreting, and the training structures do not yet serve the interests of growing excellence in these fields. We believe there is urgent development work to be done, to establish training in cultural and conceptual interpreting: however, at the moment a purer linguistic model seems to hold the ground for advanced training for community interpreters. The issues of qualification and higher-level skills are bound up with career opportunities and pay and conditions. Baker, Hussain and Saunders (1991) have valuable discussions of training for interpreters and those who work with them, codes of practice and the management of interpreting services.

Beyond survival

To conclude, we would like to return to the current policy context that defines the learning of English by speakers of other languages as basic skills. We do not wish to argue that review, investment and development are unnecessary. But the current perspective in the teaching of English as a second or other language to people settling in the UK still carries the assumptions of a society that sees itself as monolingual, and carries too the unintended arrogance endowed by the status of English as a world language. A recent publication about languages in London, *Multilingual Capital* (Baker and Eversley, 2000), challenges this by detailing the enormous variety of languages spoken in the schools and neighbourhoods of London, and recognises them as a resource and not a liability. The practice of community interpreting and cultural mediation is a striking example of work done to promote social inclusion and cohesion by people adapting the norms of multilingual societies elsewhere, or responding creatively to their own movement from one linguistic environment to another. If we are to respect and develop these practices, one field for more research is the way in which texts feature in these communicative practices alongside and in tension with the spoken word. The powerful literacies that are formed within established institutions, and which shape the ways in which even people who cannot read the texts relate to those institutions, are a necessary part of an agenda for language and literacy skills that will serve the current social demands of life in the UK.

References

Alladina, S. and Edwards,V. (1991) *Multilingualism in the British Isles* (1 and 2), London: Longman.

Baker, P. and Eversley, J. (eds) (2000) *Multilingual Capital: the Languages of London's Schoolchildren and their Relevance to Social, Economic and Educational Policies*, London: Battlebridge Publications.

Baker, P. with Hussain, A. and Saunders, P. (1991) *Interpreters in Public Services*, Birmingham: Venture.

Barton, D. (1994) *Literacy: An Introduction to the Ecology of Written Language*, Oxford: Blackwell.

Basic Skills Agency (1996) *Lost Opportunities: the Language Skills of Linguistic Minorities in England and Wales*, London: BSA.

Baynham, M. (1993) 'Code switching and mode switching: community interpreters and mediators of literacy' in Street, B. (ed.), *Cross-Cultural Approaches to Literacy*, Cambridge: Cambridge University Press.

Carr-Hill, R., Passingham, D. and Wolf, M. with Kent, S. (1996) *Lost Opportunities: the Language Skills of Linguistic Minorities in England and Wales*, London: BSA.

Department of Health (1998) *Our Healthier Nation: a Contract for Health*, London: TSO.

Faust, S. and Drickey, R. (1986) 'Working with interpreters', *Journal of Family Practice*, 22, pp. 131–38.

Fernando, S. (1991) *Mental Health, Race and Culture*, Basingstoke: Macmillan.

Gardener, S., Hossain, A. and Janssen, A. (1995) '"Grab her and have a quick word" – how some primary schools communicate with bilingual parents', unpublished.

Kress, G. (1989) *Linguistic Processes in Sociocultural Practice*, 2nd edition, Oxford: Oxford University Press.

Lakoff, G. and Johnson, R. (1980) *Metaphors We Live By*, Chicago: University of Chicago Press.

Linguistic Minorities Project (1985) *The Other Languages of England*, London: Routledge and Kegan Paul.

Nazroo, J. (1997) *Ethnicity and Mental Health: Findings from a National Community Survey*, London: Policy Studies Institute.

Rack, P. (1982) *Race, Culture and Mental Disorder*, London: Tavistock.

Raval, H. (1996) 'A systemic perspective on working with interpreters', *Clinical Child Psychology and Psychiatry*, 1 (1), pp. 29–43.

Contributors

Alan Addison graduated as a carpenter, and much later, in English Literature. He returned to work as a family literacy tutor in North Edinburgh, the place of his birth, cultural learning and setting for his chapter.

Geraldine Castleton is Research Fellow in the Centre for Literacy and Language Education Research at Griffith University, Brisbane, Australia. Her research and publications focus mainly on the relationship between literacy policy and practice across a range of contexts.

Jim Crowther was formerly a tutor and organiser of adult basic education, in Edinburgh, during the 1980s. He is currently a lecturer in adult and community education at Edinburgh University and has written various articles on class, culture and literacy. He co-edited *Popular Education and Social Movements in Scotland Today* which was published by NIACE in 1999. He is a founder member of the International Popular Education Network.

Marcia Fawns studied on the MA course in Language Studies in the Department of Linguistics and Modern English Language at Lancaster University. Her main interest is in the way in which language study can help people to identify and ultimately resist the manipulative power of language.

Fiona Frank is Communications/Co-ordination Manager of the Workplace Basic Skills Network, which is based at CSET, Lancaster University. She has been working in the field of workplace basic skills for the past 10 years and has been interested in access to learning for disadvantaged groups for much longer. She is an inveterate 'networker' and uses ICT constantly for work and leisure.

Sue Gardener has been working in adult literacy, language teaching and training for work, for at least three decades, mainly in north-east London but with wider connections. She now runs the adult continuing education programme at the Urban Learning Foundation, an educational charity.

Mary Hamilton is Professor of Adult Learning and Literacy in the Department of Educational Research at Lancaster University, UK. Her main areas of interest are in adult and continuing education: policy issues and public representations of literacy; comparative perspectives, especially across industrialised societies; processes of informal adult learning and issues of access and transition for mature students.

She is particularly involved with Adult Basic Education, both literacy and numeracy and basic skills issues across all levels of the education system. She is a founder member of the national network, Research and Practice in Adult

Literacy (RaPAL) and a core member of the Lancaster Literacy Research Group.

Roz Ivanič is a Senior Lecturer in the Department of Linguistics and Modern English Language at Lancaster University, a member of the Literacy Research Group there, and a founding member of RaPAL, with a special interest in academic literacies. She is the author of *Writing and Identity: The discoursal construction of identity in academic writing* (Benjamins), and co-author with Romy Clark of *The Politics of Writing* (Routledge).

Catherine Jamieson has first degrees in Education and Social Work. The opportunity to work alongside adults with learning disabilities, between 1984 and 1997, inspired and informed the work for an M.Ed in Special Educational Needs from Stirling University in conjunction with Moray House College in 1995. Catherine currently works for Community Education in the City of Edinburgh's Adult Basic Education Team.

Ann Janssen has been working in adult literacy, language teaching and training for work, for at least three decades, mainly in north-east London but with wider connections. Ann has the additional insight of being trilingual. She is a director of Making Training Work, a not-for-profit training provider.

Catherine Kell is a lecturer in adult education in the Education Department at the University of Cape Town, South Africa. She started off working in a Freirean literacy project in the townships around Cape Town in 1981. Since then she has researched, taught and advocated literacy. She is particularly interested in the relation between classroom-based literacy teaching and everyday literacy practices.

Hugo Kerr is a veterinary surgeon, but has had over 20 years' practical and theoretical involvement, at various levels and in various capacities, with the teaching of adult literacy. He has, apart from his veterinary degree, a Cert Ed (FE), a BA (psychologies – OU) and an MEd (literacy).

Jane Mace writes about literacy and adult life. She is a founder member of RaPAL, a trustee of World University Service (UK), a lecturer at South Bank University, London and the mother of two adult children.

Catherine Macrae has worked as a tutor and a manager in adult literacy for 18 years. She is currently working on the government-funded Adult Literacies in Scotland Project. She has a keen interest in writing and is doing postgraduate research on the teaching of writing with adults.

Ian Martin teaches in the Department of Community Education, Faculty of Education, University of Edinburgh. He has written extensively about community-based adult education and the politics of educational policy.

Mary Norton is a program co-ordinator and facilitator at the Learning Centre, in Edmonton, Alberta. She is also an adjunct assistant professor in the University of Alberta's Faculty of Education and is involved in various research-in-practice endeavours.

Habibur Rahman is the Senior Programme Co-ordinator (Materials Development) of Proshika, a large indigenous NGO in Bangladesh. He has spent his working life developing functional literacy programmes for the rural and urban poor of his own country.

Brian Street is Professor of Language in Education at King's College, London University and Visiting Professor of Education in the Graduate School of Education, University of Pennsylvania. Over the past 25 years he has undertaken research into literacy practices at home and school in a number of countries, has been consultant to a number of development projects, in both the North and South, and has a commitment to linking ethnographic-style research on the cultural dimension of language and literacy with contemporary practice in education and in development. He has written/edited 10 books and over 60 articles on these themes.

Lyn Tett worked for 10 years as the adult literacy organiser for a rural area of Scotland before moving to a post that involved establishing and supporting a Scottish Adult Basic Education Forum. She is currently head of the Department of Community Education at the University of Edinburgh and her research in adult literacy focuses on its role in challenging the processes of social exclusion.